Declaring His

GLORY

among the

NATIONS

FOREWORD BY JOHN MACARTHUR

Declaring His

GLORY

among the

NATIONS

Daily Scripture Meditations

from Pastors Around the World

FACULTY AND GRADUATES OF
THE MASTER'S ACADEMY INTERNATIONAL

THE
MASTER'S ACADEMY
INTERNATIONAL

Declaring His Glory Among the Nations:
Daily Scripture Meditations from Pastors Around the World

© 2020 The Master's Academy International
13248 Roscoe Blvd
Sun Valley, CA 91352
(818) 909-5570
info@tmai.org

Prepared for publication by www.greatwriting.org

ISBN: 978-0-9600203-9-3

Cover design: www.greatwriting.org
Book layout and design: www.greatwriting.org
Prayer profile design: Maffrine LaConte

Acknowledgments

It is no small feat to bring together the writings of more than 200 authors representing 15 countries and nearly as many languages. TMAI is profoundly grateful to the Lord for the small army of servants who dedicated countless hours to this project. We would like to thank Danny Gumprecht for his superb editorial oversight, as well as Aaron Darlington and his team of editors: Scott Lang, Aaron Shryock, and Grant Gates. We are also grateful to Jim Holmes at Great Writing for taking the project and getting it to completion; Samuel Hanchett and Jonathan Willoughby for their faithful translations; Maffrine La-Conte for her patience and professional design input; TMAI's office manager Channing Chow for her crucial administrative support and attention to detail; James L. Stamps Foundation, and other partners whose generous support made the publication possible. Lastly, we would like to thank the authors of this devotional, who—like Ezra— have given their lives not only to understanding Scripture, but obeying it, and teaching it to others.

May God bless each of these individuals for their service to our Lord Jesus Christ.

TMAI Training Center Locations
Worldwide

United States

Mexico

Honduras

GERMANY
CZECH REP.
UKRAINE
AUSTRIA
SWITZ.
CROATIA
SPAIN
ITALY
ALBANIA
RUSSIA
JAPAN
PHILIPPINES
MALAWI
SOUTH
AFRICA

Foreword

JOHN MACARTHUR

On a mountain in Galilee, the resurrected Lord Jesus Christ announced the ministry plan for His followers—they were to go into all of the world and make disciples through the proclamation of the gospel and the teaching of God's truth. Eleven disciples were to lead these followers in carrying out this Great Commission as Jesus ascended back into heaven. As ordinary as they were and as extraordinary as this commission was, the eleven, and those who followed them in faith, did indeed take the gospel to the ends of the earth within a few decades (Acts 1:8). Two-thousand years later, we look back and trace the spread of the Good News, and then look around to see how this commission is being faithfully obeyed today.

The Master's Academy International (TMAI) was officially formed over 15 years ago to train local, indigenous church leaders all across the world who would then make and equip disciples of Christ in local churches. With a commitment to expositional preaching and the authority of Scripture, more than 15 schools on four continents have trained men to be faithful to the mandate of Christ's commission in all contexts and places. As I have said elsewhere, I believe the history and impact of these schools is the greatest missions story of our time. How encouraging, then, it is to see this devotional in my hands, knowing it is fruit of these ministries and evidence of the Great Commission being faithfully obeyed.

Pastors, professors, students, and graduates of the represented schools have each contributed to this daily devotional. One entry for each day of the year has been written by individuals connected to the ministry of TMAI. As you read through the entries each day, you will be fed truth from Scripture and will be challenged—whether directly because of its implications for the Christian walk, or indirectly by hearing what ministry is like for these individuals amidst their challenging circumstances. You will also gain a glimpse into the spiritual lives of these men around the world as they minister to you personally, demonstrating their love for the truth written and incarnate. You will be reminded of the global nature of gospel ministry, and how much still needs to be done by way of prayer and support. You will feel compelled to pray for these schools and the men leading them, that our Lord who promised to be with us always, even to the end of the age, would be with them in their ministries, strengthening and blessing them for every good work.

May you be encouraged and equipped as you hear God's glory declared among the nations.

JOHN MACARTHUR

PASTOR-TEACHER, GRACE COMMUNITY CHURCH;

CHANCELLOR EMERITUS, THE MASTER'S UNIVERSITY AND SEMINARY

Introduction

MARK TATLOCK

Declare his glory among the nations,
his marvelous works among all the peoples!
For great is the LORD, *and greatly to be praised;*
he is to be feared above all gods.
For all the gods of the peoples are worthless idols,
but the LORD *made the heavens.*
Splendor and majesty are before him;
strength and beauty are in his sanctuary.
Ascribe to the LORD, *O families of the peoples,*
ascribe to the LORD *glory and strength!*
Ascribe to the LORD *the glory due his name;*
bring an offering, and come into his courts!
Worship the LORD *in the splendor of holiness;*
tremble before him, all the earth!
Say among the nations, "The LORD *reigns!"*

PSALM 96:3–10 (ESV)

God's global plan of redemption is clearly outlined in Scripture, beginning with His statement in Genesis 12:1–3 to Abram, where God declares He will bless Abram's descendants and through them extend this blessing to all the families of the earth. Paul makes clear this blessing is the blessing of salvation, as explained in Galatians 3:6–9. Therefore, from the Abrahamic covenant to the final scene in Revelation 22, where the very leaves on the tree of eternal life are described as representing the salvation of the nations forever, all human history bears testimony to what God promised to accomplish—the drawing unto Himself people from across this globe to worship Him for all eternity.

Throughout the Old Testament we see this truth confirmed. This was David's understanding as he pens a song of praise at the returning of the recovered ark of the covenant to Jerusalem (1 Chron. 16:8–36). The recovery of the ark from the Philistines was an occasion to celebrate the demonstration of God's sovereign power over the idols of the Philistines and to praise Yahweh, the one true God, who was not like the gods of the Gentiles—deaf and dumb to their prophets' prayers. David, modeling praise for the nation, bursts forth with the bold assertion that the children of Israel should "Tell of His glory among the nations, His wonderful deeds among all the peoples" (1 Chron. 16:24). This was Israel's mission as assigned by God in Exodus 19:6—to be a kingdom of priests and a holy nation. Their responsibility was to be mediators of the message of reconciliation—to turn from idolatry and to become worshippers of the only true God. Even in the Old Testament we see that God intended for this message to go to the nations and among all peoples!

David understood the redemptive plan of God, declaring this truth in multiple Psalms, such as Psalm 67, where he asks God to be gracious and bless Israel so that His salvation may be known among all nations (Psa. 67:1–3). In Psalm 97 David again references God's desire to have His glory proclaimed among the nations: "The heavens proclaim his righteousness, and all the peoples see his glory. All worshipers of images are put to shame, who make their boast in worthless idols; worship him, all you gods!"

David's son Solomon also understood that God's redemptive plan included Gentiles (the nations). When dedicating the glorious temple as a house of worship to Yahweh, Solomon does not fail in his prayer to include a reference to those Gentiles who would turn to Yahweh and call out to Him in their prayers. This public dedicatory prayer includes Solomon's appeal:

> Likewise, when a foreigner, who is not of your people Israel, comes from a far country for your name's sake (for they shall hear of your great name and your mighty hand, and of your outstretched arm), when he comes and prays toward this house, hear in heaven your dwelling place and do according to all for which the foreigner calls to you, in order that all the peoples of the earth may know your name and fear you, as do your people Israel, and that they may know that this house that I have built is called by your name.
> (1 Kings 8:41–43, ESV)

It should not be lost on us that the newly constructed temple, as designed by God, included a Court of the Gentiles—a permanent reminder that God was to be worshiped among all the peoples of the earth. It was this very court that Christ cleansed when the Jews failed to remember this truth and abused this court's original purpose (Matt. 21:12–13; Isa. 56:7).

As the Jews failed to accomplish God's purpose for the nation, He instructs the church to take on this role and responsibility of being a light to the nations. Peter, who heard Christ utter the Great Commission and had been present at Pentecost (where men from every known nation heard him preach the gospel in their own languages), wrote to believers scattered throughout the Roman Empire, "But you are a chosen race, a royal priesthood, a holy nation, a people for God's own possession, so that you may proclaim the excellencies of Him who has called you out of darkness into His marvelous light" (1 Pet. 2:9). It is now the church's mission to declare the glory of God among the nations. This is the very essence of the Great Commission from our Lord.

Mission Statement of
The Master's Academy International

TMAI is committed to fulfilling the Great Commission by training indigenous church leaders to be approved pastor-teachers, able to equip their churches to make biblically sound disciples.

The mission of TMAI aligns exactly with God's redemptive plan and purpose for His church to be built among the nations. Churches faithfully teaching the truth become disciple-making churches. Villages, towns, and cities are most effectively reached when God's people live holy lives, proclaiming the true gospel in the context of their daily work commitments and social networks. Because the Great Commission is aimed at making biblically literate disciples—not just converts to Christianity—the teaching work of the church is the primary means by which the Great Commission is fulfilled. Converts made, without a biblically sound church to teach and train them to live godly and sober lives in this present world, will leave converts vulnerable to the threats of heresy, false doctrine, or even falling away from the faith. The local church is central to the mission of God. And central to the local church is the faithful proclamation of God's word, assuring the authorial intent of every text has been rightly interpreted and taught with conviction and clarity. Declaring the glory of God among the nations is the proclamation ministry of the local church.

Today the ministry of TMAI has successfully equipped pastors from 85 nations, through established training centers in 15 countries. Our expectation is that the number of schools will double in the next decade. This is in response to the increasing demand by national church leaders who desire to preach in an expositional manner to their people. This demand is a clear indication that God is arousing His church in our generation to rightly divide the word of God. And so, as you come into the presence of God each day, devoting yourself to worshipping Him, may you be reminded that God is at work among the nations today. Pastors trained by TMAI to rightly interpret and proclaim the Scriptures are faithfully instructing their congregations to understand sound doctrine and to walk in wisdom. As you meditate on each devotional penned by these men, remember that God's plan has always been that His name and glory would be declared among the nations.

Over 200 authors from 15 countries, representing 12 languages, have contributed to this devotional—stop and marvel at the work of God's word among the nations! Each devotional indicates the name of the man who authored it, as well as the school and country in which they minister. Every devotional in this volume is a testimony of a man who pursued such training and models sound teaching in his country. As part of your daily devotions, I would invite you to pray for this pastor or church leader, his family, and his church. Pray also for the school, its faculty, and the many pastors that are being trained. Most of these leaders are bi-vocational, meaning that in addition to pastoring their congregations, they must work full time to meet the needs of their families. These families are making great sacrifices to serve the Lord and need our prayers to face the demands of ministry, work, and studies. On the last day of each month, you will find a dedicated prayer profile to guide you in prayer for a particular region or school. The ministry of intercession is essential to the progress of the gospel and the fight for truth.

The truth of God is transnational, and as you are spiritually encouraged by men from as far away as Russia, Honduras, Malawi, or Japan, know that God, indeed, is *declaring His glory among the nations.*

Mark Tatlock
President, The Master's Academy International

Commission Fulfilled

*I saw another angel flying in midheaven, having an eternal
gospel to preach to those who live on the earth, and to every
nation and tribe and tongue and people.*

REVELATION 14:6

MARK TATLOCK: PRESIDENT, TMAI HEADQUARTERS | LOS ANGELES, CALIFORNIA

John's glimpse into the eternal state reveals that the Great
Commission will be fulfilled! Those redeemed throughout history
will one day be gathered before the throne of God. This has always
been God's intended plan. When Christ commissioned His disciples
to take the gospel to Jerusalem, Judea, Samaria, and the remotest
parts of the earth (Acts 1:8), it was in complete accord with God's
plan of redemption. And it will only be in heaven where we who are
gathered from among all the families (nations and tongues) of the
earth will experience the fulfillment of this glorious mission.

This means that there is no American church or American God—
just the opposite. Whether we are American, Chinese, Indonesian,
Russian, German, Kenyan, or another ethnic believer, we follow the
same Lord. While sins of favoritism or racism seek to disrupt the unity
of believers, the fulfillment of God's mission will never be thwarted.

One day before the throne, John tells us we will see the Tree of Life,
representing eternal life, and the very leaves on that tree will represent
the nations of the world to whom the healing gospel came and fulfilled God's commission. What a great privilege to live at a time when
the making of disciples is a shared, international mission. National
pastors, equipping their congregations to reach not only their own
countrymen, but across borders, have made the missionary enterprise
a cross-cultural, shared task. That is a small picture of heaven and a
reminder that the Commission will be fulfilled.

As we start this year, pray today that God will give success to His
laborers around the world and that more from every nation, tribe,
tongue, and people will worship Jesus Christ as Lord!

A Long Line of Godly Men

The things which you have heard from me in the presence of
many witnesses, entrust these to faithful men who will be able
to teach others also.

2 TIMOTHY 2:2

CHIZASO M. G. CHUNGA: CENTRAL AFRICAN PREACHING ACADEMY | MALAWI

Pastoral ministry involves receiving and faithfully passing on the truths that Christ gave to the apostles during the foundation of the church.

In this verse, the apostle Paul instructs Timothy to train men for leadership in the local church by entrusting them with the teaching that he had received from Christ. From the time of the early church, the apostles trained up spiritual leaders by passing on to godly men what Jesus had taught them.

As a pastor, I am aware that God has entrusted me with sound doctrine that I am to pass on to others. Those who receive it, in turn, are charged to equip the next generation. A pastor, therefore, does not invent his own teaching or appoint himself; he receives training from others who have come before him. Similarly, a pastor also must have his own disciples, so that he may entrust to them what he has received himself. It is the same doctrine and same gospel that has been passed from generation to generation, which must be passed to the coming generations, as well.

Leaders must identify men who are *faithful* and *able to teach* others. Paul repeats these qualities in 1 Timothy 3:2, where he writes that an elder should be above reproach and able to teach. It is important for our church leadership to have these qualities so that they can discharge their responsibility of training up the next generation.

Pray for your spiritual leaders to receive and faithfully pass on the true words of Christ. The strength and gospel witness of our churches depend on it!

A Single Offering

For by one offering He has perfected for all time
those who are sanctified.
HEBREWS 10:14

IVAN MUSTAC: THEOLOGICAL BIBLICAL ACADEMY | CROATIA

When reading this verse we must ask, "Of whom is the writer speaking?" Who is this figure that provided such a perfect offering? Through careful reading of the context, we learn that it is Jesus Christ. The author of Hebrews is also drawing attention to two words that are crucial to our understanding. These words are *one* and *offering*. The first verse of this chapter indicates why he has done this: "the Law ... can never, by the same sacrifices which they offer continually year by year, make perfect those who draw near." We see that Jesus Christ with His one offering, His own life and death, did for humanity what was unattainable by the Law. He brought complete salvation forever.

Therefore, we can add nothing to Christ's salvation. What a relief this was in my early years as a believer, realizing that Christ did it all. As I struggled with specific sins in my early walk with Christ, I started questioning my salvation. Was it genuine? Do I need to do something more? No, Christ did it all through a single offering! This was a great discovery for me. This truth fortified my salvation that I have in Christ.

How valuable this truth is when you live in an area like Croatia where Roman Catholicism is the dominant religion. Every day, people attempt to repeat the sacrifice of Christ. This is why the church needs to believe and proclaim this clearly: "Christ did it all by one offering for all time!"

Have you trusted in this single, perfect offering? Thank Christ today for His sacrifice.

Giving for God's Glory

*Because of the proof given by this ministry, they will glorify
God for your obedience to your confession of the gospel of
Christ and for the liberality of your contribution to them and
to all, while they also, by prayer on your behalf, yearn for you
because of the surpassing grace of God in you.*

2 CORINTHIANS 9:13–14

M. S.: MIDDLE EAST (NAME WITHHELD FOR SECURITY)

The topic of giving money is nearly always taboo in Christian circles. Perhaps the subject has acquired such a poor reputation due to the inappropriate manner in which it is frequently handled. However, the apostle Paul dealt with this difficult topic in a straightforward and honest manner. Despite any prior misgivings, believers must give due attention to God's call to participate in the ministry of giving.

Paul reminded the Corinthian believers that their ministry of giving was actually evidence ("proof") of their genuine relationship with Christ. The generous believer gives tangible testimony to the work of grace that has been wrought in his heart (2 Cor. 9:14). Further, the Corinthians' giving was considered "obedience" to the gospel of Christ.

Consider this definition of the gospel: God the Father sent the Son freely, generously, under no external coercion, in order to meet the needs of others. True Christian giving will follow a similar pattern. As we respond to the gospel, by imitating the character of God, it is important that we consider how we will participate in the ministry of giving, thereby manifesting the grace of God in our lives. It is our privilege to care for others, and to support God's work, by offering up that with which we have been entrusted.

Ultimately, Christians have the assurance that their giving is not in vain. Faithful giving to sound ministries will produce "thanksgiving to God" (2 Cor. 9:12) and motivate others to glorify the name of Almighty God. If anyone needed a reason to give, he should look no further than these verses. Are you glorifying the Lord as He deserves with your giving? *Soli Deo Gloria!*

True Confession

If we confess our sins, He is faithful and righteous to forgive us our sins and to cleanse us from all unrighteousness.

1 JOHN 1:9

ALEKSEY KOLOMIYTSEV: WORD OF GRACE BIBLE INSTITUTE | USA

Freedom from sin is one of the greatest needs in people's lives. Sin deprives us of joy, brings feelings of guilt, and complicates our relationship with God. Sin makes us ineffective by creating obstacles for God's effective working in and through us. Sin also inevitably destroys life by gradually weakening our resistance to temptation.

When we do not resist sin, the problem becomes worse. We fall into sin because we make mistakes. We sin because we are careless. We sin because we succumb to the deceptive promises of sin.

Fortunately, God foresaw the way to liberation from sin: confession. The word "confess" means "to say the same thing, to agree." To confess sin means to agree with God's evaluation of sin, to acknowledge oneself as sinful and deserving of punishment.

Yet, the confession of sin consists of another aspect. True confession is linked with the realization that the Son of God died on the cross for sin. The Christian's sin is what nailed the Son of God to the cross, where He bore the full weight of the punishment we deserved. Such knowledge saddens the heart of one who loves Christ, yet confession helps us realize that we have a basis on which to seek forgiveness from God—the Lord Jesus Christ.

Thus, John writes that He who is faithful and just grants forgiveness and cleanses us from all unrighteousness because the Son who died on the cross continues to intercede for us before the throne. Thank God today for the gift of true confession—and practice it regularly.

Walking in Holiness

No temptation has overtaken you but such as is common to man; and God is faithful, who will not allow you to be tempted beyond what you are able, but with the temptation will provide the way of escape also, so that you will be able to endure it.

1 CORINTHIANS 10:13

MELVIN ROMERO: EVANGELICAL MINISTRIES OF THE AMERICAS | HONDURAS

One of the things that I've enjoyed most in life has been to teach my children to walk. To see them take their first steps and walk in a suggested direction brought satisfaction to my heart and theirs. Usually it would lead us to celebrate with laughter and a hug. Each of them faced the same difficulties, risks, distractions, and weaknesses, but they responded in different ways. Sometimes they lost sight of my hand, deviating in their own direction, but my love as a father led me to stay by them to avoid letting them fall.

In the same way, we are God's children, and He has given us a path to follow with good works that He expects us to complete until we reach His heavenly abode. During our "walk," we are constantly tempted to sin against God's holiness; however, we are called to respond to these trials and temptations in such a way that our lives reflect the holy character of God. Paul tells us in this verse that, although the temptations are many and different, none of them are out of the ordinary. Temptations are common to all mankind. If others have succeeded, so can we. The ability to defeat such temptations comes from God, who remains faithful, never allowing them to be greater than the strength He provides. He always provides a way to escape and thus succeed.

You *can* overcome temptation in your life. You *can* faithfully endure whatever you might be facing. Through prayer and Scripture, He will help you walk, like a father with his child, in the straight path of holiness.

Displaying the Gospel Every Day

[Walk] with all humility and gentleness, with patience,
showing tolerance for one another in love.

EPHESIANS 4:2

GIANLUCA POLLUTRI: ITALIAN THEOLOGICAL ACADEMY | ITALY

As each new morning dawns, we wake up ready to face the day, to get things done. Often there is a clear checklist of tasks to accomplish. In this text, Paul presents believers with a sort of checklist for daily behavior. It is meant as a guide to help the Ephesian believers evaluate their lives in light of the gospel. He implores them to follow some basic principles that will put the gospel of Jesus Christ on display.

Therefore, as we tackle our daily to-do lists, let us also meditate on *this* checklist from heaven. Let us ready ourselves to put on our new life in Christ first by walking in *humility*. Instead of placing ourselves in the center of our daily activities, let's plan ahead on how we can serve others during the day. And when things get rough and people do not respond the way we had hoped, let's follow the guidelines and respond with *gentleness* and *patience*.

Sometimes, we will be repeatedly tested with difficult people. So, we need to develop a heart of *tolerance in love*. We tolerate those who at first glance are not so loveable because we know how much God loved us while yet sinners. That tolerance reflects the gospel. These qualities spoken by Paul derive from God Himself and the way He has treated us in Christ. Therefore, when we consider our checklist of tasks to accomplish each day, let us remember the character qualities that will most beautifully put on display the gospel for all to see. This is how we walk in a manner worthy of our blessed and inestimable calling of salvation.

No Insignificant Member in Christ's Body

*For even as the body is one and yet has many members, and
all the members of the body, though they are many, are one
body, so also is Christ…. Now you are Christ's body, and
individually members of it.*

1 CORINTHIANS 12:12, 27

JESÚS ENRIQUE GUTIÉRREZ CORONA: WORD OF GRACE BIBLICAL SEMINARY | MEXICO

Christians are all members, without exception, of the one body of Christ. It does not matter our nationality, social position, economic level, academic skills, or denomination. Each one of us is an individual and equally important member of the universal church (Christ's body).

God's Spirit has provided us with specific gifts to serve the other members of Christ's body. Nevertheless, when we serve, we sometimes forget how important our God-given gifts are. We are prone to think that some gifts are insignificant or that publicly visible gifts matter more.

Consider one member of the human body, the kidney. This organ is smaller than a mobile phone, yet *every* day it can purify more than fifty gallons of blood, eliminating a wide variety of dangerous chemicals.

Our Lord made our bodies with this seemingly insignificant member that serves such a crucial function. In the same way, He outfits His body, the church, with members who are not publicly noticeable or who do not have more visible gifts, yet are vital to the proper health of the body.

Let's remember that God has placed each of us within the church, fitting us together with others in just the right place for His purposes to be accomplished. He has provided us with all we need to serve Him and our fellow believers in the most relevant and worthy way, even though sometimes it might not seem like it. Think about your interests, abilities, and the opportunities God has granted to you. Are you using them to the fullest, for the benefit of your local church?

Life in the Vine

Every branch in Me that does not bear fruit, He takes away;
and every branch that bears fruit, He prunes it so that it may
bear more fruit.

JOHN 15:2

BOB AMIGO: THE EXPOSITOR'S ACADEMY | PHILIPPINES

The apostle John records seven "I am" statements of the Lord Jesus, with the image of a vine being the last of them. This picture was familiar to the disciples, as vineyards were plentiful in Israel and important to their economy.

As the Lord made His way to Calvary, He used this picture to assure the disciples of the fruitfulness that results from spiritual union with Him. The vine represents Jesus and the branches represent His disciples. Jesus taught that the branches can only produce life when they are a part of the vine. By itself, a branch would be reduced to dead wood and completely useless.

Fruitfulness is an essential mark of saving faith, and since Jesus is the vine, it is impossible for true branches not to bear fruit. Thus, barren branches are removed and burned. Pruning also distinguishes dead branches from fruit-bearing branches, providing more room in the vine for the growth of the good branches. Furthermore, it prevents useless branches from breeding insects and blight that may ruin the quality of the good fruit. God desires to see not only quantity of fruit from believers, but quality as well.

As an act of loving concern, God the Father, the vinedresser, prunes every believer. The process is often painful, but God personally attends to this undertaking for our good and His glory.

The writer of Hebrews affirmed the same principle when he wrote, "Those whom the LORD LOVES HE DISCIPLINES, AND HE SCOURGES EVERY SON WHOM HE RECEIVES.... He disciplines us for our good, so that we may share His holiness" (Heb. 12:6, 10).

Kind in Heart, Humble in Spirit

To sum up, all of you be harmonious, sympathetic, brotherly,
kindhearted, and humble in spirit.

1 PETER 3:8

DAVID BEAKLEY: CHRIST SEMINARY | SOUTH AFRICA

Loving and caring for others is a difficult task. It is even worse when it is a command and the "others" don't particularly care for your love. But when it is done out of joy, the world takes note. When Peter wrote "to sum up" in this verse, he was summing up his instructions that were very pointed and directed toward fellow believers about submitting to bad governments, bad employers, and bad marital relationships. And, if that were not bad enough, Peter gave this call of submission to people who were already suffering and experiencing persecution for their faith! How is this possible?

South Africa is a very complex country, with a complex history that has been checkered with oppression, strife, and hypocrisy—largely in the name of the "state" church, which in the past was professing evangelical. In 1994, the government changed and the servant was now the master. Needless to say, there was a backlash against "White Christianity." But, when a student-pastor from Christ Seminary understood these words from Peter, and saw a converted "enemy" from the previous regime, he went to meet his foe only to discover a brother. After they discovered and rejoiced in their unity of mind, they both preached together in a Township church to a full house.

The result was a testimony that resounded throughout the country. A secular and polarized culture was now hearing—and intrigued by—the gospel message of peace from two unlikely brothers.

How might you demonstrate loving submission, kindness of heart, and humility of spirit to those around you today?

A Diet for the Mature

But solid food is for the mature, who because of practice have their senses trained to discern good and evil.
HEBREWS 5:14

LANEY STROUP: JAPAN BIBLE ACADEMY | JAPAN

The term "10/40 window" is a frequent buzzword in missions. Located between 10 and 40 degrees north latitude, this is the area with the largest concentration of unreached people groups in the world. Most of these lands have remained off limits to missionaries due to persecution, or simply are out of reach due to geographical challenges. The nation of Japan, however, does not fit either of these descriptions.

A coveted trading post since the 1600s, Japan is a pleasant country, readily accessible by air or sea. Opened to the West by Commodore Perry in the mid 1800s, the nation of Japan has more or less welcomed foreign missionaries for the past 150 years. Despite this opportunity, however, the nation of Japan remains one of the least-reached people groups in the world.

Theories for this riddle abound. One clue is the way that Japanese churches respond to sound, biblical exposition: they don't just listen, they hunger for it, hanging on every word like a drop of water in a desert. Despite much missionary activity, this country is still starving for the word of God.

As the author of Hebrews warns, believers cannot survive long-term on the elementary doctrines of the gospel; they need solid food to mature. Thus, while many Japanese have come to faith, the church as a whole remains stunted due to malnutrition.

Pray for us as we labor to meet the pressing needs of the Japanese church. And pray for Japanese Christians, that they would survive this famine, and grow healthy and strong, as a testimony to the power of God's word and a beacon of hope to the rest of the nation.

Fear Not! God Is with You

Have I not commanded you? Be strong and courageous! Do not tremble or be dismayed, for the LORD *your God is with you wherever you go.*

JOSHUA 1:9

LUIS MIGUEL CONTRERAS ROMERO: WORD OF GRACE BIBLICAL SEMINARY | MEXICO

In the first nine verses of Joshua 1, the Lord commands Joshua to be strong and courageous three times, and twice He tells Joshua that He would be with him. Why would the Lord repeat these words?

Probably because of the difficulty of the task. When God gives Joshua this command, he is in his upper 80s, receiving the enormous task of leading the nation of Israel into Canaan. Moses is dead and Joshua is to conquer and divide the land among the tribes of Israel.

But the Lord showed His compassion to Joshua, by reminding him twice (Josh. 1:5, 9) that He would be with him. The certainty that God was with Joshua was the basis of the strength and courage that he needed to lead Israel.

God also assures us as Christians of the wondrous reality of having His presence with us. We may trust that God is with us to give strength and courage in the face of adversity and temptation.

The nearness of God encourages many believers in Mexico to be strong and courageous in the Lord, even amid a shaky economy. The next time you are confronted with hardship or financial uncertainty, remember the promise that God is with you (Heb. 13:5). It was this promise that established Joshua's victories; and it is this promise that will keep your path straight, as well.

The Message That Saves

If you confess with your mouth Jesus as Lord, and believe in your heart that God raised Him from the dead, you will be saved.
ROMANS 10:9

MATTHIAS FROHLICH: EUROPEAN BIBLE TRAINING CENTER | GERMANY

Have you ever asked yourself what to aim for in conversations with unbelievers? This verse provides us with a simple and clear understanding of the gospel. It gives a brief description how a sinner becomes right with God.

Paul ties these two principles together throughout the whole passage: believing with the heart and confessing with the mouth. Why? Because saving faith is not merely knowing and affirming theological truth about the crucifixion and resurrection of Christ; rather, saving faith always acts upon what is believed. Saving faith that believes the substitutionary atonement and resurrection of Christ becomes visible when the sinner calls upon the name of the Lord to be saved (Rom. 10:13), and confesses Jesus as Lord.

This unsophisticated proclamation is the means by which sinners are saved. In this truth, our own soul finds rest. It is not because of our effort, but because Christ completely paid the debt of our sin, that we are saved. God attested to this by raising Christ from the dead. By calling him our Savior and Lord, we belong to Him. Christ is all we have, and Christ is all we need.

This is the only message that saves people, no matter what language they speak, what color their skin, where they live, or what experience they have. Nothing may be added to this message, but it must not be diminished, either. This is the only message we must be committed to. This message has to reach the lost. Pray to the Lord of the harvest to send out laborers into His harvest. And commit to supporting them with your physical and spiritual resources.

United by Love, Ruled by Peace

Beyond all these things put on love, which is the perfect bond of unity. Let the peace of Christ rule in your hearts, to which indeed you were called in one body; and be thankful.

COLOSSIANS 3:14–15

ASTRIT A.: ALBANIA (FULL NAME WITHHELD FOR SECURITY)

Love is a characteristic that needs to be continually present in a believer's life. Putting on love is a beautiful metaphor of a life devoted to loving others in a sacrificial way. After a list of characteristics in previous verses regarding how a Christian should live, Paul places love as the most important in a believer's life. Love is that which binds together everything else. As children of God, believers should reflect God, who is love (1 John 4:8).

It is also important that the peace of Christ should reign in our hearts. How can we understand this practically? Because of Christ, we who once were enemies of God are now reconciled. It is the same peace that characterized our Lord Jesus Christ, which He also purchased for us on the cross. This perfect peace with God is reflected in our interactions with other believers. The goal of every church is to see its congregation united by love and ruled by the peace of Christ.

Finally, Paul commands us to be grateful. Living in a fallen world, where complaining is universal, it is imperative for believers to be thankful in every circumstance. We ought to be thankful at all times because of God's great love and grace demonstrated toward us sinners.

Of course, these exhortations to put on love, to let the peace of Christ rule in our hearts, and to be thankful are only given to one class of person: "those who have been chosen of God" (Col. 3:12). The power to love, the reign of peace, and a heart of thanksgiving all come from God. For the Christian, this is not a burden; it's a birthright.

The Need to Preach the Cross

But we preach Christ crucified, to Jews a stumbling block and to
Gentiles foolishness, but to those who are the called, both Jews
and Greeks, Christ the power of God and the wisdom of God.
1 CORINTHIANS 1:23–24

JOSHUA RICHERT: CZECH BIBLE INSTITUTE | CZECH REPUBLIC

Christ as crucified should be the emphasis in every pastor's preaching and every Christian's gospel proclamation. In Paul's day, the gospel was a stumbling block to Jews and foolishness to Gentiles. Jesus Christ is fully God; everything was created through Him and for Him. That He would take on a human nature and body, and die on the cross to pay for sin is a scandalous message. This was not popular in the first century, and it's not popular today.

So why all the commotion about changing the message to make it more palatable? Paul says that the gospel is the "power of God and the wisdom of God" (1 Cor. 1:24). God has chosen to show His wisdom and power in an unlikely place—the crucifixion of His beloved Son. To stray from this message is to lose God's power that brings the spiritually dead to life.

Our goal is not to proclaim what is popular, but to proclaim the cross. In the Czech Republic, a main focus of churches and pastors is the love of God—to the neglect of God's holiness, which demands payment for sin. Thus, preaching Christ as crucified doesn't have the prominent place it should.

The gospel is where God's power and wisdom are chiefly put on display. It would be foolish to resort to human wisdom and philosophies. Are you tempted to preach a more popular message? Don't be! The gospel is "foolishness to those who are perishing, but to us who are being saved it is the power of God" (1 Cor. 1:18).

Bought with a Price, Even Your Body

Or do you not know that your body is a temple of the Holy Spirit who is in you, whom you have from God, and that you are not your own? For you have been bought with a price: therefore, glorify God in your body.

1 CORINTHIANS 6:19–20

JONATHAN WILLOUGHBY: INSTITUTO DE EXPOSITORES | USA

Since the Fall, men and women have shamelessly exposed their bodies to all kinds of sinful pleasure and vice with the rationale that we have an *innate right to do as we please with our bodies*. Society encourages the individual to pursue his wildest dreams and to experience ultimate thrill and excitement in life by indulging in any and every bodily whim. Sexual immorality is at the peak of all sinful, bodily desires.

The Latin American culture screams out for this freedom of using the body in any which way. In years past, it was considered a logical and ethical practice for parents to expose their early-teenage sons to immoral relationships with illicit women in order to stimulate "manliness" and prevent their boys from developing homosexual desires.

This shameful practice had a rationale: since man has liberty to use his body as he wishes, why not use it for a "seemingly good" cause? This depraved way of thinking is only one example of how society misuses the body.

Though the corruption of our society saddens us, it is mortifying when such thinking infiltrates our churches. Like the Corinthians, we must be reminded that the physical body is not insignificant and, thus, we cannot use it to please ourselves. On the contrary, the body is for the Lord, and the Lord for the body (1 Cor. 6:13).

Paul fortifies this argument with a final and uncontested truth—we are the dwelling place of the Holy Spirit and we have been bought with a price. Therefore, believer, your body was costly and it is significant to God; dare not to use it as you please!

The Name That Saves

For there is no other name under heaven that has been given among men by which we must be saved.

ACTS 4:12

VALERY B.: RUSSIA (FULL NAME WITHHELD FOR SECURITY)

Evangelical Christians in Russia are often accused of betrayal. Those close to us say that by embracing the evangelical faith we have betrayed the "faith of our fathers." By this, they mean the Russian Orthodox faith, or even paganism, which was the original religion of ancient Russia and its territories. Betrayal is a serious allegation, and no one wants to be a traitor. Perhaps there is truth in these accusations? Absolutely not!

Our Scripture is part of Peter's response after being questioned by the Jewish leaders about why he did not believe in the Jewish faith—what would have seemed to be the faith of his fathers. Peter's answer was a clear declaration that God has determined—for Jews and Gentiles alike—that all people must believe in only one name. The "faith of our fathers," no matter how ancient or widespread, is not able to save anyone. Only Jesus Christ can save a person from the fiery judgment. Upon hearing this answer, the leaders threatened Peter and the other apostles and forbade them to preach in that name.

Spiritually blind and perishing sinners continue to oppose the name of Jesus. Governments today, including ours here in Russia, have made stricter and stricter laws against preaching this name. But God has only given one name by which, if we call on it, we will be saved from hell.

Dear believer, the Lord has given you opportunities to bear witness to this great name. Let's stand in the line of men like Peter, declaring boldly that salvation is found in no other name than the name of Jesus Christ.

Employ Your Special Gift

As each one has received a special gift, employ it in serving one another as good stewards of the manifold grace of God.
1 PETER 4:10

RUBEN VIDEIRA SOENGAS: BEREA SEMINARY | SPAIN

As the groom's wedding day approaches, his eyes sparkle with anticipation. His eager enthusiasm grows with every tick of the clock. In the same way, the imminence of Christ's arrival should spark the fire in our hearts to keep fervent in our love for one another.

This love is not some ethereal concept impossible to grasp. Peter defines it straightforwardly—to love our fellow believers is to serve them with our unique gifts for God's glory. We are the body of Christ. Each one of us plays an important role for its edification. Therefore, there is no such thing as a small gift. Any dysfunctional human organ, regardless of its size or significance, will negatively affect the physical integrity of the human body. Likewise, any believer who does not serve the church will become detrimental to its spiritual health.

Every believer has experienced the insurmountable grace of God in salvation. And His grace is manifested as a gift that we are in turn to use in serving fellow believers. Since it is a gift, it is not ours to waste. This means that we are stewards of this spiritual endowment. Scripture is clear that when Christ returns we will face the Giver of all gifts to give an account for how we employed this grace. However, this should not cause us to serve Him out of fear, but out of love. Just as the groom cannot wait to see his beautiful bride walking down the aisle, so we should look with anticipation to see Christ's face, and praise Him for working in and through us to love and serve His people.

Do Not Let Sin Reign

Therefore we have been buried with Him through baptism into death, so that as Christ was raised from the dead through the glory of the Father, so we too might walk in newness of life.

ROMANS 6:4

OLEG KALYN: GRACE BIBLE SEMINARY | UKRAINE

As God's children, we earnestly wait for the moment of our glorification, when we will be taken from the presence of sin and will enjoy the presence of our Savior forever. This hope gives us joy and strength for each new day. Yet we are often frustrated because we continue to sin, and seemingly have no power to stop it. For this reason, Paul encourages believers to consider the fact that they cannot live under the power of sin, for they have, in fact, died to its power.

This death occurred when they were baptized into Christ. Baptism into Christ involved union in His death, burial, and resurrection, so that believers would live new lives in the present time. The power of God accomplished the resurrection of Christ; this same power has brought believers, through union with Christ, into the new state of life. God's purpose is that "we too might walk in newness of life." We are to live a certain way as a result of dying and being buried with Christ.

Beloved, sin has no power over the child of God; through union with Christ, we are able to fight and overcome sin because it is no longer our master. Christ redeemed us from its slavery and made us free. Therefore, concludes Paul, do not let sin reign any longer in your bodies. Instead, present yourselves to God as those who are alive from the dead, for such you are (Rom. 6:12–13).

Approved by Tests

In this you greatly rejoice, even though now for a little while,
if necessary, you have been distressed by various trials, so that
the proof of your faith, being more precious than gold which
is perishable, even though tested by fire, may be found to result
in praise and glory and honor at the revelation of Jesus Christ.

1 PETER 1:6–7

SANTIAGO FUENTES HERNÁNDEZ: WORD OF GRACE BIBLICAL SEMINARY | MEXICO

When I entered fifth grade, my new teacher was a friend of our family. He had taught my three older siblings, and he knew me as well. But he wasn't going to give me an easy ride. Throughout that year, he pushed me to work as hard as the other students. It was a tough year, but I look back on it with gratitude. He tested me and showed me what kind of student I was.

In today's passage, Peter talks about being tested. He explains that we will be tested in our faith, yet as believers, we can rejoice in the trials. We rejoice because we have been chosen, born again to a living hope, and made heirs. We are also guarded by God's power.

Despite these privileges of being in Christ, we go through the same trials as the rest of our society: violence, economic crises, corruption, and much more. We face personal trials like sickness, unemployment, and family issues. Peter reminds us that these trials are allowed, for a little while, by our eternal God.

We enter the furnace of trials only when our omniscient and loving God considers it necessary. Our faith is tested in many ways, but He is still sitting firmly on His throne. We can trust in Him completely.

One day Jesus Christ will praise our faith, lavish blessings upon us, and promote us to the position He has promised in His Word. There's no greater reward than that, and it is infinitely greater than passing fifth grade!

Dignified Deacons

Deacons likewise must be men of dignity, not double-tongued,
or addicted to much wine or fond of sordid gain, but holding
to the mystery of the faith with a clear conscience. These men
must also first be tested; then let them serve as deacons if they
are beyond reproach.

1 TIMOTHY 3:8–10

ALEKSANDER G.: RUSSIA (FULL NAME WITHHELD FOR SECURITY)

If you read through First Timothy, it takes little effort to discern a crisis in the Ephesian church, which was directly connected to the activity of unworthy church leaders. The apostle Paul had warned about this earlier (Acts 20:28–30). Therefore, he is insisting that candidates for the ministry (elders and deacons) be carefully examined.

What is a deacon? The term used and the list of requirements presented point to the answer. He is a servant in the full sense of the word. That is, he is first of all a man who serves with humility. Secondly, he is spiritually mature. Thirdly, he is a man of gospel convictions. It is particularly important that the life of a deacon match his Christian convictions. His actions must not contradict his evangelical confession.

Think about the fact that brethren appointed to the ministry are a huge blessing for the local church. Without them, the life of other leaders and the members of the church would be extremely difficult. Christ manifests His love to His church by sending it leaders who are called, and who, like Him, sacrifice themselves for its good.

Remember that deacons—who are still sheep of Christ's pasture—need prayer and encouragement from every other member of the church. Remembering this, spend time in prayer for the leaders of your church. Ponder how you might participate in the labor of God's field together with them. Exercise yourself to answer the call to minister for the good of the church together with those who equip you "for the work of service" (Eph. 4:12).

Sound Words, Sound Lives

If anyone...does not agree with sound words...he is conceited and understands nothing; but he has a morbid interest in controversial questions and disputes about words, out of which arise envy, strife, abusive language, evil suspicions, and constant friction between men of depraved mind and deprived of the truth, who suppose that godliness is a means of gain.

1 TIMOTHY 6:3–5

EDUARDO GONZÁLEZ: BEREA SEMINARY | SPAIN

A church without qualified leadership is like a house with a crumbling foundation—it is not a safe place to be. Without a balanced diet of sound doctrine, the local church will have a difficult time accomplishing its mission. This is why Paul insisted that Timothy carry out his work in Ephesus, putting in place right teaching. For Paul, those who taught a different doctrine contributed spiritual blindness to the church. Timothy had to protect the flock from such influence. If error surfaced, Timothy had to remain faithful as a man of God. Unlike those who had usurped leadership, Timothy needed to reject two sources of temptation: selfish ambition and empty talk—ambition being the wrong motivation, and empty talk the wrong outcome. For a man of God, it's the exact opposite: sound words are his motivation and godliness is his profit.

As men of God we must limit ourselves to preaching sound doctrine, waiting on Him, living a godly life, and not putting our hope on any recognition from men, but only from God.

Can you identify other motives in your life for serving the Lord other than His glory? Do you believe sound doctrine and a godly life are enough to discredit bad influences? Godly men, armed with the truth, are the instruments God uses to plant, strengthen, and reestablish His church—pray for them!

Submit to One Another

Be subject to one another in the fear of Christ.
EPHESIANS 5:21

LANEY STROUP: JAPAN BIBLE ACADEMY | JAPAN

One of the most difficult issues in missions is that of interpersonal relationships. Although in word, most missionaries profess to be willing to die for each other, in deed, petty differences and personal preferences often lead to the breakup of entire mission teams.

In Ephesians 5:21, though, Paul calls us to a life of mutual submission. And in the following verses, he spells out several familiar expressions of this submission. Under this heading, husbands are called to love their wives, fathers are exhorted not to provoke their children, and masters are warned not to lord their authority over their slaves. Thus the call to submit to one another in Ephesians 5:21 applies to everyone in some fashion, and we are to fulfill our part, regardless of our position in the relationship.

This is easier said than done, though, especially when we feel that the other party is in the wrong. In fact, we may often wonder, "Is this actually what Christ intended?" The answer is yes, and the key is in the latter half of this verse: "in the fear of Christ."

The reason we submit to one another is that Jesus asked us to. No more, no less. And to make sure that we understand, Jesus left us a perfect example by washing His disciples' feet.

May our Savior's example teach us to love one another, and may our love and reverence for Him overflow to the point that we in turn submit to one another—for the testimony of the church, for the progress of the gospel, and for the salvation of the lost.

Defeating Surviving Sin

If we say that we have no sin, we are deceiving ourselves and the truth is not in us.

1 JOHN 1:8

CARLOS MONTOYA: EVANGELICAL MINISTRIES OF THE AMERICAS | HONDURAS

A distorted or weak view of sin results in one of two spiritual ills: legalism or licentiousness. The Latin culture is steeped in a religion with a distorted view of sin, which teaches that man in his own effort can fulfill the demands of the law (legalism). On the other hand, in this same culture, a weak view of sin has fueled an unrestrained lifestyle of promiscuity, marital unfaithfulness, and other social and moral ills, even among professing believers (licentiousness).

The apostle John's words are clear. Any denial of surviving sin in the believer is self-deception and a sign of one's departure from the truth. There is no question. We are still affected by the principle of sin within us.

It might be argued, then, that the presence of surviving sin implies a defeated life or an unbearable burden we must live with. But this is not at all the case! The very context surrounding this verse presents the *answer* to surviving sin: grace! In 1 John 1:7, we see the grace of Christ's atoning blood that "cleanses us from all sin." In 1 John 2:1–2, we see the grace of Christ, our advocate, as "the propitiation for our sins." Though we still fight with sin, the decisive battle has been won by Christ. Now we stand as righteous before the Father, resting solely on the merits of His Son. We trust in these great truths, knowing that, "if we confess our sins, He is faithful and righteous to forgive us our sins and to cleanse us from all unrighteousness" (1 John 1:9). Trusting and confessing—that's how we avoid legalism and licentiousness and that's how we defeat surviving sin!

Amazing Fearlessness

*Now as they observed the confidence of Peter and John and
understood that they were uneducated and untrained men,
they were amazed, and began to recognize them as having
been with Jesus.*

ACTS 4:13

D. P.: MIDDLE EAST (NAME WITHHELD FOR SECURITY)

Uneducated fishermen, standing firm before the powerful religious
leaders who had killed Christ, proclaiming the gospel with boldness—this is fearlessness!

What a shock to the rulers! Who did these men think they were?
The word used for "confidence" references a state of boldness or
fearlessness. The rulers were amazed by the courage and clarity of
these two fishermen. Did these men not know that as rulers they had
the power to deliver a death sentence? *What drove these men to such
amazing fearlessness?*

Early on a Sunday morning, Fatima walks out the door of her
one-room living space in the poorest Muslim neighborhood of her
country. All her family and neighbors are Muslim, but she is going to
church. As people ask her where she is going on a Sunday morning,
her simple reply is, "I'm going to learn about Jesus. Do you want to
come?" Does she not know the danger to her life? *What drives such a
woman to amazing fearlessness?*

In both cases, it is the truth of the gospel, learned at the feet of
Christ and lived out by the power of the Holy Spirit (Acts 4:8), that
emboldens disciples to fearless proclamation.

Are *we* proclaiming the amazing, life-changing truth of the gospel?
Despite danger? Despite hardship? Despite rejection? And are *we* remaining at the feet of Christ, in awe of His glorious salvation, seeking
empowerment from the Spirit, that we might proclaim His salvation
with amazing fearlessness?

Effective Worship in the Marketplace

O Lord, who may abide in Your tent? Who may dwell on Your holy hill?
PSALM 15:1

Eric Weathers: TMAI Headquarters | Los Angeles, California

Psalm 15 motivates believers to openly praise God in the presence of their coworkers, customers, and suppliers. Our psalm describes actions of the redeemed. It demonstrates the commitment, reputation, and character of those worshiping the Lord.

The opening two-fold question is piercing: "Who may abide in Your tent? Who may dwell on Your holy hill?" David cannot be with God until he first traverses the hill upon which His tent is pitched. Do you have the credentials to be in God's presence?

Just before God gave the Ten Commandments, He warned the people, "Do not go up on the mountain or touch the border of it; whoever touches the mountain shall surely be put to death" (Exod. 19:12). Since David could not touch God's mountain, then neither could he enter His presence. The king wanted to be with God, but he did not want to die!

David then lists several characteristics of those who may dwell with God. These express themselves in the workplace as: having integrity, accomplishing righteousness, speaking the truth from the depths of your soul, fleeing from slanderous language, not harming your neighbor, not reproaching a friend, despising that which God loathes, honoring God's people, fulfilling your promises even if the consequences are severe, and, when lending to the poor, not charging interest.

Ask yourself—do these characteristics describe you as one who worships God in the marketplace?

God's Glory Comes Through Simple Men

God has chosen the foolish things of the world to shame the wise, and God has chosen the weak things of the world to shame the things which are strong.

1 CORINTHIANS 1:27

CHRISTIAN ANDRESEN: EUROPEAN BIBLE TRAINING CENTER | GERMANY

Not only did God choose to confound the wise by focusing on the repulsive message of the cross—"for the word of the cross is foolishness to those who are perishing" (1 Cor. 1:18), He continues to confound the wise by choosing foolish people to teach the message. Indeed, the wise are shamed, as well as the strong!

If it were up to us, we would choose the wise, the noble, the rich, and the powerful to lead us to success and salvation. God has another way. He helps us to understand that it is not our achievement that redeems us but the message of Jesus Christ's death on the cross.

According to His wisdom, God has chosen us who have nothing to offer to teach the greatest message in the universe, the only message that saves men from eternal damnation. We are twice privileged: first because Christ died for us on the cross and second, He chose us to preach the only saving message that exists. Yes, we are privileged!

But let us remember that we are also responsible to spread the truth of the cross near and far without hesitation and without compromise. We must do this so that everyone can hear it and also see our lives being transformed by it. May God's glory shine through simple men and women as we proclaim the saving gospel!

Live by the Spirit, Walk by the Spirit

If we live by the Spirit, let us also walk by the Spirit. Let us not become boastful, challenging one another, envying one another.

GALATIANS 5:25–26

GIANLUCA POLLUTRI: ITALIAN THEOLOGICAL ACADEMY | ITALY

The true source of godly conduct is the Holy Spirit. Just as a plant that receives nourishment from its roots will yield fruit, Paul urges believers who are indwelt by the Holy Spirit to *walk* in that reality. In other words, to yield fruit (Gal. 5:22–23) as the outworking of their new spiritual life. If we live by the Spirit, Paul argues, let us also walk by the Spirit!

In this text, Paul describes what walking in the Spirit *does not* look like. He prohibits boasting, challenging, and envying. Walking in the Spirit is deeper than external behavior. It reaches the heart motives. You and I can do all sorts of "good" deeds, but if these outward acts are polluted by our conceited and boastful way of life, they are of no value at all. Human strength may produce certain deeds, but it is only by the power of the Holy Spirit that we may produce deeds that are free from jealousy, pride, and competition.

As Charles Spurgeon once said, "Our evil desires are nailed to the cross, but they are not yet dead; we have need therefore to abide under the influence of the ever-blessed Spirit." Walking in dependency on God will never produce arrogance because the works He produces in us cannot be attributed to our own strength or merit. Abiding in the influence of the Spirit will never produce competition or envy because it is the Spirit's design to unite us in Christ.

So let us walk in the Spirit today, seeking God's help to keep us from pride, competition, and jealousy.

Godly Character

*It is a trustworthy statement: if any man aspires to the office
of overseer, it is a fine work he desires to do. An overseer,
then, must be above reproach, the husband of one wife,
temperate, prudent, respectable, hospitable, able to teach, not
addicted to wine or pugnacious, but gentle, peaceable, free
from the love of money.*

1 TIMOTHY 3:1–3

GABRIEL MARTÍNEZ GARCÍA: WORD OF GRACE BIBLICAL SEMINARY | MEXICO

A building with freshly painted walls looks impressive. But if that building rests on soil rich in salt, and there is no protection against the salinity, it will corrode the foundation and walls. No amount of paint will keep it from crumbling over time.

In a similar way, God's word teaches us that the church must have a firm foundation of godly leaders, men who are solid on the inside and not corrupted by the world.

Such a leader must be above reproach, faithful to his wife, respected by all, and hospitable as well. He must be temperate, not self-willed, and good at teaching. He must not love wine, money, or quarrels, but rather be gentle and peaceable.

It should be a priority of the church to have such leaders and also to train up men to be more and more like Christ. Being a leader shouldn't result from being the oldest, most successful in business, or the best speaker. No, it is about character and obedience to the word.

Do you have such a love for Christ and His church that you want to serve sacrificially? Do you have a life transformed by the indwelling power of the Spirit? All God's children should strive to reflect these character qualities, regardless of their position at church. Whether we are preaching or teaching the youngest of children—whatever we do—may we do it all to His glory!

Pray for Understanding

*Lead me in Your truth and teach me, for You are the God of
my salvation; for You I wait all the day.*

PSALM 25:5

BRIAN KINZEL: GRACE BIBLE SEMINARY | UKRAINE

What's behind the psalmist's plea for learning? What explains his
desire for knowledge? Context tells us that his enemies hated
him and sought his destruction. The memory of his past sins afflicted
his conscience, as well. Moreover, he wanted his family to be safe-
guarded in the truth.

In the same way, our difficulties should move us to seek the Lord,
open the Scriptures, and pray, "Teach me." As we remember our past
failures, we should ask God to lead us away from temptation. For the
good of those we love, we should plead to the Lord to guide us.

The inspired poet calls out to God, "Lead me ... teach me," but
that can only happen by means of truth. David said, "Your words
are truth" (2 Sam. 7:28); and God desires this truth to be in the heart
of His children (Psa. 51:6). The one great need for every person is to
know the truth, which is why it is my joy to train preachers, those
who convey God's truth. Without truth, we cannot be saved or grow
spiritually.

Remember, God leads and teaches His people by the truth of His
word. This psalm teaches and encourages us to pray to understand
that truth.

Central Europe

THEOLOGICAL BIBLICAL ACADEMY | CROATIA
CZECH BIBLE INSTITUTE | CZECH REPUBLIC
EUROPEAN BIBLE TRAINING CENTER | GERMANY/AUSTRIA/SWITZERLAND

Though it is the birthplace of the Reformation, Central Europe today is one of the most atheistic regions in the world. Only a return to God's word can bring the people of these countries out of their apathy and doubt. TMAI's training centers are equipping leaders who are zealous to bring a new Reformation.

TODAY, PRAY FOR

Non-believers across Central Europe to be awakened to their need for the gospel.

Perseverance and patience on the part of European Christians as they preach the gospel of hope to a largely unresponsive culture.

God to raise up many church leaders throughout Europe to plant and pastor biblical churches.

Afflicted, Comforted, Prepared to Comfort

Blessed be the God and Father of our Lord Jesus Christ, the
Father of mercies and God of all comfort, who comforts us in
all our affliction so that we will be able to comfort those who
are in any affliction with the comfort with which we ourselves
are comforted by God.

2 CORINTHIANS 1:3–4

HOMERO GONZÁLEZ: WORD OF GRACE BIBLICAL SEMINARY | MEXICO

I'll never forget my first memorial service following the death of a close friend. It was a bittersweet experience, for I knew that my dear brother was with the Lord, yet he was leaving behind a wife and four children, who would now face life without their husband, father, provider, and physical protector. How was I supposed to comfort a widow and four children who were facing the death of their beloved husband and father? We all ran together to 2 Corinthians 1:3–4.

In these verses, Paul highlights the character of God, which unexplainably drives us to worship Him, even through afflictions. We experience consolation when we behold God's comfort-drenched nature within a Father-child relationship that He has made us a part of. At the same time, His comforting character enables us to comfort others in need. Therefore, the constant aches we feel are neither fruitless nor meaningless; they are sovereignly designed by our merciful Father, who leads us to rest and to behold that He is the God of *all* comfort!

Believer, do not lose hope! We have a great and powerful God who comforts our hearts in the face of any and all afflictions. Moreover, remember that as He comforts you, He is also strengthening you so that you can comfort others who are suffering. Run to God alongside those who are afflicted or in trials! Cry with them and embrace them with the same fulfilling and overwhelming comfort that the Lord has given to you.

A Holy Calling

[God] has saved us and called us with a holy calling, not according to our works, but according to His own purpose and grace which was granted us in Christ Jesus from all eternity.
2 TIMOTHY 1:9

D. G.: ASIA (NAME WITHHELD FOR SECURITY)

Every breath that humans take proves that our Creator is gracious. But God's grace toward believers is unique, for in Christ He gives them eternal life when they deserve eternal death.

By the grace of God we are saved. When we were infinitely incapable of saving ourselves from our sins (Eph. 2:1), God sent His beloved Son to save us (Matt. 1:21). Christ is the channel for God's grace. This grace in Christ was granted for us in eternity; therefore, if you and I have repented and believed in Jesus, it is because God in eternity sealed our salvation in Christ.

God saved us and called us to a holy life. We are saved to serve God, to be His witnesses in every circumstance—not just in blessing but also in the midst of suffering.

Recently I was encouraged by my friend's faith when, strengthened by God, he stood strong amidst persecution. When a mob attacked him for being a believer, he could have denied his faith, but he did not. He prayed to his heavenly Father, "Lord, this life is Yours, let Your will be done." What an example that the God who saved us will also strengthen us when we suffer for the gospel.

Are you living for the One who died for you? Remember God saved us with a holy calling; living for yourself is sinful and an affront to God, who has showered us with grace. The more we understand the grace of God, the more we understand how much we owe God. Point people to God's grace in Christ.

No Stopping!

*Not that I have already obtained it…but I press on so that
I may lay hold of that for which also I was laid hold of by
Christ Jesus. Brethren, I do not regard myself as having laid
hold of it yet; but one thing I do: forgetting what lies behind
and reaching forward to what lies ahead, I press on toward the
goal for the prize of the upward call of God in Christ Jesus.*

PHILIPPIANS 3:12–14

CARMELO B. CAPARROS II: THE EXPOSITOR'S ACADEMY | PHILIPPINES

While our position in Christ is perfect and our eternal life is secure, our spiritual life of sanctification is a continuing process. Justification is not our final stop; it is only the beginning of our journey leading to spiritual maturity and, eventually, glorification. Growth is to be unceasing; the only time it should stop is when we stop breathing!

Paul's salvation experience had taken place about thirty years before he wrote the letter to the Philippians. He had won many spiritual battles within that time frame and had grown much during those years, but he wasn't complacent. When Paul wrote, "forgetting what lies behind," he may have been alluding to his spiritual successes or perhaps even some personal failures. Whatever the case, Paul was not going to allow any of those things to be dead weight that would prevent him from growing.

Paul was continually determined to climb greater spiritual heights and march on to spiritual progress. The verb "reaching forward" in Philippians 3:13 literally means "stretching oneself in a race." It graphically illustrates a runner who musters all of his remaining energy and propels himself toward the finish line. This is the same mindset you need to have in your Christian life! The testimony of Paul serves as a vivid reminder to all of us that there is never to be a stalemate or plateau in our spiritual lives. So press on toward the goal for the prize of the upward call of God in Christ Jesus!

No Greater Love

Greater love has no one than this, that one lay down his life for his friends.

JOHN 15:13

JULIUS MALEWEZI: CENTRAL AFRICAN PREACHING ACADEMY | MALAWI

The kind of love that Jesus has for His own is unlike any other. There can be, in fact, no greater love.

In this verse, we learn of Jesus' supreme sacrificial love, for He was willing to lay down His life for His friends. His love led Him to bear our sins. Peter writes, "He Himself bore our sins in His body on the cross, so that we might die to sin and live to righteousness; for by His wounds you were healed" (1 Pet. 2:24).

We are Jesus' friends, who have been healed by His wounds and called to follow His example. We are to love one another just as He has loved us. The apostle Paul writes, "Therefore be imitators of God, as beloved children; and walk in love, just as Christ also loved you and gave Himself up for us, an offering and a sacrifice to God as a fragrant aroma" (Eph. 5:1–2).

Jesus Christ suffered for us, shed His blood, and died on the cross to pay the price for our sins. We deserved to die, but He took our place! Instead of us receiving the punishment for our own actions and being sent to hell for all eternity, Jesus sacrificed His life for us so that we might live.

What wonderful love! May we rejoice in gratitude and follow our Lord's example, even if it involves laying down our own lives just as He laid down His for us.

Priceless Treasures from God

Grace to you and peace from God our Father and the Lord Jesus Christ.

GALATIANS 1:3

GENCI C.: ALBANIA (FULL NAME WITHHELD FOR SECURITY)

Grace and peace, the two key words of the apostle Paul's greeting, are found together in most of Paul's letters. They function as important reminders of the essentials of Christianity.

Sadly, sometimes we lay aside these truths in our daily lives. A Christian can believe that he is saved by grace, yet live as though he were saved by merit (by his good works). Though we would not admit such a thing, we may nonetheless live like it. Therefore, we need to continually remind ourselves that we have peace with God only because of the grace that He's shown to us in His Son, Jesus Christ.

Notice where the grace and peace come from. They do not originate in us. They come from God the Father and our Lord Jesus Christ! Grace has made it possible for us to have peace with God. This amazing grace, which comes from the Father through His Son, is not only justifying, but also sanctifying and glorifying (Rom. 8:29–30). We need to remind ourselves daily of the marvelous gospel of grace, and the peace with God that comes through it. We are accepted by the unmerited love of God through the sacrifice of His Son! Our sins are forgiven and we are at peace with God.

Never forget these wonderful truths. Make these two priceless treasures of grace and peace the quiet meditation of your heart today.

Persevere in Doing Good

Let us not lose heart in doing good, for in due time we will
reap if we do not grow weary.
GALATIANS 6:9

LANEY STROUP: JAPAN BIBLE ACADEMY | JAPAN

The New Testament is filled with the imagery of sowing and reaping. From Jesus' parable of the sower to Paul's final exhortations to Timothy (2 Tim. 2:6), it employs the lowly farmer as an example of hard work and the harvest as a metaphor for the end of the age. So, what makes the farmer such an important example for the Christian, and what does the harvest have to teach us regarding the Christian life?

First, the farmer must plan *diligently* to ensure that he saves enough seed for each new season. Second, the farmer must tend *consistently* to his crops to ensure that they have water and are free from weeds so they can grow. Third, the farmer must work *quickly* to bring in the harvest within the harvest window. And last, the farmer must perform all of the above *patiently* with little to no reward until his crops are harvested.

This last requirement is the point of comparison that Paul makes in Galatians 6:9. It is easy to become discouraged in life and ministry when we do not see the immediate results of our labor. And sometimes, God forbid, we may even grow weary in our fight against sin (Gal. 6:8). Like the hardworking farmer, though, we must bend our backs, we must steel our nerves, and we must set our sights on the harvest to come.

May the Lord grant us to endure, and to labor as diligently as the farmer. And may we set our sights on the task before us, so that we may one day hear the words, "Well done, good and faithful servant."

The Perfect Sacrifice

...once at the consummation of the ages He has been manifested to put away sin by the sacrifice of Himself.
HEBREWS 9:26

ALEKSEY KOLOMIYTSEV: WORD OF GRACE BIBLE INSTITUTE | USA

Perfect efficacy characterizes the sacrifice of Jesus Christ. In past centuries, the people of God had to offer sacrifices. The purpose was to remind people that they were sinful, and so they were offered continually. According to the Law, apart from individual sacrifices, a special sacrifice was offered on behalf of the entire people once a year on the Day of Atonement. On this day, the high priest took the blood of the sacrificed animal and entered the Holy of Holies, the place of the direct presence of God. The blood bore testimony that a life was given for the sins of the people.

Unfortunately, with this sacrifice and all the rest, there existed one enormous defect. They could not destroy sin. Eradicating people's sin required a ransom corresponding with the transgression.

This is the reason that the Son of God became a man. The Incarnation became a most unique phenomenon, specially ordained by God for the eradication of human sin. The destruction of sin in mankind was possible only through the sacrifice of a holy and righteous man, a person who simultaneously would possess the attributes of God. Only such a unique union could resolve the problem of man's sin once and for all. This was realized in the person of Jesus Christ. His humanity and divinity allowed Him to offer the sacrifice that truly eradicated sin.

This is why we treasure Christ's sacrifice and put our trust in Him with absolute confidence and dependence. His is the only perfect sacrifice!

The Dangerous Love of Money

For the love of money is a root of all sorts of evils, and some by longing for it have wandered away from the faith and pierced themselves with many griefs.

1 TIMOTHY 6:10

ANDREW ISIAHO: CHRIST SEMINARY | SOUTH AFRICA

Paul is clear; money itself is not the problem, nor is it evil. The issue is how money directs our desire, and where it leads. The *love* of money is a root cause of evil. And this root does not just lead to one evil, but *all kinds* of evil. This desire will lead us to shutting our hearts off to those in need, pursuing sinful practices, and worse—falsely believing that we are already blessed by God and that our actions actually please Him.

A person's desire to be rich is actually a contempt for God's present plan for his or her life. South Africa is plagued with "health and wealth" prosperity churches. Many are sucked into the vortex of this heresy, but what is worse is the plight of many young pastors who succumb to the multi-level marketing scheme of church ministry in order to enrich themselves, and are now outside the faith leading the charge against the true church.

What is the issue? This issue is one of contentment in God. God is good, and He is a rewarder. God is our treasure. Love of anything other than God Himself will create a lasting and gnawing unfulfilled craving. This leads to a crash of faith with no return. Endless wandering, looking for satisfaction, only leads to self-induced "piercings," which are blamed on God.

Hear and beware—all those who put trust and desire in money and possessions will hear the very same words that were spoken by God to the farmer who built bigger barns—"You fool!" Guard your heart from this love of money!

Confident Confession

If we confess our sins, He is faithful and righteous to forgive us
our sins and to cleanse us from all unrighteousness.
1 JOHN 1:9

MARIUS BIRGEAN: EUROPEAN BIBLE TRAINING CENTER | GERMANY

True confession of sin to—and forgiveness from—our heavenly Father are vital if we are to enjoy a normal Christian life. Sin hinders our relationship with God and fellow believers; therefore, having our sin forgiven is essential to spiritual restoration. Lack of confession leads to spiritual misery. David experienced this when he attempted to hide his heinous sin (Psa. 32:3–4). However, he came to his senses and confessed his sin, which brought forgiveness and restoration of his relationship with God.

John's first epistle teaches us the same spiritual truth. God calls Christians to enjoy fellowship with Him (1 John 1:3) and other believers (1 John 1:7), but in order to have this, we must walk in the light, as our God is light (1 John 1:5–7), and accept the truth about our spiritual condition (1 John 1:8). This means we must acknowledge the presence of sin in our lives and turn from sin as quickly is possible. For this to happen, we need to confess our sins before God.

To confess is to say the same (as God says) about our sin—to refuse to cover it or find excuses for it. There is no need to hide our sin since we have the assurance that God will forgive us, not because we deserve it, but because of His faithful and just character. God's Son is also our trusted Mediator on whose merits we can rest fully (1 John 2:1–2). There is a place for confessing sin to fellow believers (James 5:16) but, foremost, our confession should be to God. Let us be quick to confess our sin and repent from it, so we might enjoy again the Father's smile.

Resist the Roaring Lion

Be of sober spirit, be on the alert. Your adversary, the devil,
prowls around like a roaring lion, seeking someone to devour.
But resist him, firm in your faith, knowing that the same
experiences of suffering are being accomplished by your
brethren who are in the world.

1 PETER 5:8–9

EDUARDO NERIO: EVANGELICAL MINISTRIES OF THE AMERICAS | HONDURAS

Anyone would be afraid to face a lion because of its fierce and overwhelming power. Using the same imagery, Peter presents the adversary of our soul, the devil, as a roaring lion on the prowl seeking whom he will devour.

All believers are under the close watch of the enemy. He seeks the opportune moment to strike and attack with temptation. There is, however, something that every believer can do to avoid being devoured by Satan—be of sober spirit and resist his attack. Remember, then, to be vigilant and steadfast in the faith in our Lord Jesus Christ.

A woman came to our church, and with tears in her eyes she told me that her family was being destroyed by the enemy. She was fearful of his power and attack. She was desperate. Yet, she did not understand that even though the enemy has the power to attack, he does not have power to destroy. He is not invincible.

A vigilant attitude against our enemy will help us to avoid his traps, and the strength of the Holy Spirit through the word of God will help us to remain firm in our faith and resist his ambushes in the midst of trials. Remember that we don't have to defeat Satan; we just have to resist him. While this "roaring lion" is not invincible, it is wise to keep your distance. In the words of the apostle James, "Submit therefore to God. Resist the devil and he will flee from you" (James 4:7). In what areas are you vulnerable to his attack? Shore up these areas with the word of God.

The Hope of Glory

[The saints]to whom God willed to make known what is the riches of the glory of this mystery among the Gentiles, which is Christ in you, the hope of glory.
COLOSSIANS 1:27

IGOR G.: RUSSIA (FULL NAME WITHHELD FOR SECURITY)

Our God wants to be known and glorified. He wants all nations of the world to worship Jesus as their Lord and Savior. In this passage, Paul explains both to his original readers and to us that the main reason why God made him a minister of the gospel is this: to preach the good news about Jesus to the Gentiles. Paul proclaimed to the nations that through faith in Christ Jesus they can have access to the blessings of the new covenant—the indwelling presence of Christ through the Spirit, and hope for the coming glorious kingdom (Eph. 2:11–22).

Since God is omniscient, this plan has been always known to Him. Salvation of the Gentiles was never a Plan B in God's mind. But why then does Paul call it a mystery? What was earlier unknown was that both Jews and Gentiles would be united in one community where they will worship God together and there will be no ground for divisions between them (Eph. 2:14–16). Christ abolished everything that previously separated these two groups and He arranged everything for them to enjoy sweet brotherly fellowship in one body. Paul calls this news the "glorious gospel" (1 Tim. 1:11), and it's truly so.

This passage reminds all believers that Christ is in us. What an encouragement and joy this truth should produce in our hearts! We are never alone because He is always present with us. And His presence with us now is a foretaste of His future presence with His people. Jesus is truly Immanuel, God with us.

Do You Not Know?

*Do you not know? Have you not heard? The Everlasting
God, the* LORD, *the Creator of the ends of the earth does not
become weary or tired. His understanding is inscrutable.*

ISAIAH 40:28

BRANIMIR PLAVSIC: THEOLOGICAL BIBLICAL ACADEMY | CROATIA

God often brings good news amid hard circumstances. The Jewish people were about to be captured by the Babylonians and taken into captivity for seventy years because they violated God's law and broke His covenant. Amidst the bad news and hard circumstances, God spoke good news to encourage them because He already had a plan to return His people from captivity.

Most Jews forgot their God. They lost their hope and did not trust in the Lord. Unfortunately, they were trusting in the false gods around them as if they were equal with the Lord. However, God would rescue them for His own purposes, even though they did not deserve it. And in view of their promised return, they were not to be despairing because God is merciful. He is faithful to His covenant promises that He established with Israel. He will keep His word.

So what must the people of Israel do? They must remember their God—that He is powerful. He is not like the false gods who are impotent and unable to help in any way. This God is never tired nor grows weary like a man. They must remember that their God is faithful—He is mighty in power and has promised to rescue His people from their captivity. He is the Everlasting God, the One who has always existed, the great and almighty Creator of all things. Nothing is impossible for Him; no problem is too great!

That is the God we serve. If He is indeed your Savior, trust Him afresh today, for He will never forsake His people or let them down.

Motivational Forces

Set your mind on the things above, not on the things that are on earth.

COLOSSIANS 3:2

WESLEY ROBINSON: CZECH BIBLE INSTITUTE | CZECH REPUBLIC

We are living in a faster pace of life than previous generations. Without electronic devices to remind us of what we need to do today, we may forget. It is becoming increasingly easier to focus on the things of this world and not on the things above. What separates or differentiates you as a Christ-follower from your unbelieving neighbor or coworker? Although our behaviors may be similar, our heart motivations are different than the unbeliever.

Paul writes to the Colossian church to tell them to set their minds on the things above. When Scripture speaks of the mind, it includes our thoughts, beliefs, understanding, judgments, and discernment. Are our thoughts and beliefs honoring to God? Do we think about how our behavior should reflect God's glory? We must choose to be concerned about honoring Christ and not man. When we choose to set our minds on the things above, we create a God-honoring motivation that leads to God-honoring behavior. Our behavior must be motivated from a desire to honor Christ, which starts with setting our minds on the things above.

What we value in our heart will be known in how we speak and how we act. What are your words and actions saying about you? What consumes your time throughout the day? How much of your day is spent thinking about the things above? Set your mind on such things and let your heart be motivated by what honors God.

Blessed to Bless

*And God is able to make all grace abound to you, so that
always having all sufficiency in everything, you may have an
abundance for every good deed.*

2 CORINTHIANS 9:8

Gus Pidal: Berea Seminary | Spain

Early on as parents, we wanted to make our children aware of the
importance of being generous with others. One way we imple-
mented this was at birthdays. We would take the sibling shopping to
buy the birthday child a present. Ultimately, the gift was paid for by
mom and dad, but we wanted to give him the opportunity to show
kindness to his sibling.

In the same way, God is the giver of all good gifts. In His amazing
kindness, He provides us with resources and gives us opportunities to
be generous to others.

In 2 Corinthians 9, Paul is writing to believers, commending them
for their giving. At the same time, he encourages them to sow generously and tells them that God loves a cheerful giver. In our passage, he
reminds them to depend on God; Paul tells them that "God is able to
make all grace abound to you." He is speaking of material blessings—
it is God who can make grace abound. But for what end? "So that always having all sufficiency in everything, you may have an abundance
for every good deed." The ultimate end of God blessing you is that
you will have an abundance—not to hoard but to be a blessing to
others, which, in Paul's context, is supporting the advancement of the
gospel—the ultimate blessing.

Are you abounding in every good deed? Are you using God's blessings upon your life to give to others? Just as a parent rejoices in seeing
his child's kindness, God rejoices in seeing us abound in every good
deed and using our lives to bless others.

Always Ready

*But sanctify Christ as Lord in your hearts, always being ready
to make a defense to everyone who asks you to give an account
for the hope that is in you, yet with gentleness and reverence.*

1 PETER 3:15

IGOR G.: RUSSIA (FULL NAME WITHHELD FOR SECURITY)

Shortly before Peter finished his earthly mission and entered the glorious presence of his Savior, he encouraged believers to anticipate suffering for Christ's sake. Peter knew well that faith in Jesus and a life of godliness will lead to persecution (2 Tim. 3:12). In this exhortation, Peter admonishes Christians not to lose heart in view of pressure, opposition, and suffering, but to endure as they continue to live in this world as aliens and strangers (1 Pet. 2:11).

One thing that should characterize a Christian's walk is a special reverence and awe for the Lord Jesus. Peter's command to sanctify Christ as Lord means that we are to serve Christ as a loving Master, seeing our lives as belonging to Him. He has redeemed us with His blood (1 Pet. 1:18–19), and made us His possession (1 Pet. 2:9). He has ultimate right of our time, talents, strength, and resources.

Moreover, we are called to be ready to give an account for our faith in Christ. Just as Jesus predicted, believers are persecuted (Luke 21:12; Matt. 5:10–12) and oppressors demand disciples of Christ to give an account for their hope. Yet Peter is not only interested in Christians' *actions*; he is also concerned about their *attitude*. How should they respond to their enemies? How should they treat them? They are called to respond with gentleness and reverence, following the example of their Master, who, "while being reviled ... did not revile in return; while suffering ... uttered no threats" (1 Pet. 2:23).

Persecution is coming—prepare now in your attitude and actions for giving an account of the hope in you. Be always ready!

Let Integrity Guide Your Life

*The integrity of the upright will guide them, but the
crookedness of the treacherous will destroy them.*
PROVERBS 11:3

MYKOLA LELIOVSKYI: GRACE BIBLE SEMINARY | UKRAINE

The Scriptures often remind us that the inward condition of our hearts determines our external behavior. The Hebrew words translated here as "integrity" and "upright" are the most common Old Testament terms to express the concepts of justice and honesty. The former is a description of a comprehensive dedication to the Lord in all areas of life. The latter literally speaks of a smooth and straight surface in contrast to something twisted or crooked. Figuratively, it describes God's ethical standard of fairness, according to which kings, judges, and priests were measured in the Hebrew Bible.

Such character qualities guide their possessors. In Hebrew, the term for "guide" is also used to describe how a shepherd carefully directs his sheep through a dangerous passage littered with dangers. It is also used in the Psalms to describe God's sovereign protection of those who fear Him. Parents and mentors may guide the lives of young men and women for a time, but sooner or later their life choices become their own responsibilities. At that point, they will be guided either by integrity or crookedness.

Proverbs repeatedly teaches us that while fools believe their foolishness puts them in an advantageous position in life, it is precisely their foolish and wicked behavior that will be their downfall. But integrity, godliness, and wisdom—these are truly of great worth. They guide a person in the straight and narrow path. O Lord, help us to be men and women of principle, and grant us hearts of integrity that will protect us from losing our way!

Behold and Become

*But we all, with unveiled face, beholding as in a mirror the
glory of the Lord, are being transformed into the same image
from glory to glory, just as from the Lord, the Spirit.*

2 CORINTHIANS 3:18

D. G.: ASIA (NAME WITHHELD FOR SECURITY)

In the New Covenant, Christians can behold the glory of our Lord
as in a mirror. Under the Old Covenant, the glory of the Lord was
revealed yet veiled. Indeed, Moses had to keep a veil on his face for the
people could not look on the fading glory (2 Cor. 3:7, 13).

A natural man cannot understand the gospel, as it is veiled to the
perishing (2 Cor. 4:3). But if a person turns to the Lord, the veil is
removed and he can behold the glory of the Lord. But where can we
see the glory of the Lord? Creation declares the glory of the Lord, but
more explicitly the glory of the Lord is seen in Scripture.

An encounter with God will not leave us unchanged. As we behold
the glory of the Lord, we will be transformed into His image. That
transformation from "glory to glory" is not instantaneous, but rather
an ongoing process. God's purpose, then, in revealing His truth to
us is that we might be transformed to look like His Son (Rom. 8:29).
This was the goal of Paul's preaching (Col. 1:28), and thus should be
the goal of our lives.

"How can I change?" is an often-asked question among believers.
We must remember that it is the Spirit who helps bring about change
and transformation. We cannot change ourselves, but by the help of
the Spirit and by beholding the glory of the Lord in the Scriptures, we
are transformed into His image. Are you changing day by day to look
more like Christ?

Justifying Ourselves

I do not nullify the grace of God, for if righteousness comes
through the Law, then Christ died needlessly.
GALATIANS 2:21

DMITRY C.: RUSSIA (FULL NAME WITHHELD FOR SECURITY)

Have you tried to justify yourself? We can do this to ourselves, one another, our bosses, our children—even God. The desire to justify self is ingrained in the very nature of sinners, and virtually every religion banks on an effort to keep certain rules to achieve justification. Unfortunately, even those who have believed in Christ can at times live out their sanctification in works-righteousness behavior.

In Galatians 2:21, God protects us from horrific self-deception. He wants to put an end to our imagining that we can be justified by the Law (instead of Christ), even in the smallest measure and even if we try hard. He wants to seal off every passageway that leads us astray into false hope because He desires to keep us on the one true path. Can it be stated any clearer than "if righteousness comes through the Law, then Christ died needlessly"?

Unfortunately, even though I affirm this truth, I am regularly tempted to feel more justified because of my performance. When I've sinned, instead of repenting and believing in the righteousness of Christ, I catch myself simply trying to do something biblical in order to feel better. I attempt to justify myself and do not notice how that devalues Christ.

When you sin or when you see yourself as more obedient than others, turn to the text of Galatians 2:21 for course correction. Direct others to do the same. Let us beware of devaluing the sacrifice of Christ and attributing too much importance to ourselves.

Justification before God is too difficult a matter to be accomplished by us. Christ alone is our righteousness.

Hearts Corrupted and Hearts Cleansed

For out of the heart come evil thoughts, murders, adulteries, fornications, thefts, false witness, slanders.
MATTHEW 15:19

GENIS M.: ALBANIA (FULL NAME WITHHELD FOR SECURITY)

These words from the lips of Jesus are wise and penetrating. He exposes false teaching while supplying the exact truth necessary for the moment. The religious leaders taught that a person was unacceptable to God if he did not keep Jewish traditions. Jesus taught, however, that a person is unacceptable to God due to the corruption of his own heart. It is a profound indictment of all humanity. It is not what goes into man but rather what comes out of him that defiles him. We are not guilty before God because we fail to follow certain religious rituals; instead, we are guilty before God because our hearts are corrupt, the proof of which is seen in what comes out of them.

Jesus' point is that we do not need external rituals to be clean. We need new hearts. This is exactly what was promised by God in Ezekiel 36:26—"I will give you a new heart." And it is exactly what Jesus accomplishes for us by His death on the cross. For the believer, there is a new birth, a new heart, and a complete cleansing by Jesus' blood (1 John 1:7; 2 Cor. 5:17).

We continue to struggle this side of heaven because sin remains in our flesh. But sin no longer reigns in our hearts. We are no longer enslaved to evil thoughts, anger, lust, lies, envy, or gossip. So let us take full advantage of this wonderful gift and cultivate in our hearts an abundance of good treasure and good fruit (Luke 6:45).

The Curse of the Cross

*Christ redeemed us from the curse of the Law, having become
a curse for us—for it is written, "Cursed is everyone who
hangs on a tree"—in order that in Christ Jesus the blessing of
Abraham might come to the Gentiles, so that we would receive
the promise of the Spirit through faith.*

GALATIANS 3:13–14

LANCE ROBERTS: CZECH BIBLE INSTITUTE | CZECH REPUBLIC

The cross is an-oft seen symbol in our society. People adorn themselves with cross necklaces and earrings, some put it on their walls, some tattoo it on their bodies, and some put it on their graves. But why? For different reasons, of course, but the real significance of the cross and the importance of its meaning for Christians is found in these verses.

In the Old Testament, being hung on a tree was reserved for executed criminals who violated the law of God. It was a public proclamation that the lawbreaker was indeed cursed and bore his punishment. Jesus bore this public humiliation and curse on the cross for all who believe.

If you were to live a thousand years and only commit one sin, you are a lawbreaker, condemned, cursed, and under the wrath of God. And as one under the curse of the Law, you cannot redeem yourself from the curse that is upon you. You could no more reach the moon by balloon than you can redeem yourself from the marketplace of cursed sinners.

But Jesus came to redeem sinners out of the slave market of the accursed by becoming a curse for us. He died as our substitute by bearing our sin, guilt, judgment, and shame. He received the stroke of God's judgment on your behalf. He died on the cross not because He was accursed, but because you are. He died so you could receive the blessings and the promise of the Spirit. So every time you see a cross, remember that it was there that Christ redeemed you from the curse of the Law, and set you free.

Fighting Only with God's Resources

For the weapons of our warfare are not of the flesh, but divinely powerful for the destruction of fortresses. We are destroying speculations and every lofty thing raised up against the knowledge of God, and we are taking every thought captive to the obedience of Christ.

2 CORINTHIANS 10:4–5

RAFAEL SALAZAR: EVANGELICAL MINISTRIES OF THE AMERICAS | HONDURAS

John Calvin said that the gospel is a fire that ignites Satan's wrath, so every time he sees the gospel advancing he prepares to fight. We can be certain of this much: Christians *are* in a spiritual battle.

Second Corinthians is largely a defense of Paul's apostolic credentials against false apostles who had arrived at Corinth. The false apostles diabolically strategized to maliciously attack Paul in order to weaken his influence and trustworthiness as a representative of Christ. They spread the rumor that Paul's humility was a sign of his weakness. They suggested that a "true apostle" should stand out with a religious flair and attractive style, as an intellectual and moral grandstander. This was spiritual warfare, and the health of the church was at stake.

Paul responded not by defending his own ability, intellect, or eloquence; instead, he pointed to the divine resources that alone are effective in such a battle. He knew that external displays of "power" meant nothing, but that the truth of God's word was mighty to overthrow the ideological fortresses established by Satan.

In Honduras, similar attacks are made against the true church and its representatives, defaming and ridiculing any ministry that does not boast of spiritual greatness or intellectual superiority. In fact, Christians everywhere are assaulted on these spiritual fronts, but our confidence must remain in the truth, power, and effectiveness of God's word. Though it may not be popular and it might even appear impractical at times, the Bible is always the winning path. Make sure that you are fighting the fight of faith with the right weapons, with the resources given to us in God's word.

From Our Suffering to His Glory

[Jesus] said to him, "Go, wash in the pool of Siloam"
(which is translated, Sent). So he went and washed, and
came back seeing.
JOHN 9:7

AMOS MAPIRA: CENTRAL AFRICAN PREACHING ACADEMY | MALAWI

In life, suffering is real and inevitable. We have all suffered. But do we realize that God works in our suffering to manifest His glory? God may even use our suffering to drive us to believe that Jesus is the Christ and thus have eternal life.

In this passage, a blind man suffered greatly. Unlike many who are spiritually blind, this man knew his great need. Similarly, if we are to experience God's glorious provision while suffering, we too need to recognize our need.

The blind man also listened to Jesus' commands. Many suffer and don't know what God wants for them, because they have never heard the gospel. Yet others hear the word of God, and through it, they know what God wants for them in their suffering. Like the blind man, they hear and realize that God may be providing a way *out* or often *through* their painful situation.

Most important of all, the blind man obeyed Jesus' command. In the same way, when we experience trials and suffering, we need to obey God's command and adhere to His will. The blind man did not doubt or ask Jesus questions, he just went and washed. Here is a good example for us to follow. You do not always need to understand everything before you can respond in obedience—you just need to obey.

You may be experiencing intense suffering at this moment—whether physical, emotional, or spiritual. It may press in on you greatly. But take the long view of your suffering and see that God can manifest His glory amid your pain.

Home with the Lord

We are of good courage, I say, and prefer rather to be absent
from the body and to be at home with the Lord.
2 CORINTHIANS 5:8

MARIO ALVAREZ RIVERO: WORD OF GRACE BIBLICAL SEMINARY | MEXICO

Fearful moments, such as the loss of a loved one or bad news from the doctor, often awaken us to the brevity of life and the reality of death. No one wants to experience death. Better to avoid it entirely by being caught up in the clouds with our Lord Jesus Christ (1 Thess. 4:17). The idea of our soul being temporarily naked, without its body, makes us shudder. Unfortunately, we often forget that God has been preparing for us a future glory in eternity, and that it is the Holy Spirit Himself who will lead us into the presence of God when we die.

Our text today speaks of the sense in which we are absent from the Lord while remaining in our earthly bodies. This is because we await that future glory in eternity. We live as strangers and foreigners in this world. We are not centered on the visible and temporary things around us; instead, we walk by faith. We anticipate the invisible and eternal things, knowing that it is far better to be at home with the Lord, even though this implies physical death!

As believers, we need not fear death, for both life and death are protected and guided by Christ's love. We trust in that glorious future that awaits us on the other side, knowing that it is truly "home with the Lord" (2 Cor. 5:8). Knowing that we will soon enjoy the presence of our Lord in eternity, we ought to live even now in such a way that is pleasing to Him.

Bearing Burdens

*Bear one another's burdens, and thereby fulfill
the law of Christ.*
GALATIANS 6:2

DMITRY C.: RUSSIA (FULL NAME WITHHELD FOR SECURITY)

Helping someone who has fallen into sin is not any easy task. When we help an erring Christian return to the path of truth, we take on the burden of caring for them in the spirit of humility (Gal. 6:1). We don't just saddle ourselves with something that is superfluous; we do something that especially pleases Christ.

Practically, this may turn out to be a complex undertaking that we could compare to setting a broken leg. Most likely, the injured party would not trust us to treat them right away. He might be afraid of pain or complications that go along with the healing process. It's possible that he might behave badly or be hostile. We need to abundantly exhibit the fruit of the Spirit (Gal. 5:22–23) in order to not only begin to help, but see the whole matter through to the end. Otherwise, we would be tempted to move on as soon as possible from the difficulty (there's a reason it's called a burden!).

What if we don't want to burden ourselves with the problems of people in our church? If that's true, we need to honestly ask ourselves one uncomfortable question and answer it honestly—what if Christ had not lifted your burden of sin and carried it on Himself? What if He had simply said, "That's not my problem. After all, that fellow has only himself to blame!"? What would have happened if He had not come down, taken up your case, and straightened your path? You would have perished under sin's weight. Remember that you could fall into sin at any moment—then you would need help from someone else.

Protecting Our Homes

For speaking out arrogant words of vanity they entice by fleshly desires, by sensuality, those who barely escape from the ones who live in error.

2 PETER 2:18

SANTIAGO ARMEL: INSTITUTO DE EXPOSITORES | USA

A father is a shepherd of his own home. He has been called to guide and nurture in love a small and precious flock. As part of his calling, he cannot ignore the great threat posited by fierce wolves who are eager to devour his little sheep. His task is to defend his family from the imminent threat.

Peter warns his audience that false teachers are stalking their flocks, hoping to captivate the young believer with their arrogant yet attractive words. They use boisterous language, flattery, and big promises to lure the weak into their traps. Today, your children may be the target of the treacherous system of this world. Boys and girls who are on their way to know Jesus Christ, or young converts in the faith are some of Satan's favorite victims.

Parents must be alert and drive away from their homes any influence that stinks of false teaching. Television, the internet, a tablet, or a close family member may be the open door into your home. These evil influences will not always knock at your door as obvious bearers of false teaching. The wisdom of this world and the excessive desire to satisfy lusts for fame, wealth, and power are threatening to enter your Christian home every day.

Parents should exercise discernment and diligently filter out the enemy's influence, which is designed to hinder the spiritual growth of our little disciples. Ask God for discernment and wisdom to recognize the inappropriate influences that are knocking at the door of your home. Be in tune with your family's spiritual heartbeat and take time to nurture everyone in your care through prayer and meditation on the word of God.

One Flock with One Shepherd

I have other sheep, which are not of this fold; I must bring them also, and they will hear My voice; and they will become one flock with one shepherd.

JOHN 10:16

ROBBIE CASAS: THE EXPOSITOR'S ACADEMY | PHILIPPINES

After declaring "I am the good shepherd" (the fourth of Christ's seven "I am" statements in John's gospel—statements that describe the fullness of His character as the God of redemption), Jesus announces to the Jews that He has "other sheep, which are not of this fold." This reference to "other sheep" speaks of the Gentile elect who are not of the Jewish fold.

Whenever I come across verses like this, which make reference to the salvation of the Gentiles, I cannot help but be profoundly moved and humbled by God's graciousness to reach us non-Jews who "were at that time separate from Christ, excluded from the commonwealth of Israel, and strangers to the covenants of promise, having no hope and without God in the world" (Eph. 2:12). How can I not live my life for the glory and pleasure of God? Jesus, the good shepherd, was sent to be *my* shepherd, too!

It is motivating to consider that God has redeemed people from every tribe, tongue, and nation to become one flock in Christ's excellent care. Whenever you are tempted to relax your commitment to Christ, ponder deeply the sweet and lavish grace of God to bring you, who were once far from Him, into His fold. A sheep without a shepherd is doomed to destruction, but God has given us a good shepherd in Christ Jesus. Remember this glorious privilege and press on with renewed devotion to follow Him.

Your Sins Are Forgiven

*And Jesus knowing their thoughts said, "Why are you thinking
evil in your hearts? Which is easier, to say, 'Your sins are
forgiven,' or to say, 'Get up, and walk'?"*
MATTHEW 9:4–5

MISKO HORVATEK: THEOLOGICAL BIBLICAL ACADEMY | CROATIA

Several men brought a poor paralytic man to Jesus so that He would
heal him. This man was not only physically incapacitated, but also
spiritually dead, which was his paramount problem. We admire the
men for their compassion on their friend. Obviously, they wanted him
to be made well, so that he would not depend on others to carry him
around, and that he would be able to take care of himself and even
care for other people's needs. However, one thing his friends did not
know was his greatest need—forgiveness of his sins.

Forgiveness of sin is the number one need of every person. Regrettably, countless professing Christians do not know their need or the
real reason why Jesus came to this earth. His coming was not to heal
bodies, but save souls. Estimates are that 81 percent of the population
in Croatia claims to be Roman Catholic. They will sadly hear the
same expression as these men but from the wrong person—from their
priests, and not from the Lord. This is nothing new under the heavens. When scribes (predecessors of Roman Catholic priests) heard Jesus say, "Your sins are forgiven, get up and walk," they were so upset,
that they accused the Lord of blasphemy. The Lord had to confront
and correct their error.

Pray with us that the countless deluded Croats would believe that
only the Lord Jesus has the authority to say, "Your sins are forgiven."
And may all of us endeavor to confront and correct false teaching,
which keeps people from experiencing the great joy of having their
sins forgiven.

Albania

SCHOOL NAME CLASSIFIED

The gospel first came to Albania (New Testament Illyricum) through Paul's missionary efforts (Rom. 15:19). After decades of Catholic and then Islamic domination, in the 1940s communist dictator Enver Hoxha declared the nation atheistic, brutally wiping out all religion. When the regime collapsed in 1991, religious freedom returned and Islam took back its historic roots in the country. In a twist of irony, today TMAI's member school is training pastors in the former home of the dictator who once persecuted Christians.

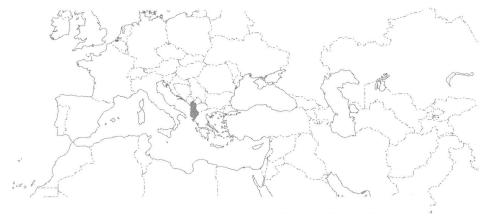

TODAY, PRAY FOR

The church in Albania, as it is made up of nearly all first-generation believers.

More church leaders to be trained so that the church would be rooted and grounded on God's word.

The gospel to pierce through the deception and slavery of cultural and religious Islam.

Love One Another

*A new commandment I give to you, that you love one another,
even as I have loved you, that you also love one another. By
this all men will know that you are My disciples, if you have
love for one another.*

JOHN 13:34–35

ALEKSEY KOLOMIYTSEV: WORD OF GRACE BIBLE INSTITUTE | USA

Of Christ's many attributes that made deep impressions on unbelievers, Jesus highlights perhaps the greatest one in this passage. Neither theological knowledge, nor religious activity, nor acts of
sacrificial giving reveal true Christianity to the same extent as when
believers love one another with the love of Jesus Christ. As He was
training His disciples, Jesus presented love as the most reliable sign of
the presence of true faith.

There is a serious reason for this. Christians can truly love only
when they do it with the love of Jesus Christ, when they are truly
saved by Him, know Him, and are filled with Him. People express
love in diverse ways. Man's love—regardless of how it's shown—is
radically different from the love of God. God's love arises from the
loving heart of the Father, and does not depend upon external factors
and conditions. It utterly stems from the goodwill and kind disposition of a loving heart.

Only this type of love is capable of overcoming evil, which fills
the world surrounding it. Only this type of love can bring light and
warmth amid darkness and the cold of humanity oppressed by sin.
Only this type of love can overlook the faults of others, patiently bearing in oneself their burdens, and helping others to overcome them.

The heart capable of generating such love must be extremely strong
and perfectly independent of someone or something. This is why it
is impossible to learn such love. People are incapable of practicing
it. Such love can only fill our hearts when we have received it from
Christ. Friend, do you have this love for Christ and His people?

Light in the Darkness

For so the Lord has commanded us, "I HAVE PLACED YOU AS
A LIGHT FOR THE GENTILES, THAT YOU MAY BRING SALVATION TO
THE END OF THE EARTH."
ACTS 13:47

MIGUEL ÁNGEL PRADO: BEREA SEMINARY | SPAIN

Often the people with whom I share the gospel reject its message, and for different reasons. The rejection comes in various ways: indifference, skeptical arguments, confrontation, and sometimes even verbal and physical abuse. These reactions come from both believers and unbelievers.

For Christians, such times test our faithfulness and motivations. How do you respond in those situations? Do you respond with personal pride or non-biblical arguments? Do you change the message in order not to offend someone?

In this passage, we find a good example of how Paul and Barnabas reacted when they faced rejection. Jews, filled with jealousy, were blaspheming God and contradicting Paul. But what was Paul and Barnabas's reaction? They were faithful to God's commandment. Paul chose to be faithful to his Master by being faithful to His word. They fulfilled the task they were given. They relied on the power of the word of God. Scripture was their guide.

In the same way, we must obey God before men. The Lord is our Master and we are accountable to Him. This must never change, even in the face of opposition. God's word, through His Spirit, brought light to our darkened hearts. We, in turn, are to let that light shine in the midst of this generation (Matt. 5:14–16). Our message must be Paul and Barnabas' message—salvation in Christ as revealed in Scripture.

As believers, we must have Christ's mind and daily depend on God's wisdom. We must light up this world through a faithful witness to God's word, for His glory.

Truth about Love

In this is love, not that we loved God, but that He loved us and sent His Son to be the propitiation for our sins.
1 JOHN 4:10

Tomasz Krazek: European Bible Training Center | Germany

Essentially everywhere we look, love is a response to a perceived worthiness of its object. Thus, we are tempted to think that God loves us because of something valuable in us, or simply in response to our love toward Him. Some even go so far as to say that the cross is actually the revealing of our value.

However, all John has to say about our part in the love relationship with God is that we did not love God. Furthermore, we were sinners in need of propitiation—guilty, rebellious, undeserving. There was nothing attractive about us that generated God's love toward us. Love was God's initiative. And the ultimate, most wonderful, awe-inspiring expression of this love was the giving away of His only-begotten Son to die in place of sinners.

These truths, understood and embraced, leave no room for pride nor for despair. There is no room for pride because the love of God, expressed in the sacrificing of His Son, points not to the magnitude of our worth but to the magnitude of our sin. There is no room for despair because neither our failures nor our doubts, nor any other un-loveliness in us, can destroy God's love toward a believer. The love of God is not found in our loveliness. Its measure and certainty are not found in our feelings. It is found in the historic event, in which "He made Him who knew no sin to be sin on our behalf, so that we might become the righteousness of God in Him" (2 Cor. 5:21).

Apply this truth to your heart—may God's love humble you and assure you this day.

The Spreading Word

*The word of God kept on spreading; and the number of the
disciples continued to increase greatly in Jerusalem, and a
great many of the priests were becoming obedient to the faith.*

ACTS 6:7

D. G.: ASIA (NAME WITHHELD FOR SECURITY)

The church-growth movement has done more harm than good.
In many mega-churches, pastors become celebrities and worship
becomes idolatrous.

Believers desire to have their churches grow, but before thinking of
implementing man-made ideas, we should remember that it is God
who causes the growth (1 Cor. 3:6–7). Christ promised that He will
build His church, and the growth is not in question (Matt. 16:18).

In Acts we learn God's strategy for church growth—it is by the
proclamation of God's word. As the apostles devoted themselves to
prayer and preaching, the word of God kept on spreading. A pastor's
primary responsibility is to preach the word (2 Tim. 4:2).

As the word of God spread, the number of disciples continued to
increase. Yet, notice that it is not only the apostles who spread the
gospel; fellow believers started spreading the gospel. We are all to
make disciples who will then make more disciples.

When the word of God spreads, it converts all sorts of people.
Luke mentions that a great many priests were becoming obedient
to faith (Acts 6:7)—those who recently were hostile to Christ (John
19:6). This hit me hard, and I was personally humbled, when God
saved my colleague. I thought she would never accept Jesus as Lord,
as she used to rebuke me at work when the gospel was shared.

Throughout church history it is clear that the spreading of the
word brings growth in the church. Remember that God rewards us
according to our faithfulness (Matt. 25:23), not according to the size
of our church or number of converts. Remain faithful in spreading
the word!

The Race of Faith

Therefore, since we have so great a cloud of witnesses surrounding us, let us also lay aside every encumbrance and the sin which so easily entangles us, and let us run with endurance the race that is set before us.

HEBREWS 12:1

GIANLUCA POLLUTRI: ITALIAN THEOLOGICAL ACADEMY | ITALY

Hebrews 11 details a list of saints, such as Abraham, Moses, and Noah, who reached the finish line of faith. These provide for us a great legacy of faithfulness to follow. In our text today, the author of Hebrews explains that these examples surround us and motivate us to imitate their lives of faith. To live a victorious life in Christ is possible, and we are not the first ones to run in such an honorable race. They stand as trophies of God's grace and proof that God can and does preserve His own to the very end.

To win this race we are required to obey three direct commandments: (i) lay aside every encumbrance; (ii) lay aside sin; and (iii) persevere to the end.

Laying aside every encumbrance requires discernment to recognize what is essential to the race and what just weighs us down. The same spiritual discernment is required when it comes to laying aside sin. Only by learning God's word are we made aware of the subtleties of sin. Though the various impediments and sinful patterns may differ slightly among believers, we can still learn from those who have preceded us as both positive and negative examples—for they all struggled with similar trials and temptations to those that we experience.

So let us put on our marathon attire and put off every non-essential or sin, and let's run the race God has set before us with endurance. Never forget that God has granted us victory in Christ. Let us learn from the saints who have gone before us and persevere in this race to the end.

From Darkness to Christ

For He rescued us from the domain of darkness, and
transferred us to the kingdom of His beloved Son.
COLOSSIANS 1:13

ALFRED GOLIATH: CENTRAL AFRICAN PREACHING ACADEMY | MALAWI

How dark the world is! How dark many lives are! Sin and its consequences—poverty, disease, and war—are all around us. Many are fleeing their homes to escape fighting and famine. Others might have a measure of prosperity but lack true peace in their hearts. There are so many who need rescuing.

In Colossians 1:13, the apostle Paul reminds us that our heavenly Father has already worked out His plan of redemption. He sent Jesus to rescue us from this terrible dominion of darkness! We were living in sin and despair, following the course of this world, but through the death of His own beloved Son, God delivered us from sin and gave us spiritual life.

There are only two realms of humanity in Scripture: the domain of darkness and the kingdom of Christ Jesus. These two realms have different masters. The first is characterized and ruled by darkness. The second is characterized and ruled by the King of Light, Jesus. For those of us who have been rescued from the domain of darkness, we now have a new master and a good king. This verse reminds us that Jesus both *rescues* and *reigns*.

Dear brother or sister in Christ, you have been rescued and now belong to a new kingdom. Satan no longer has dominion over you. Do not let sin rule over you! You have the power in Christ, by His Spirit, to overcome temptation and to live victoriously even amid the darkness all around (Heb. 2:14–15). Praise be to God!

Scripture: God's Multi-Tool

All Scripture is inspired by God and profitable for teaching, for reproof, for correction, for training in righteousness.
2 TIMOTHY 3:16

SANTIAGO FUENTES HERNANDEZ: WORD OF GRACE BIBLICAL SEMINARY | MEXICO

The Bible is God's inspired book. He breathed it out and His servants wrote it down. Because it comes from God, it is profitable for teaching and imparts the necessary knowledge to live a godly life. It reproves by confronting sin, dragging it out from its hiding place, so that we can repent of it. The Bible also corrects. To correct means to straighten out, like putting a bone back in its place. The Bible likewise sets us straight so that the body of Christ can function properly. Lastly, the inspired word of God is profitable for training in righteousness. It is God's tool to produce in us desires, attitudes, and actions that are fitting for children of God.

Recently, someone gave me a Swiss Army Knife, something I had seen used by survival experts on television. I was excited to discover all the tools in it, and imagined myself using it in various survival situations. But how much more excited should we be about Scripture, seeking to discover all the useful truths that God has provided for our lives? The Bible does not just help us survive, it enables us to live an abundant life of victory even in enemy territory!

Though I've imagined myself in various survival situations, I've only in fact used my knife twice, both times at home. I even forgot it during my last camping trip. I can, it turns out, live without it; but we cannot live without God's word. It is vital for our daily lives and our ultimate good. Let's learn to use it.

March 8

Do You Love Me?

So when they had finished breakfast, Jesus said to Simon Peter, "Simon, son of John, do you love Me more than these?" He said to Him, "Yes, Lord; You know that I love you." He said to him, "Tend my lambs."

JOHN 21:15

ALEKSEY KOLOMIYTSEV: WORD OF GRACE BIBLE INSTITUTE | USA

What is the most significant attribute a Christian should possess for ministry? Effective service requires much: giftedness, humility, knowledge of the Lord, willingness to serve, and dedication. Each of those qualities helps shape the overall fruitfulness of the Christian in ministry. But there is one attribute that exceeds them all—love for Jesus Christ.

After trying to take matters into his own hands in the Garden of Gethsemane, and denying the Lord at the house of Caiaphas, Peter might rightly expect a difficult conversation with His Master. But instead of reproaches, Jesus Christ focused on one issue with His most zealous apostle—Peter's love for Him. Pointing at a nearby boat and nets, Jesus asked Peter three times: "Do you love Me more than all these?" After a positive answer, Jesus repeated His main assignment for Peter every time: "Feed My sheep."

To a large extent, our love determines our personality, our character, and our activities. It often determines the focus of thoughts, feelings, desires, and actions. It is a source of strength to overcome difficulties, a generator of inspiration and creativity, and a ray of hope and encouragement. This is why the main condition qualifying a Christian for ministry is his love for Jesus Christ.

Jesus is the perfect embodiment of love. If you're a Christian, you responded to His love in faith when He saved you. Look to Him daily to be the source and example of your love for the church and the world in need around you.

Freedom of Redemption

*In Him we have redemption through His blood, the forgiveness
of our trespasses, according to the riches of His grace which
He lavished on us.*

EPHESIANS 1:7–8A

JONATAN RECAMÁN: BEREA SEMINARY | SPAIN

Few things are more heartbreaking for a believer than seeing people fall for the fraud of false religion. This is the reality for disciples of Jesus in countries where many people profess Christianity as their religion. A good example of this is the celebration of Holy Week in Spain. For seven days, the devotion for false religion is on display in every street in every city. Sadly it's one "holy" week, and fifty-one unholy weeks.

The problem is ignorance of the gospel. At the beginning of his letter to the Ephesians, Paul is displaying the results of the gospel, the spiritual blessings we have in Jesus. One of these blessings is redemption, which means that, by the grace of God, we are made free from the consequences of our sin against God. Instead of suffering the eternal punishment we deserve, Christ suffered it for us, and we receive His righteousness and an eternity with the Father that only Jesus deserves (2 Cor. 5:21).

In Paul's times, a slave couldn't earn his own freedom; someone else had to pay a ransom. In the same way, we can't earn our freedom from sin. False religion seeks its own redemption. In Spain, the ransom is Holy Week. But the gospel shows that God is the One seeking the redemption of sinners because He paid the ransom. Through the substitutionary death of Jesus, He redeemed us from our trespasses.

So, the death of Jesus is not something to be remembered one week per year; it's something to be proclaimed every day and celebrated weekly on the Lord's Day. Jesus is not a moral reference; He is a mighty Redeemer.

We need to preach Jesus. We need to expose the fraud of false religion, and proclaim the freedom of redemption.

Sending Beautiful Feet

*For "*Whoever will call on the name of the Lord will be saved.*" How then will they call on Him in whom they have not believed? How will they believe in Him whom they have not heard? And how will they hear without a preacher? How will they preach unless they are sent? Just as it is written, "*How beautiful are the feet of those who bring good news of good things!*"*

ROMANS 10:13–15

MARCUS DENNY: CZECH BIBLE INSTITUTE | CZECH REPUBLIC

Rebellion is man's natural habitat. But when, like Balaam, a sinner sees the angel of death standing in his way, when he sees God's sword against his throat and God's wrath above his head, he will not put out his hand to God and say, "Let's make a deal." He will bow in fear and trembling and *call upon the name of the Lord*. Submission to Christ as Lord is not merely essential to conversion, it is the *essence* of it.

But how can men call upon and submit to the Lord if they know nothing of Him? Who will go? And just as importantly, who will send? The church must always be holding up these questions to her people and must always remember that *sending* means sacrifice.

Nothing saddens me more than seeing churches send out those who will least likely be missed and those who are easiest to replace. Antioch sent out Paul and Barnabas. They sacrificed their right arm because of the needs of a perishing world. Few things prove the lordship of Christ over a local church more than the willingness to sacrifice to Him our most precious servants. These individuals have the beautiful feet that Paul speaks of. Those ministers and servants that are most beautiful to us will be most beautiful to the lost and waiting world. And this sacrifice is most beautiful to our God, who sent His most precious Servant to us.

Pray that the Lord will place in your heart, home, and congregation a greater burden for the lost and perishing. And pray that you would take greater part in either sending or going.

Wolves in Disguise

Beware of the false prophets, who come to you in sheep's clothing, but inwardly are ravenous wolves.

MATTHEW 7:15

IGOR BODUN: GRACE BIBLE SEMINARY | UKRAINE

The people of God in every age must be on guard against imposters. Jesus warns that imposters disguise themselves in order to be heard, to gain trust, to find entrance into the sheepfold. They look like the *shepherd* but they are more like the *wolf*. Sheep's clothing refers to the woolen outer garment that would identify a shepherd. The frightening picture that Jesus paints is of a wolf who puts on this clothing.

False teachers may appear to be genuine, but they are not. They are not in the church to feed and protect the sheep, but to *devour* them. They come to satisfy their own selfish appetites. Their inward motives are in conflict with their outward appearances. For this reason, Jesus explains that we must judge not by mere appearances—for appearances can be deceiving—but with righteous judgment (John 7:24).

We must be alert for false teaching. Beware! The savage wolves may penetrate your church not only through its doors but also through the Internet, TV, and books. Look past appearances and judge the fruits. The appetite of a wolf cannot be hidden. Materialism and greed are common characteristics of wolves (2 Pet. 2:3). Also, their teaching will not accord with sound doctrine. Paul exhorts us to "examine everything *carefully*; hold fast to that which is good" (1 Thess. 5:21).

A true shepherd will be like Christ. He will be temperate and free from the love of money (1 Tim. 3:2–3). He will not teach of his own authority but will be faithful to the word of God.

Pleasing Men or Pleasing Christ?

For am I now seeking the favor of men, or of God? Or am I
striving to please men? If I were still trying to please men, I
would not be a bond-servant of Christ.

GALATIANS 1:10

ANDREY GORBAN: WORD OF GRACE BIBLE INSTITUTE | USA

What a shame it is when a person who belongs to Christ chases after the fleeting praise and approval of men! In this passage, the apostle Paul points to the absurdity of this pursuit, for it will surely prove fruitless. Note this important truth from the text: it will always be one or the other, the approval of man or of God, pleasing man or serving Christ; there is no middle ground.

What better person to bring our attention to this reality than the apostle Paul himself. He was once the ultimate man-pleaser—a Pharisee. However, after his encounter with the risen Christ, he was completely changed. Our human instinct is to seek to be loved and accepted by others, but as followers of Christ that desire changes to seek to honor and glorify Him in everything. The born-again person becomes completely new, and can in turn fully understand and agree with that which the apostle Paul writes regarding the former sins and lusts of the believer in 1 Corinthians 6:11, "Such were some of you; but you were washed, but you were sanctified, but you were justified in the name of the Lord Jesus Christ and in the Spirit of our God." Having been washed, sanctified, and justified, how can we then return to seeking the approval of men? How can we be set on pleasing men, rather than serving Christ?

May our hearts be fixed on honoring Christ, exalting His name, and serving only Him. As believers, our affections are to be for Christ, and our ultimate joy is found in a deeper relationship with Him.

Nothing Is Impossible

For nothing will be impossible with God.
LUKE 1:37

OLEG KALYN: GRACE BIBLE SEMINARY | UKRAINE

God can do whatever He wills. This concept is clearly presented in Scripture, and it serves as a great encouragement for His people. In Genesis 17:1, He said, "I am God Almighty." He revealed Himself to Abraham in this way just to prove to him that nothing can stop His plans.

In the same way, God sent the angel Gabriel to Mary to announce that He was about to accomplish a wonderful thing—that she, being a virgin, would give birth to the promised Messiah. When she was puzzled by how this could be, the angel from the Lord reminded her of this vital lesson: that nothing is impossible with God.

The tasks that God gave to His people, recorded in Scripture, reveal His greatness and power. They were always beyond human capacity, since God wanted to demonstrate His strength to His people and to the world around them, "that all the peoples of the earth may know that the hand of the LORD is mighty, so that you may fear the LORD your God forever" (Josh. 4:24). His mighty deeds were monumental witnesses of His unique power, for surely He can do whatever He wills, and nothing can stop His plan.

Let us remember this truth in our own lives. Often we are discouraged because everything He calls us to do looks impossible for us. Even the smallest thing in our ministry cannot be done by our own strength and effort; we are totally dependent on Him. Those who understand this dependency are used by Him to achieve the impossible by His power and strength—for nothing is impossible with God!

How May I Help You?

Now we pray to God that you do no wrong; not that we
ourselves may appear approved, but that you may do what is
right, even though we may appear unapproved.

2 CORINTHIANS 13:7

MELVIN ROMERO: EVANGELICAL MINISTRIES OF THE AMERICAS | HONDURAS

Paul's pastoral heart is consumed by the spiritual life of his sheep. In his ministry, there existed nothing more important. In this verse, Paul prays to God for the obedience and holiness of the Corinthians: "Now we pray to God that you do no wrong." In addition, Paul tells them the reason for which he makes this request: "Not that we ourselves may appear approved, but that you may do what is right, even though we may appear unapproved." Paul is not interested in receiving the approval of his critics; his interest is in the well-being of God's flock.

We find this attitude throughout Paul's letters. In Philippians 4, he expresses his joy and gratitude for the care and help that their church had sent, but his joy was not on account of his personal gain. Rather, he rejoiced because such generosity benefitted the Philippians themselves as they did what was pleasing to the Lord.

The Lord Jesus said it this way: "Greater love has no one than this, that one lay down his life for his friends" (John 15:13). Few of us are ever put in a position to literally die for another, but we each have countless opportunities to move into the background and allow others to benefit before ourselves, more than ourselves, and instead of ourselves.

This is our calling as believers. We are to imitate Christ's humility with the same love that led Him to die on the cross. Brothers and sisters, the best way to demonstrate such love is to help others to be found faithful daily before God, even as Paul desired and prayed that the Corinthians "do what is right."

In Weakness Lies Our Strength

And He has said to me, "My grace is sufficient for you, for power is perfected in weakness." Most gladly, therefore, I will rather boast about my weaknesses, so that the power of Christ may dwell in me.

2 CORINTHIANS 12:9

RALPH KNOLL: EUROPEAN BIBLE TRAINING CENTER | GERMANY

Our society pretends to be strong. We want to do things in our own strength and we want to be trouble free all the time. We want to remove weakness and suffering from our dictionaries. But the Bible draws a different picture.

Long ago there was a group of people who spoke against the apostle Paul. They argued that he wasn't a strong person, that he wasn't one of the great speakers they knew, and that he was weak. Paul had to defend his apostleship and taught his opponents that he is a servant of Christ. He suffered in different ways in his ministry, and he even boasted about his weakness—because he knew that the power of Christ rested upon him in his weakness. He wrote that he is content in weakness, hardships, and persecution because he knew: When I am weak, then I am strong, because Christ's power dwells in me.

We are often influenced in our daily life and ministry by society. We can think that we are strong in ourselves and able to do all things. But this is a lie! We fully depend on Christ. We need His strength and His wisdom. His grace is sufficient for us! This is one of the most beautiful and joyful principles for daily ministry. It's not me nor my strength—it is Christ—and when I realize and accept the truth that I need Him and His grace every second of my life, then His power will be perfected in my weakness.

Do you believe God's grace is sufficient? Boast in your weakness and Christ's power.

Whom Shall I Fear?

Do not fear those who kill the body but are unable to kill the
soul; but rather fear Him who is able to destroy both soul
and body in hell.

MATTHEW 10:28

LANCE ROBERTS: CZECH BIBLE INSTITUTE | CZECH REPUBLIC

When Jesus sent out His disciples in Matthew 10, He warned them of dangers and trials to come—He sent them out as sheep among wolves, warning they would be scourged, answer to kings, experience betrayal, be hated, and even be persecuted. Such pressures naturally bring about fear, which can result in forsaking or compromising one's ministry.

So Jesus sought to instill in His disciples the fear that drives out all other fears. It is the fear of God—a holy awe and reverence of God that fears offending or displeasing Him. It is rooted in a confidence in God's character. When you fear God, you fear nothing else—not even death.

Though you may not fear physical persecution or scourging, you and I have feared much lesser things, have we not? Maybe you have struggled to share the gospel with someone, to preach a controversial passage, or to confront someone in sin? These fears are rooted in a fear of man. This is the contrast in Matthew 10:28—fearing man or fearing God in your ministry.

The fear of man slams the brakes on evangelism. It is the kill switch to authoritative preaching. It works as a poison that saps the strength and life out of God's minister.

To cultivate a healthy fear of God, we must meditate on His character and grow in our knowledge of Him. It results in being more concerned about being approved by God than accepted by man, and being more concerned with God's view of our ministry than man's.

Your ministry will stand or falter by how you deal with fear. Will you fear God or man?

The Commission of a Compassionate King

Then He said to His disciples, "The harvest is plentiful, but the workers are few. Therefore beseech the Lord of the harvest to send out workers into His harvest."
MATTHEW 9:37–38

GENIS M.: ALBANIA (FULL NAME WITHHELD FOR SECURITY)

Here we have a window into the heart of God's appointed King, the Good Shepherd Jesus Christ. Jesus' compassion motivates Him to invite and exhort His disciples to participate in the ministry of saving lost souls. "Seeing the people," Matthew writes of Jesus, "He felt compassion for them, because they were distressed and dispirited like sheep without a shepherd" (Matt. 9:36). His love moves Him to action.

We need a heart like that of the King in order to see that the harvest is indeed great and that the workers are few, a heart like that of the King who went so far as to give His own life as a ransom for many. Only a heart of Christlike compassion will join in this work. An indifferent heart, unfeeling and cold, will not give as Jesus gave, will not see as He saw, will not speak to people about their needs as Jesus did, nor will it invite others to join the harvest work as Jesus has done.

Help our weak hearts, O Lord! Incline them to Your words, even these words of compassion from Your beloved Son. Help us to behold the glories of our King, and to see His compassionate heart so that ours might be conformed to it. It is Your desire that workers be sent out into the harvest, please make it our desire, as well. Whether we go into the harvest or support others who go, may we reflect the compassionate heart of our King and Shepherd, Your Son Jesus Christ.

Our Lord's Neglected Example

For I gave you an example that you also should do as I did to you.
JOHN 13:15

MYKOLA LELIOVSKYI: GRACE BIBLE SEMINARY | UKRAINE

One of the most shared memes last year in the Russian-speaking world was a side-by-side comparison. On one side, the kneeling Christ washing the apostles' feet; on the other side, the lavishly dressed Patriarch of the Russian Orthodox Church extending a hand from his throne to a man kissing his ring. The caption says, "Can you feel the difference?"

While Evangelicals are rightly appalled by such perversions of the biblical picture, we should ask ourselves whether *we* are ready and willing to follow the example that our Lord set. While the Son of Man came to serve, most of us, in all sincerity, would prefer to be served. Although Jesus existed in the form of God, He did not regard equality with God a thing to be grasped, and humbled Himself by becoming obedient to the point of death. We, on the other hand, are naturally inclined to vehemently grasp at every accolade, taking every opportunity available to be exalted.

But Christians should never be thus characterized. Instead, we should reflect Christ's own sacrificial love as we fulfill His law by loving one another even as Christ loved us. As a young seminary graduate entering the ministry, this has been (and continues to be) a painful but wonderful lesson to learn.

We must not neglect our Savior's example. And we will be grateful in the end if we don't. For, as we humble ourselves to serve others for their benefit and for God's glory, we will find, in the end, that it is truly more blessed to give than to receive.

Christ Is the Head of the Church

He is also head of the body, the church.
COLOSSIANS 1:18

ASAEL HERNANDEZ LUGO: WORD OF GRACE BIBLICAL SEMINARY | MEXICO

There is only one Lord who is over everything. In the context of this passage, Paul describes Jesus Christ as Lord over creation (Col 1:15), over all spiritual power (Col. 1:16), and as the eternal God and Sustainer of the universe (Col. 1:17). But here Paul goes further and describes Jesus Christ as the only one who has the right and power to rule the church. Just as the body receives orders, coordination, and growth from the head, so the church is dependent on Christ. The church is a body that cannot die, for it has its origin, foundation, and permanent life in Jesus Christ, who rose again and will live forevermore.

There are many churches today that claim to be subject to Christ, but which in practice prefer to obey their traditions, emotions, or founding fathers. But Christ is the head of the church, and He rules and nourishes His church through His word. For this reason, every local church must have as its highest priority the study, practice, and proclamation of Christ's word (Col. 3:16), so that its development and practice may be according to Him, its only rightful head.

If the body does not obey its head's instruction, development and productivity are hindered. In the same way, a church that does not listen to Christ's word cannot fulfill His purposes. But when a church lives in subjection to the Scriptures, it reflects the rule of Christ and is effective in accomplishing all that He desires.

How do you arrange your daily routine? If you want to make sure that Christ reigns in your life, make sure that you listen to His word.

The Truth Is Our Approval

But we have renounced the things hidden because of shame,
not walking in craftiness or adulterating the word of God, but
by the manifestation of truth commending ourselves to every
man's conscience in the sight of God.

2 CORINTHIANS 4:2

MICHAEL LEISTER: EUROPEAN BIBLE TRAINING CENTER | GERMANY

Have you ever felt pressure because sowing the word of God did not produce a great, visible, or instantaneous harvest among the people you were ministering to? Welcome to Paul's world. In his second letter to the Corinthians, amid defending his apostleship, Paul also gives a personal letter filled with comfort and direction in difficult situations like preaching the word to hardened hearts.

Paul offers a most important principle that we must follow when we communicate the gospel: *speak not for the applause of people, but for the approval of God.* God is the One who has made us sufficient to be ministers of a new covenant (2 Cor. 3:6). It is a ministry of the Spirit and of righteousness (2 Cor. 3:8–9), and a ministry that is enduring (2 Cor. 3:11).

Ministering in Germany can be discouraging. Hearts are hardened by materialism and the *Zeitgeist* (spirit of the age). Yes, our country is the country of the Reformation, and yet it is also the country of the Enlightenment, higher criticism, and postmodernism. Therefore, there is a temptation to adapt the content or high standards of the gospel message to make it more acceptable.

Yet, what great comfort we find in that God has entrusted to us His truth. It is God who calls people to himself. It is God who lets light shine out of darkness (*ex nihilo*), and it is God who approves our reputation by applying the truth to the conscience of man. Let's fully trust in God by using His potent word of truth. Speak and communicate God's truth for *His* approval, not that of men.

The Substitute

But He was pierced through for our transgressions, He was crushed for our iniquities; the chastening for our well-being fell upon Him, and by His scourging we are healed.

ISAIAH 53:5

GIAMPAOLO NATALE: ITALIAN THEOLOGICAL ACADEMY | ITALY

This verse begins and ends with the language of substitution. Christ was wounded, bruised, and punished for our sin, so that we might live through Him. The theme of substitution is found throughout the Old Testament. In Exodus 12, for example, it is through substitution that the people of God escape the judgment that was coming to Egypt. They were to sacrifice an unblemished lamb and put its blood on the doorposts of their houses. Lambs were slain in the place of the Israelites' firstborn sons, and God therefore *passed over* them (Exod. 12:13).

But the Passover that the Israelites celebrated in Egypt was only a shadow of the reality yet to come. Christ Himself is the reality, as John the Baptist knew. When he saw Jesus, he cried out, "Behold, the Lamb of God who takes away the sin of the world!" (John 1:29). In 1 Corinthians 5:7 we learn that "Christ our Passover also has been sacrificed." And the apostle Peter speaks of the redemption that we have been given through "precious blood, as of a lamb unblemished and spotless, the blood of Christ" (1 Pet. 1:19).

Take time to delight in the doctrine of substitution. You possess the greatest and most important message in the world. Christ died as a substitute for sinners! Because of this, forgiveness and eternal life is opened wide to all who would believe. When was the last time you shared with someone about the remarkable substitute that God gave to this world? This is a truth that truly changes lives.

God Is Worthy of Genuine Worship

"For from the rising of the sun even to its setting, My name will be great among the nations, and in every place incense is going to be offered to My name, and a grain offering that is pure; for My name will be great among the nations," says the LORD *of hosts.*

MALACHI 1:11

VALERY B.: RUSSIA (FULL NAME WITHHELD FOR SECURITY)

In Malachi, God contends with His people who complain to Him. The people of God accuse the Creator of not loving them, neglecting them, and treating them unfairly. In actual fact, all of these complaints are nothing more than a poor attempt on the part of the people to find a justification for their sinful deeds. The priests deplorably neglected the service of the Lord—they were sacrificing lame and sick animals, and presenting defiled food upon His altar. At the same time, they had the gall to question God: "How have we despised Your name?" (Mal. 1:6). God knew, however, that the priests were not ashamed to utter blasphemy among themselves, saying, "The table of the LORD is to be despised" (Mal. 1:7).

Does the Lord deserve such worship from His people? Our verse answers this question. A time will come when the whole planet will reverently honor the name of God, the Creator of heaven and earth. Many nations who would never think to serve the Lord, or would do so carelessly or hypocritically, will see God's greatness.

We Christians, representatives from all peoples, serve the great God of the Bible. Our ministry, in part, fulfills the prophecy of Malachi 1:11. Over the face of the whole earth, from east to west, triumphant hymns of praise and worship to the Triune God can be heard in Christian churches. The time will come when the name of God will be praised among all nations, completing the prophecy of Malachi. As a foretaste of that glorious time, we must sincerely and continuously sanctify the name of God by worshiping Him in spirit and truth.

Christian Maturity

But speaking the truth in love, we are to grow up in all aspects into Him who is the head, even Christ, from whom the whole body, being fitted and held together by what every joint supplies, according to the proper working of each individual part, causes the growth of the body for the building up of itself in love.

EPHESIANS 4:15–16

S. R.: ASIA (NAME WITHHELD FOR SECURITY)

Every Christian ought to grow in maturity. God wants us to mature that we would no longer be children in our Christian walk. Christ called us out from our sin and has given gifts to His church for the purpose of growth in maturity. But one may well wonder what does maturity look like? Our passage answers that question—a key characteristic of a mature Christian is speaking the truth in love under the lordship of Christ.

However, there are few things more difficult to practice in our Christian life than to speak truth boldly (without compromise) and to love lavishly (without hypocrisy). It is not easy in church or in the workplace, and sometimes even in our homes. However, these virtues were manifested by our Master to hostile sinners in equally hostile environments.

There is no Christian growth without truth and love going hand in hand. I have seen over the years in different churches in Asia that truth without love drives away people from church; and love without truth does not transform the church. Without both, there is no growth in maturity.

We who have been born of the Spirit are to grow up like Christ, following our Master who spoke truth in love irrespective of circumstances. We must do this even if it costs us our lives. Are you a maturing disciple of Christ? Do you speak the truth in love? Is this key characteristic true of you? The next time you speak the truth, ask yourself, "Am I really seasoning this with love?" Remember, truth without love is *brutality*; love without truth is *hypocrisy*.

All-Out War

For our struggle is not against flesh and blood, but against
the rulers, against the powers, against the world forces of
this darkness, against the spiritual forces of wickedness in
the heavenly places.

EPHESIANS 6:12

JONATAN RECAMÁN: BEREA SEMINARY | SPAIN

Many people today do not think there is a spiritual dimension. Many believe that the battle between good and evil is just something we see in movies. The devil loves that many people think this way. Yet, the Bible tells us that there is an intense struggle between spiritual truth and the spiritual forces of wickedness, and part of the devil's strategy is to keep people ignorant of or indifferent to such a struggle.

In Paul's letter to the believers at Ephesus, he is encouraging them to live in a manner worthy of their calling; this means to live according to the spiritual blessings they have in Jesus. But Paul knows the schemes of our enemy, and he wants to prepare them for the battle against the devil's powers.

This struggle is a "face-to-face" battle. Paul uses a word that refers to a fight between two people, until one hurls the other down and holds him down. The image is quite clear: the devil tries to hurl us down so that we don't stand firm in our faith. We face a powerful enemy, and not of flesh and blood. The fight starts and must be fought in the mind, for that is where our battle begins.

We are called to stand firm, and we can only stand firm if our minds are filled with truth. This is the only way we can identify and defeat the schemes of the forces of darkness. We must follow Jesus' example when He was tempted by the devil (Luke 4:1–13). Let us fight with our minds filled with truth, for it is all-out war.

Worship Pleasing to God

Therefore I want the men in every place to pray, lifting up holy hands, without wrath and dissension. Likewise, I want women to adorn themselves with proper clothing, modestly and discreetly, not with braided hair and gold or pearls or costly garments, but rather by means of good works, as is proper for women making a claim to godliness.

1 TIMOTHY 2:8–10

LEWIS M. CHIRWA: CENTRAL AFRICAN PREACHING ACADEMY | MALAWI

Order is very important. A community without order is a community in chaos. There is to be order in the church. In God's lovingkindness, He seeks order among His children in worship.

In this passage, we see Paul urging men to pray with their hands lifted and their hearts set right. As the heads of families, men must be exemplary in their prayer lives. Their prayers must not be characterized by anger or division but by love and unity. The point is not so much the posture of the hands but the position of the heart. Men, let your prayers model a right relationship to God.

Paul also explains how godly women should adorn themselves. Their clothing should be respectable and modest. Their dress and adornment must not rob the church of its focus; women dressed in showy clothing, decorated with ostentatious jewelry and makeup, will detract from the church's goal of worshiping God. But the internal beauty and good works of godly women greatly aid in bringing Him glory.

Godly men of prayer who seek peace and unity bring order to our churches; modest women of good works help maintain it. Let us remember that God shares His glory with no one. He must be the center of our attention and our worship. Let us never allow fighting, disunity, or immodesty to take center stage in our churches. Let us do all for the glory of God as we worship in an orderly way.

What Good Is the Law?

Because by the works of the Law no flesh will be justified in His sight; for through the Law comes the knowledge of sin.
ROMANS 3:20

LANCE ROBERTS: CZECH BIBLE INSTITUTE | CZECH REPUBLIC

Every generation has had to define, defend, and declare the gospel of Jesus Christ. The apostle Paul in his letters to the Romans and Galatians addressed the error of adding works to faith in order to merit one's salvation. The Protestant Reformers fought the same battle with the Roman Catholic Church, and even today this false doctrine is making attempts to creep into the church. Man's natural tendency is to want to have a part in his salvation. But as Jonathan Edwards rightly stated, "You contribute nothing to your salvation except the sin that made it necessary."

Romans 3:9–20 describes the anatomy of man's depravity, and shows the impossibility of doing anything to merit one's salvation. Every part of us is tainted and corrupted by sin. Therefore, no amount of obedience to the Law or maintaining good works can persuade God to declare us righteous and worthy of entering His glory. Even our most righteous deeds are stained with sin and are no more than filthy rags in His eyes (Isa. 64:6).

The purpose of the Law was never to justify a depraved sinner, but to pull back the curtain and show him his sin and condemnation before a holy God. It was given to reveal man's need for a Savior.

The next opportunity you have to the share the gospel, include the Law and the impossibility of keeping it. It shows a sinner he is guilty before the righteous Judge, and can only leave God's courtroom justified by trusting Christ for his salvation. Jesus fully satisfied the justice of God by dying as our substitute. Only faith in Him saves.

Retribution and Rescue

The Lord knows how to rescue the godly from temptation, and to keep the unrighteous under punishment for the day of judgment.
2 PETER 2:9

MIGUEL APARICIO: EVANGELICAL MINISTRIES OF THE AMERICAS | HONDURAS

The false notion that we are exempt from judgment has plagued mankind since the Fall. The natural man tends to believe that he won't receive any just retribution for his evil deeds. Someone *else* might be guilty, we reason, but *we* are not. As a result, many live according to the philosophy that existed in the days of Zephaniah: we can do what we want because the Lord won't do anything about it (Zeph. 1:12).

2 Peter 2:9, however, teaches that God in His sovereignty will hold people accountable for their actions, and that He also gives grace to some in order to keep them from sin. In the immediate context, Peter gives a couple of examples of God's sovereign justice. He *did* judge the world in Noah's day, though sparing Noah and his family. And He *did* condemn Sodom and Gomorrah to destruction, though He rescued righteous Lot and his family.

We can learn from this passage that God is sovereign and just, and the unrighteous *will* face their judgment. God has not abandoned the earth after creating it, as the deists believe, leaving all things to chance. He will "keep the unrighteous under punishment for the day of judgment," but He will also rescue the godly, knowing exactly how to protect them.

Though our society may be corrupt, and though evil may surround us on all sides, God knows how to rescue the godly from temptation. The world will ultimately be judged by fire (2 Pet. 3:7), but we who are in Christ Jesus will escape that judgment, since our Savior was judged in our place. May we honor Him, therefore, with our lives.

Your Will Be Done

And He went a little beyond them, and fell on His face and prayed, saying, "My Father, if it is possible, let this cup pass from Me; yet not as I will, but as You will."

MATTHEW 26:39

ANDREY GORBAN: WORD OF GRACE BIBLE INSTITUTE | USA

How incredibly humbling it is to read about the Savior in His humble state, not only as a man, but a man going through intense pain and suffering. In His deepest distress, the Lord cries out to His Father, and what is the essence of His prayer? His desire for the Father's will to be done.

Man often seeks to find a way out of his suffering, to ease the pain and difficulty which come with living in a sin-drenched world. In our day, it seems that nearly everyone is looking to take the easy way out of difficult situations, and there's seemingly an easy solution to every one of life's problems. What Jesus was preparing to go through, the "cup" of which He speaks, was no mere earthly difficulty. It was the very wrath of God which He, as the sin-bearer, would drink on behalf of those whom He would save. As awful and terrifying as this is, Jesus understood that the will of the Father is always best and He relied upon the reality of who God is in order to find strength to persevere and complete His Father's plan.

As we seek to honor God with our lives, may we be encouraged in knowing that, as is written in Hebrews 4:15, our High Priest *can* sympathize with our weaknesses. Moreover, may we, in the midst of trials, trust in the will of our heavenly Father, knowing that all He does is good.

The Footprint of Jesus Christ

For it was the Father's good pleasure for all the fullness to dwell in Him, and through Him to reconcile all things to Himself, having made peace through the blood of His cross; through Him, I say, whether things on earth or things in heaven.
COLOSSIANS 1:19–20

DEXTER CHUA: THE EXPOSITOR'S ACADEMY | PHILIPPINES

A genetic footprint is a term used in obtaining a DNA profile to verify the identity of human remains. On the other hand, the term footprint can also refer to the impression that our character leaves behind in a particular place and time. It is what other people remember and treasure about us.

Our world has come up with many ideas about the identity of Jesus Christ. Some say that Jesus was a moral teacher, a miracle worker, a revolutionary hero, or a savior who can bring us to heaven if our good works outweigh our sins. None of these identities, however, match the footprints that Jesus Christ has left.

We see Jesus' footprints in the Bible. This verse teaches that the *fullness* of deity dwells in Jesus. He is truly man and truly God. It also teaches that His life was offered as a complete and perfect payment to reconcile us to God, bringing back the former state of creation which was defaced by our sin. Jesus' footprints—the biblical records given to us—reveal that He is more than a moral teacher, more than a miracle worker, more even than a champion of the downtrodden. He is God in flesh, and through Him all things are reconciled to the Father.

The real footprint of Christ reminds us that God is no longer angry with us who believe. We enjoy the favor of God because Christ has made peace through the blood of His cross. He is our Savior. He is our Prince of Peace. He is our God!

Walking Contradictions

For everyone who does evil hates the Light, and does not come to the Light for fear that his deeds will be exposed.

JOHN 3:20

MARKO PETEK: THEOLOGICAL BIBLICAL ACADEMY | CROATIA

Sin makes a person irrational. It turns someone into a walking contradiction. John the apostle explains that people do evil, love darkness, and yet do not want to be exposed for who they truly are—wicked evildoers. They want to enjoy sin and avoid being exposed as sinners. Moreover, evil always wants to dress in the garments of goodness to mask its true nature.

This verse reveals many truths about sinners. Sinners practice evil and are, therefore, evil. If they were good, then they would come to the Light because they would not be ashamed. Not only do they avoid the Light—the Savior Jesus—but they also hate Him. They hate Him because they know they are guilty and they fear being exposed. Sinners love secrecy. It is a breeding area for further sin. The ideal situation for a sinner is that he would be allowed to indulge himself in sin and be perceived as a good person at the same time.

People reject the gospel because it reveals the truth and destroys their idolatrous images of themselves. But Jesus will not settle for anything less than full confession of one's spiritual state. Therefore it is the gospel preacher's duty to shed light on the sinner's heart and demand full compliance with the Savior's assessment of man's problem and the solution for sin.

There is freedom and salvation in admission of sin. The Holy Spirit mercifully and constantly exposes sin both in the lives of sinners and confessing believers because of the Savior's love. May we preach and pray that people would see their sin and not be turned into walking contradictions.

March 31

Italy

ITALIAN THEOLOGICAL ACADEMY

Italy's capital city, Rome, played a prominent role in the New
Testament, being the location of Paul's imprisonment and later Peter
and Paul's martyrdom. Today, though most Italians identify with the
Catholic church, the gospel message has been buried under centuries
of traditions and error. Italian Theological Academy is training a
generation of pastors to proclaim the good news of Jesus Christ
across this difficult country.

TODAY, PRAY FOR

The country of Italy, that God would save many people who
are deceived by the Catholic church.

Local churches across Italy, that they would have a strong
gospel witness among their unbelieving community.

God to raise up many men to model biblical preaching and
shepherding among the young Italian churches.

April 1

True Prayer Flows from a Bible-Filled Heart

In the first year of [Darius'] reign, I, Daniel, observed in the
books the number of the years which was revealed as the word
of the LORD to Jeremiah the prophet for the completion of the
desolations of Jerusalem, namely, seventy years.

DANIEL 9:2

GREG WHITE: GRACE BIBLE SEMINARY | UKRAINE

When I first arrived in Ukraine, I was amazed at how much Scripture the people in the churches had put to memory. It seemed that every believer had a small lined notebook filled with hand-written verses, which they would review on the bus or as they traveled about. It demonstrated to me that these believers truly held God's word in honor and wanted their minds to be filled with it.

Our verse today introduces what is perhaps the prophet Daniel's greatest prayer. It reveals the remarkable insight that Daniel had into the nature of Scripture; and it reveals just how much his heart was consumed with God's word. This opening verse shows that Daniel's prayer life—as ours should be—was built upon the word of God. As Daniel prays, his mind is filled with Scripture, for there are at least ten different Old Testament books referenced in this prayer.

His direct reference to Jeremiah in this verse reveals that he held Jeremiah's prophecies to be the very words of the Lord. Daniel believed in the verbal inspiration of Scripture, that it is without error in whole or in part, the very word of God.

As we consider the opening of Daniel's prayer, it drives us to ask these questions: How do *we* respond to God's word? Intellectually, we believe. But in practice, how do we treat the Bible? How often and how long do we think about it? Would we find ourselves memorizing Scripture while waiting in a line or in the passenger seat of a car? Do we, like Daniel, seek to have God's perfect word fill our hearts and minds?

True Prayer Is Serious

*So I gave my attention to the Lord God to seek Him by prayer
and supplications, with fasting, sackcloth and ashes.*

DANIEL 9:3

GREG WHITE: GRACE BIBLE SEMINARY | UKRAINE

I didn't know what to expect, but I was excited for my first visit to a Ukrainian Baptist church service. Shortly after finding a place to sit in a completely packed church, everyone stood up and the pastor started to pray. I asked a friend why everyone was standing. He explained that when he was in the military, every soldier would stand out of respect when an officer walked into the room. How much more, he asked me, should we stand in respect when we come into God's presence through prayer? Prayer was a serious matter.

In this verse we see that prayer was a serious matter to Daniel, as well. He states, "I gave my attention to the Lord God to seek Him." He is determined to be fully engaged, focused, and consumed in his prayers. We see this earnestness at the end of the verse, as well. His fasting shows deep concern, whereas the sackcloth and ashes express his humility. Daniel knows whom he seeks. His God is the sovereign Lord over all, with power to direct the affairs of the world. He did not, therefore, take prayer lightly.

This should lead us to consider our own prayer lives. Do you begin your prayers with a solemn acknowledgment that your Father is in heaven, ruling the universe with unlimited power at His disposal? Are you willing to take your prayer life seriously, to make it an uncompromising action of faith? May we keep the name of our God hallowed in our hearts as we approach Him in our prayers.

True Prayer Involves the Heart

I prayed to the LORD *my God and confessed and said,*
"Alas, O Lord, the great and awesome God, who keeps His
covenant and lovingkindness for those who love Him and
keep His commandments."

DANIEL 9:4

GREG WHITE: GRACE BIBLE SEMINARY | UKRAINE

Daniel's prayer gives rich insight into the nature and practice of God-honoring prayer. Daniel's focus is toward the LORD, or Yahweh, using the name of God that speaks of His relationship to His people. Daniel knew he could approach God because he was a child of God. Daniel had a personal relationship with God. Daniel quickly confesses that he believes in the God who is revealed in Scripture, that he believes in what God has revealed about Himself.

Before communicating any request, Daniel is moved to express his heart of adoration to God, who is superior to any human, whose acts of redemption, compassion, goodness, and judgment bring Him due reverence and honor. As Daniel surveys God's works in relation to his frail humanity, as he thinks upon God's greatness and power, it produces awe and wonder in his heart.

Sometimes we think that prayer is only requesting things from God, but some of the greatest joys of prayer are those moments in which we simply praise Him. Daniel was not reciting facts about God without believing and cherishing them. His whole heart was involved, as he had come to worship this great God that he now sought in prayer. Whenever you come to see something amazing or wonderful about God, take a moment to praise Him. And whenever you have an urge in your prayer life to proclaim His greatness, obey it!

True Prayer Contains Confession of Sin

We have sinned, committed iniquity, acted wickedly and rebelled, even turning aside from Your commandments and ordinances. Moreover, we have not listened to Your servants the prophets, who spoke in Your name to our kings, our princes, our fathers and all the people of the land.

DANIEL 9:5–6

GREG WHITE: GRACE BIBLE SEMINARY | UKRAINE

Have you ever been so concerned with God's honor that you were led to confess not only your own sin but also the sins of those around you? Have you ever prayed, "Lord, *we* have sinned"?

In this passage, Daniel identifies with his people and confesses on behalf of the nation. He confesses sin of which he had not personally partaken—at least not that we know of from the Scriptures. And yet he is moved to confess these sins with the hope that God would have compassion and the nation would be reconciled to God. It is the heart of a repentant man who cares deeply about God's honor among the people.

Daniel includes himself in the confession. He acknowledges that he is no better than anyone else. He admits his own sinfulness, having fallen short of God's standard of holy living. He repents, which means that he willfully turns away from sin and toward obedience. And he hopes the same for his nation.

Though true prayer may contain many elements, one of the most vital is confession. To confess is to acknowledge our failures to honor God as He deserves. This can include, as it did with Daniel's prayer, sin and iniquity, acts of rebellion, disobedience to known commandments, or a dismissal of the clear teaching of God's word. Like the men of God who have come before us, make confession a regular part of your prayer life. And remember: God will not despise a contrite heart (Psa. 51:17).

True Prayer Acknowledges the Results of Sin

Righteousness belongs to You, O Lord, but to us open shame,
as it is this day....Open shame belongs to us, O Lord, to our
kings, our princes, and our fathers, because we have sinned
against You.

DANIEL 9:7–8

GREG WHITE: GRACE BIBLE SEMINARY | UKRAINE

God always does what is right, but sadly, we do not. Daniel points out in his prayer that sin results in open shame, disgrace, and destruction. Though the faithful are spared eternal condemnation, no one escapes all the temporal consequences of sin in this life. Past sin can continue to bring dishonor upon a person. Nonetheless, God acts with kindness even amid our messy lives, disciplining His children in love rather than in anger.

I remember my first counseling session as a pastor in Ukraine. A woman in the church asked why God would not allow her to get pregnant. She went on to explain that before she became a Christian, she had been pregnant no less than seven times, each one ending with an abortion. Tragically, this was considered the preferred method of birth control under the Soviet Union. But as a result of the many abortions in her past, doctors confirmed that she could no longer get pregnant.

Like many of us, this woman struggled to understand that the forgiveness of sin does not necessarily mean that we will never experience any temporal consequences of it. But, as Daniel acknowledges, there are real consequences to sin. There is no more condemnation for the believer, yet we still experience some consequences of it (not least of which is physical death). We must acknowledge this in our own prayers. Only then can we begin to understand that God works through these situations for our good and His glory, using these consequences to mature us in the faith and grow us more into the image of His Son (Heb. 12:6; Rom. 8:29).

True Prayer Includes Reflection

To the Lord our God belong compassion and forgiveness, for
we have rebelled against Him.
DANIEL 9:9

GREG WHITE: GRACE BIBLE SEMINARY | UKRAINE

As Daniel thinks deeply about God, God's compassion and forgiveness flood his thinking. In his prayer, then, Daniel emphasizes God's great and manifold compassion and His abundant forgiveness. Even amid his nation's active rebellion against God, Daniel had hope, for he knew that the sovereign God of the universe is compassionate and forgiving.

When my wife, our two-year-old daughter, and I first arrived in Kiev, Ukraine, the country was in an economic depression. It seemed they lacked almost everything, including basic food items. Milk, cheese, and sugar were being rationed. But one thing that was not lacking among our brothers and sisters in Christ was their commitment to prayer and their trust in God and His mercies.

Understanding the character of God is vital for prayer. Perhaps the aspect most lacking in prayer today is that of godly reflection or contemplation. In our busy schedules, it is hard to find time to pray, let alone to think deeply about God while we pray. In this verse, however, Daniel reflects on God's great and diverse compassion and the richness of His forgiveness. Like Israel, a nation prone to rebellion, we too are inclined to rebel against God. Also like Israel, our only hope is in the sovereign God who is compassionate and forgiving.

In your prayer life, do you find time to contemplate the majesty of God, the mercy of God, and the great and marvelous forgiveness that God extends to us in Christ? Daniel took time to do this, even (especially!) in a time of trouble.

In His Image

Then God said, "Let Us make man in Our image, according to Our likeness; and let them rule over the fish of the sea and over the birds of the sky and over the cattle and over all the earth, and over every creeping thing that creeps on the earth."

GENESIS 1:26

JUAN PABLO CARMONA MEDINA: BEREA SEMINARY | SPAIN

Mankind is undoubtedly the jewel of God's creation. We are the only creatures created in His image, in the image of the Father, the Son, and the Holy Spirit. Mankind was created by the will of God, and to be fulfilled in serving God with all the abilities to discern, decide, chose, and love.

Yet, people seek to be fulfilled in many different ways. In order to feel good about themselves, human beings claim to need some sort of extra motivation, regularly resorting to their own strength and knowledge, or to other humanistic techniques.

Yet, the Bible tells us that we are created in God's image, according to His likeness with the purpose of ruling over all the creatures on earth. God created us with many different skills and abilities, and we can and must use them. Our true value is not in what we are capable of doing. Our ultimate value rests in the fact that God made us in His image, according to His likeness. God has ultimately gifted us with the ability to relate to Him and enjoy an intimate and particular communion with Him. No other created being has that kind of privilege. And though sin has marred this image, all humans nonetheless still bear this image, and through the gospel this image is renewed in believers.

Do you need anything else in order to feel fulfilled? If you're a Christian, the God of the universe created you in His image to be His herald and steward. Let us give thanks to our good Creator and mirror His character as those made in His image.

Worshiping the Creator God

In the beginning God created the heavens and the earth.
GENESIS 1:1

DAVID BESTER: CHRIST SEMINARY | SOUTH AFRICA

This is the first sentence of God's revelation to you. It is His first creative act and the origin of all material existence. Sadly, many respond to this claim with skepticism, but the proper creaturely response is worship. God reveals that unless He acted first, nothing would exist. Time as we know it commenced with His creative act, since it took place "in the beginning." No building materials are mentioned in the verse, because God created out of nothing. Though impossible for man, God's supernatural power achieved it. "The heavens and the earth" include all spheres of existence, but also emphasize how central earth is as the setting for God's redemptive history.

In our local church plant, we open every Sunday service with a call to worship, because our hearts are prone to lethargy and amnesia. Here is your call to worship today.

First, consider God's power to achieve whatever He wills. Join in with the heavenly throne room, where the living creatures and elders worship God saying, "You created all things, and because of Your will they existed, and were created" (Rev. 4:11). Next, consider God's eternality, since He created "in the beginning." Rightly the living creatures worship Him as the one "WHO WAS AND WHO IS AND WHO IS TO COME" (Rev. 4:8). Finally, consider God's goodness in providing the setting for redemptive history. On the earth God created, man sinned. In love, God sent His Son to die and rise again, securing redemption for His elect. Glory to God!

Worship Him in song, in prayer, in obedience, and in proclaiming Him to others. The Creator is worthy of praise!

Sealed with His Spirit

In Him, you also, after listening to the message of truth, the
gospel of your salvation—having also believed, you were
sealed in Him with the Holy Spirit of promise, who is given as
a pledge of our inheritance, with a view to the redemption of
God's own possession, to the praise of His glory.
EPHESIANS 1:13–14

GABRIEL MARTINEZ GARCIA: WORD OF GRACE BIBLICAL SEMINARY | MEXICO

During biblical times, important men carried with them their personal seal on a ring or on a cylinder hanging around the neck. To imprint their seal meant ownership and personal certification. It served as a warranty that the person himself backed what was sealed.

Scripture claims, "You were sealed in Him with the Holy Spirit." God sealed us *with* His Spirit, certifying that we belong to Him and are united to His Son. And the seal *is* the Holy Spirit, who is "a pledge of our inheritance." He is an advance payment, the certainty that God will personally ensure that no believer will ever be lost. The presence of God's Spirit is the most intimate guarantee that we will inherit all that God has promised.

As God's personal seal, the Spirit is a sign of God's ownership of the believer. What God owns, He will not abandon! Our salvation, from beginning to end, depends not on our own efforts but on God. His Spirit cannot be lost and will not be taken away. We who are sealed with the Spirit will share in the inheritance of Jesus Christ. We who believe in the gospel will never be put to shame. Though adversity may come, and though sorrows like sea billows may roll, God will protect His own possession to the very end.

Hence, being sealed, we may be confident, waiting for our appearing before the Lord, enjoying the advance payment of our inheritance today, and living to the praise of God's glory and grace.

Be on Your Guard

You therefore, beloved, knowing this beforehand, be on your guard so that you are not carried away by the error of unprincipled men and fall from your own steadfastness.

2 PETER 3:17

SERGEY K.: RUSSIA (FULL NAME WITHHELD FOR SECURITY)

We like security systems. The more security, the safer we feel. Perhaps this is why sermons and hymns about our eternal security are extremely loved by us. The doctrines of eternal security and the perseverance of saints help us to love and glorify God more for His mighty and eternal love to us (Rom. 8:26–39). Such is our God to whom we entrusted our lives—reliable.

But Peter wants one truth to always stir up our mind. What is this thing? Our verse tells us, as it is the climax of the letter. Peter calls us to be on our guard and then encourages us to continue to grow in grace and knowledge, lest we fall. In other words, part of being on guard is to live righteously, remembering the coming of the Lord who will punish and judge all evil (2 Pet. 2:9–10; 3:7).

Warnings in the Bible foster security. Why? Because they're a way to show how our assurance becomes a reality. The greatest security systems require our using them. Similarly, these warnings stimulate our perseverance. As someone once said, believers maintain their secure position by heeding warnings, not by ignoring them.

Are you growing spiritually? Sure, it is God who is at work in you for His good pleasure (Phil. 2:13). However, on your part, do you apply all diligence (2 Pet. 1:5)? Do you make every effort to live righteously? If not, you're not on your guard. Don't reject God's instrument to preserve you. Heed warnings, reflect on Scripture constantly, and pursue living righteously so you're not carried away. Praise the Lord for His security system.

United in Christ

For, in the first place, when you come together as a church, I hear that divisions exist among you.

1 CORINTHIANS 11:18

DENNIS ALEXANDER BANDA: CENTRAL AFRICAN PREACHING ACADEMY | MALAWI

The rich, educated, and politically connected are in the driver's seat of many churches in Malawi, while the poor are regarded as second-class believers. In such churches you find that poor believers are not allowed to take any positions of leadership, even if they are biblically qualified. They are even expected to give their seats to their rich brethren if all the chairs are occupied during a worship service. Worst of all, these elites form their own class, leaving the poor to form another, never truly associating with each other, even though attending the same church.

In this first letter to the Corinthian believers, Paul rebukes them for tolerating divisions among themselves. During the Lord's Supper, the rich were getting drunk and eating all their food without considering their poor brothers and sisters. As a result of this ungodly behavior, some became sick and even died. God was judging them for their disregard of others in the body of Christ.

Brothers and sisters, are we not all united in Christ? There is no such thing as a second-class believer in the kingdom of God. We all have one Spirit. This makes all who believe in Jesus Christ to be equal, regardless of our education, possessions, or influence in society.

Remember that our true identity is in Christ, not in what we have or do not have. Let us love one another from our hearts, just as Christ loved us.

Prayer in the Warfare

*But the prince of the kingdom of Persia was withstanding me
for twenty-one days; then behold, Michael, one of the chief
princes, came to help me, for I had been left there with the
kings of Persia.*

DANIEL 10:13

S. R.: ASIA (NAME WITHHELD FOR SECURITY)

There is the reality of ongoing spiritual warfare which we often
do not notice. Despite Satan's influences upon the earth, God's
power sustains the universe and He uses the active working of His
angels. Christians are also engaged in this battle, and those who do
not know Christ are under the influence of demonic forces (Eph. 2:2)

Sometimes we fall in this battle because we stray from Christ and
fail to take up our spiritual armor. When we fall, we are not forsaken
by God—but we must repent of our sins before Him and then press
on in the battle.

Yet, let us remember that unexpected things can happen in this
warfare—things we may never be aware of. Daniel, a righteous man,
was troubled in heart concerning the future of God's people. He
humbled himself and prayed to God for twenty-one days. God heard
His prayer and dispatched an angel to help him, who was then delayed
by a demonic being. The devil and his forces are powerful, but God
is more powerful—His angel prevailed and then helped Daniel. Then
God revealed to Daniel much more than what he asked for.

Are there times you feel like God does not hear you? God hears
you immediately and will answer prayer, though the answer may seem
delayed. Follow Daniel's example—keep waiting on God, humble
yourself before Him, and remain in constant prayer. The battle and
warfare rages, so beware of the enemy's schemes. Trust in the great
grace and power of God. Be of good courage! With Christ, we are
more than conquerors! (Rom. 8:37).

God's Loving Protection

But the Lord is faithful, and He will strengthen and protect you from the evil one.

2 THESSALONIANS 3:3

CARLOS NUNEZ: EVANGELICAL MINISTRIES OF THE AMERICAS | HONDURAS

This text vividly reminds me of my childhood when my mother took us to church, walking almost four miles each way. Fourteen of us traveled by foot to morning and evening services almost every Sunday. It wasn't easy, but it was worth it because we learned about the gospel, and I was able to see the providential hand of God caring for us as we walked through the rain, the heat, and, frequently, real danger. I still thank God for His care and faithfulness.

In this passage, the apostle Paul speaks of his own life experiences and afflictions. The brethren at Thessalonica had come to his aid to encourage him through his difficulties and temptations, but Paul assumed the work of a pastor even with the existing dangers. In doing so, he thought more of the sheep than himself. He was more interested in what God could do for the Thessalonians than what God might have done for him.

It is remarkable that God gives us His strength to guard and preserve us in the faith. Paul here is convinced that the Lord will strengthen us in our weaknesses and shelter us from evil; and because of this, believers are able to obey the apostles' teaching.

Though Honduras is one of the most violent countries in the world, we still have the responsibility to live out the gospel in our daily lives without fear. In this way, our testimonies shine as lights and bring God glory, as we entrust ourselves to the faithful care of our Lord. No matter what your circumstances are, God is faithful, and He will protect you from the evil one.

Remember Those Who Labor for Your Soul

*For you recall, brethren, our labor and hardship, how working
night and day so as not to be a burden to any of you, we
proclaimed to you the gospel of God.*

1 THESSALONIANS 2:9

NICK KALENA: EUROPEAN BIBLE TRAINING CENTER | GERMANY

Many quickly conclude that this text is just for pastors. However, you ought to read this text and see that it's just as much for church members. Paul affectionately addressed his Thessalonian brothers and sisters in the faith. With a fond familial love he calls them to remember what he, as a church-planting pastor, endured for their sake. Establishing the church was a difficult task punctuated with persecution (1 Thess. 2:2). He toiled so that the Thessalonians could hear and learn the word of God unencumbered.

In most Western contexts today, pastors are not afflicted by first-century kinds of persecution (though we must not forget those who are). But pastoring is still a difficult task. Maintaining a deep love for Christ, striving after spiritual maturity, preparing and delivering sermons, and helping individuals overcome sin with the Bible are demanding tasks. When criticism, financial strain, and physical exhaustion compound, pastoring a modern-day church requires much labor and toil. We ought to also consider and pray for the pastors in lands that are hostile to Christianity or in lands in which few healthy churches thrive.

Do you considerately remember the labor and toil that your pastors have exerted so that you might be rooted and built up in Christ (Heb. 13:7; Col. 2:7)? Does your thankfulness for your local church pastors overflow in thankful prayer to the Lord, our Chief Shepherd? In what ways does your thankfulness move you to serve for the sake of the gospel and God's glory?

The Truth about Apostasy

But the Spirit explicitly says that in later times some will fall away from the faith, paying attention to deceitful spirits and doctrines of demons.

1 TIMOTHY 4:1

P. S.: MIDDLE EAST (NAME WITHHELD FOR SECURITY)

Anyone who has been a believer for some time knows at least one person who has denied the faith. Sometimes people who once faithfully attended church, read the Bible, and served in various ministries reject Christ altogether. How should believers react to this kind of apostasy?

First, we should not be surprised. The Spirit has told us that apostasy will happen. There will always be some who look like true Christians, but have a counterfeit faith. Second, we should not be discouraged. We know that only some will fall away, and that all those who are kept by Christ's power will endure. Christ is building His church, and will continue to build it until He returns. Third, we should not be deceived. If apostasy can happen to others who have professed Christ, it can happen to us. We should not be arrogant and over-confident concerning our own salvation. We must be wary of all forms of false teaching, which ultimately find their source in Satan, the deceiver.

In the country where I minister, there are a large number of officially recognized religious sects, including both Christian and Muslim groups. Though it is a very religious place, there are very few gospel-preaching churches. Most of the religion that is practiced here does not honor Christ and it leads people to destruction. And the Holy Spirit, speaking through the apostle Paul, tells us that the source of all false doctrine is deceitful spirits and demons.

Are you trusting in Christ to keep you in the faith and to protect you from all error?

All Things for Good

*And we know that God causes all things to work together for
good to those who love God, to those who are called according
to His purpose.*
ROMANS 8:28

LANCE ROBERTS: CZECH BIBLE INSTITUTE | CZECH REPUBLIC

This verse is one of the mountain peaks of Scripture, towering in its usage above many others to encourage those in the valleys of life. As one of the *most quoted* verses in the Bible, it is also one of the *most misquoted*. Rightly understood it serves to provide hope and endurance for the troubled soul.

The promise contained in this verse is to those who love God and are called according to His purpose. Those who are called are those who are foreknown, predestined, called, justified, and ultimately glorified by God (Rom. 8:29–30). It is a message of comfort to believers who love God and are being conformed to the image of His Son.

The promise is that God is working all things together for good. *All things* includes our strengths and our weaknesses, our sickness and our health, our poverty and our riches, our pains and our pleasures, the calm and the storm. God even used the death of His own Son for good.

God's purpose in working all things together for good is for us to be conformed to the image of His Son that culminates in our glorification. As you face your next trial, remember that the Refiner's fire is working to eliminate the dross in your life to purify you and make you shine more brilliantly for the Lord Jesus Christ.

What this good God has in mind for you may not be what you think is good. But in His perfect wisdom and goodness, you can be assured that no matter what may be your earthly path or outcome, the future glory that awaits you is far surpassing.

The Priority of Preaching God's Word

So then, those who had received his word were baptized; and that day there were added about three thousand souls. They were continually devoting themselves to the apostles' teaching and to fellowship, to the breaking of bread and to prayer.

ACTS 2:41–42

EDUARDO IZQUIERDO: INSTITUTO DE EXPOSITORES | USA

The *preaching of God's word* is essential to the life of the church and the Christian. In today's passage, the apostle Peter preached the word of God at the start of the church era and it was incredibly effective—three thousand souls were added to God's universal church! Numbers aside, Peter's preaching was the means that God used to produce precious, long-lasting, spiritual fruit in thousands of lives.

When Peter saw that the multitudes were confounded by the multi-language ministry of the Spirit, he stood up and *preached God's word*. His sermon focused on the good news of the gospel as evidenced by the Old Testament Scriptures. This preaching led to the salvation, baptism, and fellowship of those who repented in faith (Acts 2:37–42).

The *preaching of God's word* went on to transform the desires of those converted. There was a desire to be nurtured with the teachings of Jesus; there was a desire to edify and exhort one another with the goal of becoming more like Christ; there was a desire to share God's physical provision with others; and there was a desire to fellowship with God through dependent prayer. All of this was the fruit of preaching God's word.

The *preaching of God's word* must be a priority for the church and the Christian. It transforms our lives and those whom we interact with. Nothing else will create a love for the Scriptures, a desire for genuine fellowship, and a dependence upon God through prayer in the hearts of God's people. Thank God for your pastors who preach God's word and pray for them.

A Perfect Exercise of Power

Then the soldiers of the governor took Jesus into the
Praetorium and gathered the whole Roman cohort around
Him.... After they had mocked Him, they took the scarlet robe
off Him and put His own garments back on Him, and led Him
away to crucify Him.
MATTHEW 27:27, 31

GENIS M.: ALBANIA (FULL NAME WITHHELD FOR SECURITY)

It is common in Albania for spiritual authority to be abused. It is often used to maintain power or to gain influence and status at the expense of others. But Jesus, the King of Glory, revealed something during His earthly life that the world had never before seen: a perfect exercise of true power.

In human terms, it would be unfathomable to endure what King Jesus endured. It would have been unheard of for a Roman officer to be mocked by his own cohort. It would be outrageous for a general today not to be recognized and saluted by those under him. How much more shocking the treatment of the King of kings at the hands of ungodly men! Jesus was rejected, mocked, humiliated, and finally crucified naked on a tree.

Nevertheless, this King, unlike all other kings, allowed such infinite injustice to occur. He allowed Himself to be led into the Praetorium, allowed Himself to be mocked, and allowed Himself to be led to the slaughter. Why? It was the perfect exercise of His true power and authority. And He explained it ahead of time, for He came to suffer and to die so that others might live (Matt. 17:22–23).

What an example the King of the universe sets to Albanian church leaders, and indeed to rulers and powers and authorities everywhere! While it is our nature to abuse influence given to us, Jesus demonstrated the absolute perfection of leadership: "For even the Son of Man did not come to be served, but to serve, and to give His life a ransom for many" (Mark 10:45).

Rejecting God's Revelation

And just as they did not see fit to acknowledge God any longer,
God gave them over to a depraved mind, to do those things
which are not proper.

ROMANS 1:28

DANIEL HERCEG: THEOLOGICAL BIBLICAL ACADEMY | CROATIA

Paul's letter to the local church in Rome is a part of the general letters written to specific churches. This means that this letter, along with others in the New Testament, is for every local church in every place. This includes churches in Croatia.

Evil is everywhere around us! A few minutes ago, I read about a man who murdered six people; among them was a 10-year-old child. Just a few weeks ago, a member of a local church committed suicide. Evil pervades society. One of the reasons why we have evil in this world is because sinners do not see fit to acknowledge God. How do they do that?

Primarily, they reject God's revelation (Rom. 1:18–20, 28–32). People by nature simply do not want to think about God, to serve Him, or to worship Him. But they cannot blame God saying, "He did not reveal Himself to us!" He did reveal Himself, but sinners reject that revelation. When mankind continues in rejection, God gives them over to a depraved mind.

Depraved minds are everywhere. If you come to Croatia, you'll find them. Truth to be told: you do not need to come to Croatia. Look in the mirror and consider your own tendency toward sin. With little thought, we all see the remaining effects of our own depravity.

How can we, then, keep our minds clean? We should stick close to God's revelation. We should know that the gospel is the power of God for salvation (Rom. 1:16) and the only cure for the remaining evil in our sinful hearts.

Great Is Your Faithfulness

The LORD's lovingkindnesses indeed never cease, for His compassions never fail. They are new every morning; great is Your faithfulness.
LAMENTATIONS 3:22–23

MISKO HORVATEK: THEOLOGICAL BIBLICAL ACADEMY | CROATIA

Jeremiah was heartbroken over the tragedy of his nation and city, Jerusalem. His soul was shattered, even though he understood why thousands of his countrymen were killed, deported, and enslaved. Israel's many transgressions caused her tragedy. Now the nation bitterly wept, her priests groaned, and many were humiliated and homeless. Israel's enemies were now her masters.

The prophet's agony forced him to cry out to God. He had lamented, "Oh that my head were waters and my eyes a fountain of tears, that I might weep day and night for the slain of the daughter of my people!" (Jer. 9:1). He knew that the only solution for Israel was repentance, a return to her covenant God in faith and a rejection of her idols.

Jeremiah's prayer demonstrates hope. Every morning he arose, asking God to reverse the nation's tragedy and knowing that "His compassions never fail." His confidence was in God's character. Though God is just to punish, His compassions never fail and one day He will redeem His people with His never-failing lovingkindness.

My country, Croatia, suffers from the influences of a godless communism, as well as the false gospel of Catholicism. Many lives are destroyed from personal sin and national unbelief. But this is true in every nation. As Christians, we must remember God's character and agonize before Him in prayer, that He would make many spiritual slaves free. We should pray every morning that God might use us to brighten the gloomy existence of our fellow citizens through the gospel. May He reveal His lovingkindness, compassion, and faithfulness so that the lost might worship Him and find, in Christ, true comfort and joy.

Tested, Not Tempted

Let no one say when he is tempted, "I am being tempted by God"; for God cannot be tempted by evil, and He Himself does not tempt anyone.

JAMES 1:13

LANEY STROUP: JAPAN BIBLE ACADEMY | JAPAN

The pages of history are filled with stories of Christians who suffered for their faith. From the stoning of Stephen to the death of William Tyndale, the stories of these heroes call out to us and encourage us to keep our focus, to continue running, and to finish well (Heb. 12:1–2).

In fact, as Paul promised Timothy, "all who desire to live godly in Christ Jesus will be persecuted" (2 Tim. 3:12). And in no case is this truer than in that of a missionary, as God often uses trials specifically to prepare them for His service (1 Thess. 2:1–4).

The sad truth, however, is that most of us will never reach this level of suffering, nor—more importantly—this level of service, because we fail to recognize God's purposes in our life. Instead of giving thanks for our trials, we complain about the people or the circumstances around us. And since we know God is sovereign, then when we do that, we are falling into the same trap as Adam: blaming God for our sin (Gen. 3:12).

As James reminds us in this verse, we must never blame God (or the circumstances He ordains) for our temptations. Yes, He tests us, but the temptations we feel and the sin that comes out when we are tested come from one source only: our internal sin nature (James 1:14–15).

Let us "consider it all joy" when we fall into such trials (James 1:2), no matter what form they take. And may God raise up a new generation of servants who are tested and ready to do His work.

Delighting in the Truth

*I find then the principle that evil is present in me, the one
who wants to do good. For I joyfully concur with the law of
God in the inner man.*

ROMANS 7:21–22

MARK TATLOCK: PRESIDENT, TMAI HEADQUARTERS | LOS ANGELES, CALIFORNIA

Prior to conversion, no one could claim to "joyfully concur with
the law of God." We were at war with the truth and found pleasure in selfish and vain pursuits of fleshly happiness. Though sin can
reign in our mortal bodies (Rom. 6:12), the gospel ignites a new appetite, a longing that can only be satisfied by God Himself. So, Paul can
write, that though he battles with temptation and weakness (Rom.
7:15–16), he has confidence in the gospel's transforming work, as his
heart—once dead to godly appetites—now hungers and thirsts for
righteousness.

When exposed to God's word, by studying, sound preaching and
teaching, or in conversation, does your heart drink deeply and find
greater satisfaction in the law of God? Those who are redeemed know
this satisfaction, and increasingly starve themselves from the lesser
delights of this world.

Those who reside in tropical contexts like India, Pakistan, or the
Philippines know that the mango is the sweetest fruit on earth. Its
popularity far outweighs the other naturally grown fruit, karela, a
gourd, which has the distinction of being the world's bitterest fruit.
If given the choice, mango will always prevail. Even as believers
we sometimes feast on the worldviews, false teachings, and secular
philosophies which are bitter to our taste. These things are to be rejected for the sweet fruit of God's truth.

Do you, as the psalmist claims, find the law of God more desirable
than gold and sweeter to you than honey (Psa. 19:10)? Check your diet
and exchange all the bitter fruits of this world for the truth, which is
sweet to the soul.

People of Mercy, Peace, and Love

May mercy and peace and love be multiplied to you.
JUDE 2

RAYMOND C. DIANGO: THE EXPOSITOR'S ACADEMY | PHILIPPINES

God is merciful, peaceful, and loving. His love moved Him to show mercy to sinful men and women, making peace with them through the blood of His own Son. He showed undeserved kindness by granting forgiveness to His people, sparing them from the punishment their sins deserved. The salvation of sinners puts the mercy, peace, and love of God on clear display!

Jude's greeting in this verse is meant for those who already believe the gospel and know, to some extent, these qualities. Jude's desire is that God's mercy, peace, and love would continue to be known by them. Every believer experiences the mercy, peace, and love of God when we trust in Christ. And every believer continues to know these qualities of God as we grow in Him.

As God transforms us by His word and Spirit, we can in turn multiply His mercy, peace, and love to others. We do this when, for example, we show mercy to the weak and needy. We do this when we proclaim to sinners the way to achieve peace with God in Christ Jesus. And we do this when we explain to sinners the love that God has shown the world by sending His only Son to die so that we who believe might live.

Just as Jude desired that his readers continue to know God's mercy, peace, and love, so we should desire to express these qualities to the world around us. Keep your eyes open today for an opportunity to show mercy, or to share about the peace of God in Christ, or to love someone even as Christ has loved you.

The Perfect High Priest

Therefore He is able also to save forever those who draw near to God through Him, since He always lives to make intercession for them.

HEBREWS 7:25

DOMI BOSQUET: BEREA SEMINARY | SPAIN

In the Old Testament, the high priest was appointed by God to offer sacrifices to atone for the sins of God's people. But the problem the priests faced was that they were all sinners themselves, and therefore they could not bring anyone nearer to God—they needed atonement too.

In light of this reality, the author of Hebrews demonstrates that even though the Levitical priesthood was necessary and instituted by God, it was inherently insufficient. Nevertheless, the priesthood of Christ is not subjected to any such limitation.

Christ, the perfect High Priest, made possible the impossible: He opened the door that led to God forever through His blood. And now, He lives forever to guarantee His people access to God. In Paul's words, "For there is one God, and one mediator also between God and men, the man Christ Jesus, who gave Himself as a ransom for all, the testimony given at the proper time" (1 Tim. 2:5–6).

Unfortunately, in Spain many prefer to rely on their own human efforts in hopes of getting closer to God, instead of relying on Christ's perfect sacrifice and on His all-sufficient work as High Priest.

Praise the Lord that we, His children, have been saved forever and that He is now interceding for us before the Father. We can come straight to Him to receive comfort and help, for there is no need of anything else—no more incomplete sacrifices, no more imperfect priests.

Consider the Great Things

Only fear the LORD and serve Him in truth with all your heart;
for consider what great things He has done for you.
1 SAMUEL 12:24

SERGEY K.: RUSSIA (FULL NAME WITHHELD FOR SECURITY)

Times of troubles, anxiety, and worry—these are realities in life we are well acquainted with. These times are fertile soil for panic, rash decisions, and sin.

Being in a season like this, Israel decided to ask for a king to reign over them (1 Sam. 8:1–6). God considered their request as a rejection of Him. They wanted a king to be a source of deliverance for their nation, so they would be like all the nations.

So, God gave them a king but admonished them in our verse to trust in and worship Him, because He's the only One who demonstrated a power to support and change life. We, too, can be in a hurry to seek deliverance outside of Him—we can forget what He has done for us.

In times of trouble we tend to forget who is the King. In such times, it is so easy to panic, to start grumbling at God, to be angry, and even to solve the problems in a wicked way. All of this is sin against Him. In cases like this my wife often says to me, "Look what God has done for us. All the good we have thus far is because of His care. Are you sure that He wouldn't care about us further?"

What problems do you have today? Is your work difficult? Is your family in shambles? Stop panicking. Consider what great things He has done for you. Then you'll have the right perspective, and will find the strength to fear the Lord and serve Him in truth with all your heart.

Tender-Hearted Forgiveness

Be kind to one another, tender-hearted, forgiving each other,
just as God in Christ also has forgiven you.
EPHESIANS 4:32

ENRIQUE GODOY CASTILLON: WORD OF GRACE BIBLICAL SEMINARY | MEXICO

Ephesians begins with three chapters about *who we are* in Christ. The rest of the book explains, in light of these truths, *how we walk* in Christ. Paul unfolds in these final chapters the magnificent ways that God's gift of salvation affects our daily lives. In this text, he encourages kindness and tender-hearted forgiveness as the appropriate response to God's own kindness and tender-hearted forgiveness toward us.

Consider the extraordinary gift of forgiveness that God has granted to you through the sacrifice of His only Son, Jesus Christ. Do you see God's kindness in sending His Son to die in your place so that you may live? Then be kind, argues Paul, to others. Do you understand that your innumerable sins are freely forgiven by God's grace in Christ Jesus? Then be forgiving toward others.

God is kind even when we are undeserving of His kindness. His heart is tender, eager to forgive the unworthy sinner who would come to His Son in faith. Is there anyone whom you have refused to show kindness? Is there anyone whom you have refused to offer forgiveness? Let your heart be tender, like God's own heart. Remember the wonderful forgiveness you have received through faith, and express your gratitude to God not by words alone, but by forgiving others their trespasses, just as your heavenly Father has forgiven you.

The Unpardonable Sin

Therefore I say to you, any sin and blasphemy shall be forgiven people, but blasphemy against the Spirit shall not be forgiven.
MATTHEW 12:31

S. R.: ASIA (NAME WITHHELD FOR SECURITY)

Have you ever been troubled regarding the unpardonable sin? It's understandable because Jesus talks about the impossibility of forgiveness for this sin. In other words, the one who commits this sin seals himself to eternal doom. This is a scary reality, yet let us remember there should be no comfort from any sin. Each of our sins should trouble us and prompt confession and repentance for forgiveness (1 John 1:9).

Yet, there is this sin that will not be forgiven. This sin is committed as a result of ongoing habitual sin. It is committed when one deliberately rejects the work of the Spirit, or the testimony of the Spirit concerning Jesus Christ. The one who commits this sin has reached the point of no return, thus is bound for eternal hell. If you are troubled and fearful that you have committed this sin, take heart—that is a good indicator you have not. A genuine Christian who is indwelt by the Spirit has never and will never commit this sin.

Jesus is warning us that Christians must not sear their conscience. We should renounce and repent from all sins so that we will not be carried away by any sin. A real Christian will also persevere in following Christ, and not turn away from Him. Let someone like Judas be a warning to us of not being a genuine disciple.

Beloved, you must be sensitive to the leading of the Spirit and take care not to grieve Him (Eph. 4:30). Confess any known sin and ask God for grace to repent.

Counting All Loss

More than that, I count all things to be loss in view of the
surpassing value of knowing Christ Jesus my Lord, for whom I
have suffered the loss of all things, and count them but rubbish
so that I may gain Christ.

PHILIPPIANS 3:8

ALEKSANDER G.: RUSSIA (FULL NAME WITHHELD FOR SECURITY)

Every person, at some time, will ask difficult questions about the meaning of life: "What am I living for? Why do I do this or that? Is there any meaning in life? What is most important in my life?" It's possible that Saul, who later became the apostle Paul, at some time looked for the answer to these questions. But once he met the resurrected Christ, everything in His life changed. What happened to the former persecutor of the church? He died to himself and was resurrected with Christ to a new life—a life of joy, filled with intimate fellowship with Jesus.

Describing this change, he was not afraid of using strong language. He declared that everything he did to justify himself in the eyes of God was nothing more than manure, rubbish, and garbage. He did not trust in his good deeds or his services, which were in God's eyes like rotten food discarded in the garbage. He understood that only Jesus Christ, through faith in His death and resurrection, can remove the guilt of sin and deliver us from judgment and eternal destruction.

Following Paul's example, reject trusting in yourself and everything that springs from your pride for the sake of Christ. Turn your gaze upon Jesus and reckon Him to be the *only* foundation for your justification before God. He is the singular source of genuine joy—everything else is loss! This is why the apostle could boldly declare: "For to me, to live is Christ and to die is gain" (Phil. 1:21)! Are you prepared to repeat these words with the apostle Paul?

Wash Their Feet

If I then, the Lord and the Teacher, washed your feet, you also ought to wash one another's feet.
JOHN 13:14

TAN MOLINA: BEREA SEMINARY | SPAIN

Recently, an extravagant farewell party was thrown by a very powerful man. Every celebrity, the *crème de la crème* of society, attended it. Tens of thousands of dollars were spent for the occasion: the most expensive suits, dresses, and jewelry were purchased; the finest foods were offered; the decor was second to none. In a word, it was sumptuous.

Jesus' farewell party, in the Upper Room, was quite different. No special guests; only fishermen, a tax collector, and even one who would go on to betray Him. Only simple food in an equally simple setting. In a word, humble. And the guest of honor, the Lord, washed the dirty feet of His guests—an illustration and contrast to their sinful longings to be recognized as great. None of them deserved such high honor.

The Lord, the Teacher, the Savior, although aware of His supremacy over all, did what was reserved for the lowliest slave—wash feet. And He did so to undeserving people. He did so to set the greatest example, an example whose pinnacle is found at the cross.

The lesson for the disciples then, and the lesson for us, His undeserving disciples today, is to have a proper view of ourselves, and to love and serve one another in a spirit of humility—perfectly exemplified by the Lord Himself. If He served others, how much more should we, even those we deem unworthy. Watch what blessings it will bring! May His Spirit help us serve others in the same way He served us.

South Africa

CHRIST SEMINARY

A former British colony, South Africa gained independence in 1961. Segregation was enforced by the colonizers and was formally structured into state policy from 1948 to 1994. Though it was officially abolished in 1994, segregation still plagues the society and church, as does syncretism between traditional African religions and Christianity.

TODAY, PRAY FOR

The gospel of Jesus Christ to bring about peace and unity among the South African church, which faces much division over issues of skin color.

Christ Seminary students as they learn a biblical worldview. Many African Christians come from a background influenced by traditional African religions.

All Sub-Saharan Africa, which is languishing spiritually under the deception of the prosperity gospel.

Restoration in the Family of God

Brethren, even if anyone is caught in any trespass, you who are spiritual, restore such a one in a spirit of gentleness; each one looking to yourself, so that you too will not be tempted.

GALATIANS 6:1

JULIO ALFONSO GARCÍA CRUZ: WORD OF GRACE BIBLICAL SEMINARY | MEXICO

Biblical spirituality is opposed to pride and contempt. It seeks not to reject and refuse, but rather to renew, rebuild, and restore. Those who are spiritual will not treat a fellow believer who has sinned with harsh words or haughtiness; instead, they will carefully and gently consider how to help such a one be turned from sin and nurtured back to strength.

The focus is not on other Christians' faults, but rather on how we respond to them. God commands us to help those who fall into sin with gentleness and humility. How do you react when you see others fail and sin? Are you impatient, frustrated, disgusted, or worn down by it? Or are you gentle with their shortcomings, eager to see their hearts renewed and their relationship to God restored?

This really matters. Disobedience at this point can divide a church, but faithfulness to the biblical way brings healing and life to a congregation. Paul said, "Now we who are strong ought to bear the weaknesses of those without strength and not just please ourselves" (Rom. 15:1). Use your spiritual strength not to crush the sinner but to help him stand.

There are many injured saints who need to be restored, and we must carefully watch ourselves, lest we find ourselves tearing them down rather than building them up. We are a family. We should treat one another as beloved siblings. "So then, while we have opportunity," adds Paul just a few verses later, "let us do good to all people, and especially to those who are of the household of the faith" (Gal. 6:10).

Look Forward to That Day

*... with a view to an administration suitable to the fullness
of the times, that is, the summing up of all things in Christ,
things in the heavens and things on the earth.*

EPHESIANS 1:10

AUBREY GULUMBA: CENTRAL AFRICAN PREACHING ACADEMY | MALAWI

No matter how bad it is today, let's look forward to the day when God unites all things in Christ. As Paul reminds us in this verse, at the right time, the "fullness of the times," God will repair all that has been broken.

We know from Scripture that all things were once united together in one perfect order. Everything was beautiful to behold; it was very good (Gen. 1:31). But then sin came and broke the unity. Now there is disunity and conflict in the spiritual realms and on earth. We even see disagreements and factions in the church, the body of Christ. And our own hearts are often divided.

But in the fullness of time, at a time and hour appointed by God, He will unite all things in Christ. There are things in heaven and things on earth that God will unite. Believers, angelic hosts, and all creation will join in praising God and Christ as He reigns.

Although we do not know exactly when this day will come, we know that the one who promised is faithful and will fulfill His Word. As we live in the Lord, no matter how tough and painful life in this world may be, let us not falter but continue in our faithful walk in Him.

Brothers and sisters, let's look forward to that day.

Peace in Every Circumstance

Now may the Lord of peace Himself continually grant you
peace in every circumstance. The Lord be with you all!
2 THESSALONIANS 3:16

CARLOS AGUILAR: EVANGELICAL MINISTRIES OF THE AMERICAS | HONDURAS

"Peace? Who can have it?" asked Juanita, holding a crying child who was hungry with nothing to eat.

"Peace?" asked Pedro. "Who can have it if we live in a corrupt country full of gangs, and we are without work?"

The people in my country look for peace, but too often in the wrong places, thinking that peace means being physically safe and comfortable.

The apostle's desire in this text, however, is that we see our Savior as the true source of peace—not our circumstances. Notice that it is a divine peace because it comes from the Lord Himself, a peace that He has purchased on the cross for all who would believe. It is a peace that means all is well with your soul. It is a peace that means God is happy with you because your sins were forgiven in Christ Jesus. It is a peace that endures, for it is rooted in eternal realities that can never change.

As believers, we must daily remember that God has graciously given us His peace, a peace that remains through any and all circumstances. Meditate on this today. Thank the Lord that your sins have been forgiven and that you have peace with God in Christ Jesus. Consider what it would be like if God hadn't sent His Son to make peace. But praise God He has!

"Peace I leave with you," Jesus said. "My peace I give to you" (John 14:27).

The Indispensability of the Local Church

*Let us hold fast the confession of our hope without
wavering, for He who promised is faithful; and let us
consider how to stimulate one another to love and good
deeds, not forsaking our own assembling together, as is the
habit of some, but encouraging one another; and all the
more as you see the day drawing near.*

HEBREWS 10:23–25

MOJMÍR ADAMEK: CZECH BIBLE INSTITUTE | CZECH REPUBLIC

The tenth chapter of Hebrews presents the climax of an apologetic argument that characterizes the whole letter. After showing the superiority and finality of Jesus' high-priestly death, the author exhorts his audience to remain unwaveringly faithful to the hope they professed. He encourages them to rely on their faithful God in the midst of persecution and subsequent doubts.

After pointing out that God is the only source of their hope, the writer turns to the role of local gatherings—showing that they are the means of mutual encouragement, exhortation, and strengthening. He shows them that they cannot survive persecution without a God-given local congregation. So as they live in "these last days" (Heb. 1:2), eagerly expecting the second coming of Christ (Heb. 9:28), they are to grow and serve within the context of their Christian fellowship.

The Czech evangelical church is so tiny that to live as an active member of a church is often viewed with suspicion by outsiders. Just recently I was told by one of the new believers in our church that he had to explain to his mom that Baptists really do not use different Bibles than other Christian traditions. I also remember that my high school classmates confused several times (perhaps on purpose) Baptists with the Ku Klux Klan. In other words, it is not uncommon to be associated with some form of cult. Yet, we know that fellowshipping in a local congregation is indispensable for the healthy growth of every believer. Do not neglect corporate gatherings and local church ministry, no matter what others may think or what it may cost you.

The Danger of Abandoning God

For this reason God gave them over to degrading passions; for their women exchanged the natural function for that which is unnatural, and in the same way also the men abandoned the natural function of the woman and burned in their desire toward one another, men with men committing indecent acts and receiving in their own persons the due penalty of their error.

ROMANS 1:26–27

GENCI C.: ALBANIA (FULL NAME WITHHELD FOR SECURITY)

Every person knows the truth about God because His eternal power and divine nature are clearly understood through creation (Rom. 1:19–20). Though all people know God exists, they don't worship or give thanks to Him (Rom. 1:21).

So, what happens when man refuses to acknowledge and depend upon God? He doesn't stop worshiping, but he does change the object of that worship. He worships creation in place of its Creator, believing a lie in place of the truth (Rom. 1:22–23). Man is created to be a worshiper. If he will not worship God, he will worship something else. And if man consistently abandons God, God will give man over to his sinful desires. This is the judgment of God upon man, as these sinful desires do not and cannot ever satisfy. Instead, they enslave.

Homosexuality is one of the frightening evidences of this judgment, whereby men and women exchange what is natural for that which is unnatural and impure (Rom. 1:24–27). The consequence is a terrible captivity to immoral sexual desire that is never satisfied.

There is, however, escape from this downward spiral! One must acknowledge God and honor Him as the one true God. How? By repenting of sin and believing in His Son, Jesus Christ, who offers forgiveness and eternal life (1 Cor. 6:9–11). This is what God asks of us today. In Jesus Christ we are set free from all of our wicked desires, and our worship is restored to the one true God. Through Christ, God is brought back in view as the supreme object of worship and our hearts are satisfied with everlasting joy in Him.

Delight in Doing His Will

I delight to do Your will, O my God; Your Law is within my heart.
PSALM 40:8

DANIEL HERCEG: THEOLOGICAL BIBLICAL ACADEMY | CROATIA

This is a truth for all of God's children! When our hearts are filled with His word, our delight is to do His will. The Lord's will is going to be our will. His delight is going to be our delight! Those who find delight in God's will are cheerful and willing to obey all that God commands them.

My grandmother recently gave her life to Christ and she was baptized. She is 65 years old, and lived her life before as a Roman Catholic. From time to time I read the Bible with her and we talk about the gospel. She always has the same reaction: tears of joy. She knows her name is written in the Book of Life. She is joyful and she now joyfully obeys God's commands. She delights to do God's will, and God's Law is her joy.

The greatest example is our Lord Jesus Christ. He always found delight in doing the will of His Father. He did not stay in a manger, nor stay in the Temple when teaching teachers. He did not stay on the mountain of transfiguration where His glory was shown. On the contrary, when the days were approaching for His ascension, He was determined to go to Jerusalem (Luke 9:51). Why? To die on the cruel cross in order to save those who are going to believe in Him, for the joy set before Him (Heb. 12:2).

Do you delight to do God's will? Consider this: If His will for your life is to die in a foreign place in order to bring the gospel to those who never heard it, would you willingly subject yourself to His will?

He Is Our Peace

*For He himself is our peace, who made both groups into one
and broke down the barrier of the dividing wall.*
EPHESIANS 2:14

VITALIY PELIKHATYY: WORD OF GRACE BIBLE INSTITUTE | USA

What is it that makes the church simultaneously one of the sweetest and most challenging places on earth? People. Every believer knows the beauty of fellowship among believers, and the pain of sin that ruins this experience. Human conflict was one of the first signs that sin had entered the world. In Genesis 3 we see how Adam and Eve go from Eden to shame and blame within a few verses after the Fall. Such has been the reality of human relationships since the Fall, the church not excluded.

What is our hope out of this brokenness? In our text, Paul is describing how the vast differences between the Jews and Gentiles are brought to peace rather than hostility. The "dividing wall," which brings about hostility, is removed through the sacrifice of Jesus Christ. While the cross of Christ is rightly thought of as bringing peace between man and God, it also brings peace between people. In fact, it is the only hope to have unity and peace in our congregations.

In our Slavic community we see the power of this peace playing out beautifully. As tensions among the Russians and Ukrainians persist, the churches whose focus is on the cross of Jesus Christ are able to minister to those who are hurt, regardless of their nationality. And at the same time, the church can be an example to the world at war that our Savior has the power to break all barriers and bring true peace among the peoples. May we then demonstrate this peace as we enjoy sweet fellowship with believers in the church.

Glory and Security

Now to Him who is able to keep you from stumbling, and to make you stand in the presence of His glory blameless with great joy, to the only God our Savior, through Jesus Christ our Lord, be glory, majesty, dominion and authority, before all time and now and forever. Amen.

JUDE 24–25

RAYMOND KWAN: JAPAN BIBLE ACADEMY | JAPAN

In this world, it's so easy to get distracted and discouraged with regard to our faith. There are enemies from within, namely our own sins and insecurities, which cause us to doubt our salvation. There are enemies from without, those who attack our faith with lies—both obvious and subtle. There are even those who fall away from the faith, people we once looked up to as examples, but now make us wonder whether or not we ourselves will finish the race as believers. However, the Lord's half-brother, Jude, reminds us that we should not focus our attention on human ability (or inability), but on the all-powerful God who guards and guarantees our salvation.

If we turn our attention to this God, what do we see? We see glory. We see the glory that Moses wanted to see in greater fullness even though he had already spoken to God face to face. We see the majestic glory that still gripped Peter even decades after he had first seen it. The God who saves and secures us is the King of glory, and no words will ever do justice in describing His glory. The world did see a veiled image of God's glory during Jesus' first coming, but when He comes again, the world will see glory in a way it has never known.

This world is filled with false, lesser, and temporary glories. However, God's glory is true, greater, and eternal. When we struggle with our faith, may we remember to look to God and His majestic glory, and rest on the truth that He can and will bring us to glory.

Suffering Unjustly

For Christ also died for sins once for all, the just for the unjust,
so that He might bring us to God, having been put to death in
the flesh, but made alive in the spirit.

1 PETER 3:18

P. S.: MIDDLE EAST (NAME WITHHELD FOR SECURITY)

Have you ever been treated unfairly? More specifically, have you ever been mistreated for the cause of Christ? Peter wrote the words of this verse to believers who were suffering for the sake of righteousness. Christ is the supreme example of one who suffered unjustly. Our Lord is the only one who never committed any sin, so His suffering and death were completely undeserved. Yet He suffered for those who were unjust, so that He might give them His righteousness. His suffering was full and complete—He gave His very life.

I live and minister in a region of the world where Christians are often persecuted for their faith. Some are forced to flee their homes to avoid violence or death. Often, persecution comes from within one's own family. Even in places where there is an official policy of religious freedom, true believers can suffer for their faithfulness to their Lord. Some professing believers are unwilling to tell their own families that they are attending an evangelical church or reading the Bible. Yet there are many who boldly proclaim Christ and live according to His word in spite of the difficulties they face.

When we suffer for our faith, we should look to the One who suffered to give us life. And we should remember that He is alive today, and He is with us in our tribulations. And because He is alive, we know that we too will one day be raised with Him. In the meantime, may we be faithful to Him.

Are you willing to obey Christ, even if obedience leads to suffering for His sake?

Our Great High Priest

Therefore, since we have a great high priest who has passed through the heavens, Jesus the Son of God, let us hold fast our confession.

HEBREWS 4:14

ALEKSANDER G.: RUSSIA (FULL NAME WITHHELD FOR SECURITY)

The Russian Orthodox Church instructs people to pray to the saints, who are looked upon as advocates and intercessors able to appease God for our sake. However, the author of Hebrews informs us that there is only one Intercessor and He is perfect. The writer turns our attention to Jesus Christ, the *faithful* and *merciful* High Priest, who gives us access to the throne of grace through prayer.

This can radically change your relationship to prayer, which is a privilege you have obtained through the blood of Jesus Christ! When you stumble and fall in your prayer life, raise your head once again and look to Christ, for He alone is your salvation—both in the present and in the consummation in the future. Turning to Jesus Christ, we don't pray to or rely on the services of a human intercessor, but we open our hearts to God's Son!

However, let's not forget that the intercessory ministry of Christ arouses us to faithfulness: "Let us hold fast our confession." This faithfulness is born out in obedience, dedication, responsibility, stability, conviction, and boldness.

The author of Hebrews purposefully places Christ at the center of our faith. Christ Himself, His superiority and His sacrifice for salvation, is the main object of our confession. As this truth is attacked by enemies of the gospel, it is imperative that we are convinced of it. This truth is necessary so we can make use of His exceptional high priestly ministry before God in prayer. Our faithfulness to Christ is manifested in a daily choice to be constant in prayer and to strive to glorify God in our lives.

The Right Investment

For whoever wishes to save his life will lose it, but whoever loss his life for My sake, he is the one who will save it. For what is a man profited if he gains the whole world, and loses or forfeits himself?

LUKE 9:24–25

STANLEY DUMANIG: THE EXPOSITOR'S ACADEMY | PHILIPPINES

In the Philippines, it is not uncommon to see televangelists or so-called outreach ministries trying to entice people to believe that God will fulfill all their felt needs, making them healthy, rich, and powerful. In a country that has a large population of poor and needy people, who would not happily receive a message like that? Even the middle class and rich are quick to believe in a god who guarantees to give them everything their lustful hearts already desire.

But that kind of teaching leads to hell. It runs contrary to what Christ has said in the text above. The true gospel that saves is a call to self-denial. This is also seen in the verse immediately prior to ours, where Jesus said, "If anyone wishes to come after Me, he must deny himself, and take up his cross daily and follow Me" (Luke 9:23). The gospel is not a worldly promise about acquiring health, wealth, and happiness. According to our text, it is possible to gain the *whole world* and still not have Christ or salvation at all!

The Christian life is lived by dying. He who wants to follow Christ must *lose* his life for His sake. Pursuing Christ requires a willingness to sacrifice physical things in this life, or even life itself, for the greater value of eternal life in Jesus Christ. Commitment to Christ requires our all. Don't invest in the things of this world. Invest in Christ and you will reap profits for all of eternity!

The True and Perfect Standard of Love

This is My commandment, that you love one another, just as I have loved you.

JOHN 15:12

RAFFAELE SPITALE: ITALIAN THEOLOGICAL ACADEMY | ITALY

This verse introduces us to a key truth of the gospel. We, Christ's disciples, are called to love one another in the same way Christ loved us. In today's world, the word "love" often simply refers to an emotion derived from circumstances. It is, in other words, a temporal and conditional feeling.

In this verse, however, Jesus calls us not simply to love one another, but specifically to love *as He loved us*. Jesus Christ is the only true and perfect standard of love. This love was manifested in His willingness to lay down His life for undeserving sinners. The love of this world has nothing to do with the love of Christ.

The love of this command is an unconditional willingness to sacrifice oneself for the benefit of others. In fact, we are even called, if necessary, to lay down our lives for the brethren (1 John 3:16), just as Christ did for us. This is the true Christian love that contrasts the selfish, temporal, and conditional love of this world.

But what is the aim of this command? It's not only to instruct believers to love, but to lead them to proclaim the true and only God by reflecting His love in this world. In fact, by loving one another all men will know that we are His disciples (John 13:35). By this love we manifest the glorious nature of God's love and the evidence of God's saving work in us (1 John 4:7), to the praise of His glory.

How to Encourage and Build Up

Therefore encourage one another and build up one another,
just as you also are doing.

1 THESSALONIANS 5:11

Matthias Frohlich: European Bible Training Center | Germany

In order to finish the race well which is set before us (Heb. 12:1), we need the fellowship of believers. Believers do not flourish apart from a local church. If they separate from the local body of Christ, they expose themselves to great danger and spiritual famine. We need encouragement and exhortation. We need to bear one another's burdens. We need to stir and build up one another.

How can believers encourage and build up one other? The context of this passage makes it clear. First, by reminding each other of the goal we are destined to by God. We have a heavenly calling! "God has not destined us for wrath, but for obtaining salvation through our Lord Jesus Christ" (1 Thess. 5:9).

Second, believers build up one another by reminding each other how to achieve this goal: "put on the breastplate of faith and love, and as a helmet, the hope of salvation" (1 Thess. 5:8). Everything Paul labored for centered around these characteristics. He wanted to see faith, love, and hope developed in the lives of believers. For this goal he prayed, taught, wrote letters, and modeled with his life. Faith, love, and hope need to grow in our personal lives, as well as in the life of each believer around us.

Praise God for the believers whom God has placed around you, to encourage you in your race. Pray and think about others whom you can encourage today, whom you can help to overcome discouragement, frustration, weariness, or sin. Help others not to despair in sanctification but to walk with endurance in a manner worthy of the God who called us.

The Gospel of Peace

The word which He sent to the sons of Israel, preaching peace through Jesus Christ (He is Lord of all).

ACTS 10:36

KGOMO THOMAS MAKGABO: CHRIST SEMINARY | SOUTH AFRICA

Perhaps you have not heard the word of God and your life is in a mess; you are discouraged, you went everywhere searching for peace in your heart but with no success. Even your good works and offerings cannot bring sustainable peace in your life. Let me introduce to you the God-man called Jesus Christ of Nazareth, who was crucified, killed, buried, and resurrected, then ascended to heaven. He is Lord of all and Savior of those who believe and accept Him, and has given them the right to be called sons of God (John 1:12).

It is not the state of your nationality that determines your relationship with God, but it is your relationship with Jesus Christ. He went around preaching good news, proclaiming the peace of God freely available to those who accept Christ as Lord and Savior. You need to repent of sin and believe in Him. It is great to know that God favors no one; He accepts whomever receives the gospel with fear and responds in faith (Acts 10:34).

Perhaps you are a believer and have strayed from fellowship with God, hence the peace of God is far from you, and it seems your Christian life is fading. The truth is, you cannot find sustainable peace parallel to the word of God and without Jesus Christ, who freely brings peace into life. He is the God of peace and you need Him. "How lovely ... are the feet of him who brings good news, who announces peace, who brings good news of happiness, who announces salvation, and says to Zion, 'Your God reigns!'" (Isa. 52:7).

Caring for our Spiritual Siblings

*Now accept the one who is weak in faith, but not for the
purpose of passing judgment on his opinions.*
ROMANS 14:1

JOHN HUGHES: TMAI HEADQUARTERS | LOS ANGELES, CALIFORNIA

This verse reminds me of parents who are constantly challenging older siblings to treat their younger siblings with kindness and care. They say things like "Be nice to your sister and watch out for her on the walk to school," or "Don't tease or ignore your brother, and don't let him get bullied on the playground."

I am so thankful that after God saved me as a young person, He graciously placed me in a church where our pastor capably taught the word and challenged us to faithfully study it for ourselves. There was a high value placed on biblical knowledge and theological precision.

Unfortunately, for me this had the unintended consequence of thinking of people as: a) those who are lost, b) those who are saved but don't correctly understand spiritual truth, or c) those who are like me and have a clear understanding of God's word.

In short, I ignored the principle in this verse and viewed my brothers and sisters in Christ as either first-class or second-class Christians. I would do my best to distance myself from those second-class believers. When I had spiritual conversations with them, my words and attitudes would let them know that they had significant deficits in their understanding of God's word and His will. In pursuing a strong understanding of biblical content and correct theology, I disregarded the truth of 1 Corinthians 8:1 that "knowledge makes arrogant, but love edifies."

Remind yourself often of the truth that any person whom God calls His child is your brother or sister in Christ. Our heavenly Father expects us to love and care for them like a good sibling should.

Don't Wait for a Bolt from Heaven

Now to Him who is able to establish you according to my gospel and the preaching of Jesus Christ, according to the revelation of the mystery which has been kept secret for long ages past, but now is manifested, and by the Scriptures of the prophets, according to the commandment of the eternal God, has been made known to all the nations, leading to obedience of faith; to the only wise God, through Jesus Christ, be the glory forever. Amen.

ROMANS 16:25–27

GENCI C.: ALBANIA (FULL NAME WITHHELD FOR SECURITY)

The gospel *is* the preaching of Jesus Christ (Rom. 16:25). It is the good news of God revealed in God's Son (Rom. 1:3–4). It is the message that was "kept secret for long ages past, but now is manifested" (Rom. 16:25–26). It was promised beforehand by the prophets of the Old Testament and revealed by the Spirit to the apostles of the New. It is a universal declaration of forgiveness and eternal life in the name of Jesus for all who would repent and believe, regardless of family, background, or status.

The gospel *accomplishes* salvation in those who believe (Rom. 1:16). Moreover, it is the way God establishes us and strengthens our faith. Do you want a more vibrant faith, firmer convictions, and greater trust in God? These all come by the gospel, by the preaching of Jesus Christ. We don't try to discover a magic formula or wait for a bolt from heaven. We don't look for a mountaintop experience or a burning in the bosom or writing on the wall or a slaying of the Spirit. We look to the gospel of Jesus Christ; and by it, we are firmly established and led to greater obedience of faith (Rom. 16:26).

There is no greater relief for the downcast soul, no greater answer to the heart of doubt, and no greater encouragement to the weak of faith than a reexamination of the gospel of Jesus Christ. Whether through the inerrant word of God or through sermons faithful to it, keep the gospel near!

Faithful Perseverance in Afflictions

*Therefore, we ourselves speak proudly of you among the
churches of God for your perseverance and faith in the midst
of all your persecutions and afflictions which you endure.*
2 THESSALONIANS 1:4

THOMAS HOCHSTETTER: EUROPEAN BIBLE TRAINING CENTER | GERMANY

What comes out when God turns up the heat in your life through persecution, temptations, infirmities, or major disappointments? What is the light at the end of the tunnel for you? The exit? A train? Something more hopeful?

In his second letter to the Thessalonians, Paul commends the believers for their exemplary character in the midst of trials. We do not know the details of the trials, but they certainly involved personal hostility from their unbelieving countrymen (1 Thess. 2:14). They received this opposition not because of wrongdoing, but because "the word of the Lord has sounded forth from" them (1 Thess. 1:8).

What makes them such a wonderful example? If you look at the verse, you will note two outcomes: perseverance and faith. They were hard pressed; they were squeezed. But, instead of faltering, they grew in their faith toward God and their love for one another (2 Thess. 1:3)!

"How can that happen?" you may ask. They endured because they had their eyes set on their only hope: Jesus Christ. They knew that home was still to come.

Whatever trials you may be going through, whether it is persecution or personal troubles, know this: Jesus is the light at the end of the tunnel. He is in the midst of it all, refining your faith to bring about supernatural, spiritual fruit. Trials test true faith. But true faith perseveres, because the One in you is greater than the trial.

The next time you face hardship, consider the example of the Thessalonians. Look ahead to Christ, so that "God will count you worthy of your calling" (2 Thess. 1:11).

Proven Love

I in them and You in Me, that they may be perfected in unity, so that the world may know that You sent Me, and loved them, even as You have loved Me.

JOHN 17:23

JOSE MANUEL ROBLES SANTOS: BEREA SEMINARY | SPAIN

The church I attend is constructing a new building. Since the building has a very nice design and is in the city center, we are now all the more visible for everyone. During construction, many have shown interest: When is the new church going to be ready? Can we attend the opening ceremony? Having faced a lot of indifference in the past, this obviously encourages us, but we are well aware that the modern design of the building or its beauty can only have an impact on their senses, never on their hearts.

In this text, Christ tells us what will really be an effective testimony to our city, what is going to really reveal Him as the Savior sent by the Father. Our church's main characteristic must be that Christ rules in our lives. This is proven when we, empowered by the Spirit, demonstrate the salvation that God has granted us in His love. We do this through our love for one another and through our obedience to Christ and His word.

Our new building may gain us some visitors, but what will gain us brothers and sisters in Christ is God working in the hearts of those visitors, making known His Son as the sinner's Savior. More than a beautiful building, our prayer is for people to see the gospel lived out through a group of sinners, now saved and transformed, living in harmony, and showing God's love in word and deed.

Do others see Christ ruling in your life through your love for other Christians and obedience to God's word?

Living Up to Your Transformed Life

So, as those who have been chosen of God, holy and beloved, put on a heart of compassion, kindness, humility, gentleness and patience.

COLOSSIANS 3:12

JOSE ALCIVAR: INSTITUTO DE EXPOSITORES | USA

A well-known preacher once shared that it was impossible to be hit by a truck and leave the scene unchanged. He explained that it would be absurd to expect anything other than obvious physical trauma from such a great blow. In the same way, he expressed, it is not possible to have an encounter with Christ, to say that He has changed your life, and not have obvious, real marks to prove it.

In today's passage, Paul is using a similar argument. In verse 10, the apostle explains that believers have "put on the new self," which indicates a renovation that takes place in every believer. The author emphasizes that, since Christ has transformed them, there will be noticeable marks all over, which will differentiate them from the rest of the world.

These obvious marks are lives characterized by compassion, kindness, humility, meekness, and patience. If we have been justified and loved by our Father, then, transformed behavior is the only proper response to His work in us. Moreover, Paul takes it a step further and motivates us to live out these characteristics each day. We must constantly remember that we ourselves have experienced the forgiveness of Christ, and, thus, we should strive to bear our marks boldly before the world—a testimony of His work in us.

Putting on the new self is not something that you do only once; rather, it is a constant discipline that can only be achieved when your heart has passed from death to life (Col. 2:13). If God has done this work within you, what other motivation do you need to live up to your transformed life?

The Compassionate Shepherd

Seeing the people, He felt compassion for them, because they
were distressed and dispirited like sheep without a shepherd.
MATTHEW 9:36

VITALIY PELIKHATYY: WORD OF GRACE BIBLE INSTITUTE | USA

A.W. Tozer wrote that what we think of God is the most important thing about us. Tozer rightly perceived that our view of God defines us and how we relate to Him. If God is seen like Santa Claus, then we work hard to make sure that by year's end we have been more nice than naughty to earn His favor. If He is like a benevolent heavenly grandfather, then it doesn't matter how we live; He doesn't care. If God is like a cosmic watchmaker who made the world and left it, then He is far away and irrelevant.

What we think of God becomes even more significant when life is difficult. When that happens, is God punishing you? Is He able to help? Does He even care? In those moments, how you view God will determine your whole reality—giving you hope or driving you to despair, to God or from God. Jesus, God in human flesh, tells us that He looks to our condition, not with judgment, simple acceptance, or disinterest, but with compassion. He cares about our pain, is aware of our suffering, and is concerned for our plight. He is the loving shepherd who gave His life for the sheep.

Whatever your situation or circumstance, Jesus calls you today to turn to His compassion, to trust His care, to rest in His promises. He is there. He loves His sheep and wants to shepherd you in and through every circumstance of life. In family life, let Him be your loving Leader; in work, let him be your caring Master; in ministry, let him be your all-sufficient Shepherd.

Love One Another

Beloved, let us love one another, for love is from God; and everyone who loves is born of God and knows God.
1 JOHN 4:7

ALEX CHIRWA: CENTRAL AFRICAN PREACHING ACADEMY | MALAWI

I often hear people complaining that no one loves them. Spouses, children, students, professionals— many people feel unloved. Love certainly does not characterize our fallen world. So, where does it come from? According to the Bible, love is from God.

This love of God toward mankind was demonstrated once and for all at the cross. We see it in Jesus' willing sacrifice of love to become sin on our behalf so that we might live in Him. What God has done through His Son Jesus Christ is the greatest demonstration of selfless, life-promoting love that the world has ever known. Jesus said, "Greater love has no one than this, that one lay down his life for his friends" (John 15:13).

In the verse above, the apostle John encourages us to love one another in this way. If we are born-again Christians, then it will follow that we will show others the same love of God that we found in Christ. We cannot truly love and fulfill God's word without His love first working in our hearts. That's why John says that love is from God.

Friend, do you have love in your heart for others, especially for the family of God? It is this kind of love—not simply knowing facts about God—that proves that you know God. Anyone can recite truths about God, but not anyone can love others as Christ loved us. Only those who are born of God and know God truly love. If you know Christ's love, make an effort today to share it with others.

Spiritual Fruitfulness

But the fruit of the Spirit is love, joy, peace, patience, kindness,
goodness, faithfulness, gentleness, self-control; against such
things there is no law.
GALATIANS 5:22–23

S. R.: ASIA (NAME WITHHELD FOR SECURITY)

We all want to overcome sin and live a spiritually fruitful life. Many times, we devise strategies and make resolutions but fail to keep them. Prior to this passage, Paul tells us to keep walking in the Spirit because it is the Spirit that bears fruit in us: love, joy, peace, patience, kindness, goodness, faithfulness, gentleness, and self-control. What a package of virtues! Think how each is displayed in full in our Lord Jesus Christ.

Many churches in our region are carried away by charismatic excesses in looking for miraculous gifts. They believe miraculous gifts are the means to have revival in the church and society. But we do not need miraculous gifts to have revival—we have the Spirit of God in us to produce the fruit that demonstrates Christlikeness. The church will be revived, and society will be impacted, when we bear this fruit by the Spirit.

Remember, we cannot truly produce this fruit by ourselves. We must have the Spirit of God indwelling us to produce this fruit. And as He permanently dwells in a Christian, so we must continually walk in the Spirit so these virtues can be manifested.

How can you walk in the Spirit and see Him bear fruit? Study the Scriptures to know and apply its truth in your life in every circumstance. The Spirit only works in accordance with Scripture. Remember also what Christ has done for you. He demonstrated all these virtues toward you in fullness while you were a wretched sinner. Show then His fruit today. Be kind to your neighbor. Show love to those infected with a selfish attitude. Bear much fruit for Christ!

Spiritual Boldness in Evangelism

And when they had prayed, the place where they had gathered together was shaken, and they were all filled with the Holy Spirit and began to speak the word of God with boldness.

ACTS 4:31

ROBERT KENSINGER: EVANGELICAL MINISTRIES OF THE AMERICAS | HONDURAS

My adopted country of Honduras is known for having one of the highest crime rates in the world, especially murder. Gangs, drugs, and vengeance plague the impoverished and often helpless people. Yet, I have been amazed by the boldness of many believers, especially pastors, as they seek to win the lost and share the only hope for change in such a lost and dangerous world. On motorcycles and bicycles they go into villages along unprotected and hazardous paths, at times infested by thieves, for the sole purpose of obeying the Great Commission.

How do they do this? From where do they get their boldness and strength? Acts 4:31 tells us that it comes directly from God through the Person of the Holy Spirit. Before receiving the Holy Spirit, when faced with a threat of danger from those around, the disciples scattered and fled (Matt. 26:56). But now, having received the Holy Spirit, they were once again facing a life-threatening warning from the rulers not to preach the gospel. This time, however, their response was entirely different. This time they stood their ground, saying, "We cannot stop speaking about what we have seen and heard" (Acts 4:20). And according to Acts 4:31, they prayed and, having been empowered by the Holy Spirit, they "[spoke] the word of God with boldness."

If we know Jesus Christ as our Lord and Savior, then we have this same Holy Spirit dwelling and working within us to empower us to obedience, especially obedience to the Great Commission. Pray to God that His Spirit would strengthen you today to speak the word of God with boldness.

Draw Near in Prayer

Therefore let us draw near with confidence to the throne of grace, so that we may receive mercy and find grace to help in time of need.

HEBREWS 4:16

ALEKSANDER G.: RUSSIA (FULL NAME WITHHELD FOR SECURITY)

J. C. Ryle once pronounced these sobering words: "In the Christian life there is no more neglected duty than personal private prayer." Neglect of prayer shows itself in its absence or irregularity, in feebleness or apathy, or in its empty or formal character. Although there may be many reasons why the wind of prayer has stilled, one of the most serious is a gaze turned away from the Savior that neglects His priestly ministry performed before the throne of God.

Think about your prayer life. Have you noticed that your prayers have turned into formalities, becoming dry and lifeless? Have you observed that your prayers even weary you, because they sound like empty words which rise no further than the ceiling? Do you notice that your prayers have become a boring duty which no longer brings the joy of fellowship with God?

If this picture depresses you, and you have stopped praying, perhaps you have given in to your feelings. You have moved your gaze from Christ to your circumstances, and your fellowship with God has grown cold. But despite your feelings, your heavenly Father is right where He has always been. The barrier to prayer is not to be found in God, but in the sin that besets us. Therefore, when we are not able or do not desire to pray, we need the truth of the Scriptures, which restore the joy of our fellowship with God.

The truth regarding our merciful High Priest, who continually petitions the Father on our behalf, motivates us to pray and to hurry into God's presence to receive the blessings that we need: mercy, grace, and relief.

What Does the Lord Require of You?

He has told you, O man, what is good; and what does the
LORD require of you but to do justice, to love kindness, and to
walk humbly with your God?

MICAH 6:8

MOJMIR ADAMEK: CZECH BIBLE INSTITUTE | CZECH REPUBLIC

It has been suggested that this text is one of the best one-line sum-maries of the whole Old Testament Law. The prophet Micah was sent by God to deliver a message of judgment on God's people, whose worship degenerated into mere ritualism. They disregarded the Lord so deeply that they acted as if the God of the universe would be pleased by empty rituals. How foolish! After many years and many prophets, who proclaimed that God does not want mere formalism, the people of God still did not listen.

So here again, God sends Micah to remind them what He demands from them. He does not want empty words and empty deeds. God wants their hearts and lives to show that they truly love Him. To act justly toward others, to love others faithfully, and simply to live the way God wanted them to live—this is what God wanted.

Jesus pronounced similar words in Matthew 23:23 on account of religious hypocrites who, for the sake of their pedantic ritualism, neglected justice, mercy, and faithfulness.

Let us be reminded, brothers and sisters, that what we attempt to do for God is not the end goal in and of itself. We can be so easily consumed by daily ministry and forget that without true love for our God, our ministry can be worthless. God wants us to live our lives as a continual act of worship, which does not come out of formalism but out of our born-again identity. Consider and ask if the Lord would make the same pronouncement on you.

Banking on Contentment

Make sure that your character is free from the love of money,
being content with what you have; for He Himself has said, "I
WILL NEVER DESERT YOU, NOR WILL *I* EVER FORSAKE YOU."

HEBREWS 13:5

JAMES DONALD DOWDY: WORD OF GRACE BIBLICAL SEMINARY | MEXICO

It is easy to love money. Not only can we pay our bills with money but we can also buy more "stuff" with it. And this stuff makes us happier, right? We think the equation goes like this: more money equals more stuff equals more happiness. But this is contrary to biblical wisdom. Whoever loves money will not be satisfied with it (Eccles. 5:10).

God alone satisfies the true needs of body and soul. He is the one who gives us the power and ability to obtain wealth (Deut. 8:18). He always provides what we need (Matt. 6:25–31). Sometimes this provision is more and other times less, but it is *always* sufficient (Phil. 4:11–12).

It is common for us to think that only the wealthy struggle with greed. However, during many years of missionary service among both poor and rich in multiple countries, I have observed that dissatisfaction with how much money and possessions we have is common to all men, *even* missionaries! The love of money can afflict anyone—rich or poor—because it is simply an attitude whereby we set our hearts on material things.

Jesus warned us to be on guard against this: "For not even when one has an abundance does his life consist of his possessions" (Luke 12:15). Therefore, live your life free from the love of money, be content with what God has given you, and thank Him every day for His provision.

Rich in Grace

For you know the grace of our Lord Jesus Christ, that though
He was rich, yet for your sake He became poor, so that you
through His poverty might become rich.

2 CORINTHIANS 8:9

ALEKSANDER G.: RUSSIA (FULL NAME WITHHELD FOR SECURITY)

The Incarnation of the Son of God reminds us of the amazing grace that transforms a spiritual pauper into someone who is spiritually rich. We never cease to marvel at the Son's willingness to sacrifice Himself. Grace was displayed in this sacrifice! Yet these words, mixed with Paul's call to mutual service, intimate that the grace that was given to us puts on us the responsibility to be rich in the area of practical righteousness, to be generous and sacrificial, storing up treasure in heaven.

Paul reminds us about the grace of Christ with the words "for you know." Addressing the Corinthians, whose willingness to sacrifice was waning, he appeals to their knowledge of gospel truth. There are times that we are like the Corinthians. We know about the grace given to us by the Lord Jesus, but we act as if struck by spiritual amnesia and forget that the grace of Christ demands sacrifice, as the apostle admonished, "See that you abound in this gracious work also" (2 Cor. 8:7). When we turn our gaze away from Christ, we undoubtedly fix it on something temporary or material.

Take time to meditate on Christ, who secured salvation for us by giving Himself for us. Even though grace, by definition, is given to us freely, that doesn't mean it didn't come at a high cost. The Lord Jesus, taking on bodily form and dying on the cross, paid a dear price. Remind yourself that the grace of God compels us to give of ourselves—first of all to the Lord and, secondly, to the work of the Lord (2 Cor. 8:5).

The Lord Removes All Reasons for Fear

The LORD is my light and my salvation; whom shall I fear?
The LORD is the defense of my life; whom shall I dread?
PSALM 27:1

VINCENT GREENE: THE EXPOSITOR'S ACADEMY | PHILIPPINES

A re you curious about what it is like to live in another country? Have you ever thought of the adventure of tasting new foods, seeing new places, and meeting new people? If your answer is "yes," it might surprise you that some would answer "no" because they fear the idea of living in a new country. They fear meeting new people who look different and speak a different language. They fear living in a place that is unfamiliar to them in almost every respect.

In this Psalm, David places his confidence in the Lord because it is the Lord who gives him reason not to fear (2 Tim. 1:7). He did not just clench his teeth and generate bravery from within; he looked to God! David, knowing the Lord's power, had no reason to fear because he knew his life was in the Lord's hands (Psa. 23:4; 46:1; 1 Pet. 5:6–7).

We, too, can trust in the Lord to lead and guide us in all of life's situations. We can have faith in His sovereignty to oversee everything. We can overcome the anxieties involved with evangelizing our neighbors, the panic of struggling finances, the worries of illness, or the threat of enemies. Whether we are missionaries on a foreign field or the salt and light in our own country, if we look to God, He will be our defense!

Are there any responsibilities or challenges in your life that cause you dread? Keep your eyes on God and He will lead you through them, for He is our light and our salvation.

Worthy Virtues

Walk in a manner worthy of the calling ... with all humility and gentleness, with patience, showing tolerance for one another in love.

EPHESIANS 4:1–2

ERNEST KANZANGAZA: CENTRAL AFRICAN PREACHING ACADEMY | MALAWI

Is your life different from those around you? Do you live in a manner worthy of your calling? In this verse, the apostle Paul presents the virtues that should characterize our lives as we follow the Lord Jesus.

First, we should be humble and gentle. Paul is echoing the words of Jesus in Matthew 11:29, where He says that He is gentle and humble in heart. Humility is to be our basic orientation toward God and others (James 4:6; 1 Pet. 5:5). Gentleness is also vital to expressing our love for others. We are to learn from our Lord, the perfect picture of these attributes.

Second, we are to add patience to our humility and gentleness. Patience is the ability to withstand provocation without losing our temper. Patience is a fruit of the Holy Spirit (Gal. 5:22); those who are chosen of God are to put on a heart of patience (Col. 3:12).

Third, we are to bear with each other in love. We should be motivated by love because Jesus first loved us when we were undeserving sinners (Rom. 5:8). He demonstrated true forbearance and love, leaving us an example to follow.

Let us look continually to Christ as our model. And as we do, we will receive grace each day to walk in a manner worthy of our calling.

Serving God or Serving Idols?

You cannot drink the cup of the Lord and the cup of demons; you cannot partake of the table of the Lord and the table of demons.

1 CORINTHIANS 10:21

D. B.: ASIA (NAME WITHHELD FOR SECURITY)

Here we are challenged and exhorted to have fellowship with the Lord Jesus Christ and His church rather than idols. This is because no one can truly have fellowship both with God and with idols. As Jesus Himself declared, no one can serve two masters. The context of this verse encourages us to prioritize Christ and His body, and avoid all other priorities which do not encourage a greater intimacy with God.

The Corinthians were saved from worshiping a pantheon of idols (1 Cor. 12:2), and some of them were now being divisive by flaunting their freedom in eating food sacrificed to idols. The man who says he is loyal to God and yet still continues to publicly support idol worship provokes God's jealousy (1 Cor. 10:22). How quickly one can hurt other Christians or hinder one's witness to a watching, unbelieving world.

Paul states that a Christian cannot drink the cup of the Lord and the cup of demons, especially in a public way. In the country that I live in and serve, many of us are saved from the worship of actual idols. As believers, we must separate ourselves from any form of participation with those idols that were followed before salvation.

Yet this is not an issue only in the East. In the West, the idols are worldviews or pursuits, such as entertainment, fashion, and materialism. This text should make us examine our witness. Does a watching world see the contrast of your life in loving Christ more than former lusts and idols you once served?

Middle East

In this region where false religions can inflict major persecution, pastoral training can be more challenging. In some cases, neighboring countries that are more open to the gospel can be used as strategic locations for training pastors to reach more hostile contexts.

TODAY, PRAY FOR

Inroads into the Middle East so that pastors can be trained and underground churches can be strengthened.

Believers who are persecuted daily for their faith. Pray for perseverance and courage to face attacks from a hostile world.

Strong churches in the Middle East so Muslims who are coming to faith in Christ may learn to be faithful disciples.

Preventing Tunnel Vision

"For My thoughts are not your thoughts, nor are your ways My ways," declares the LORD.

ISAIAH 55:8

JOSE CARLOS MARTINEZ CRISTOBAL: WORD OF GRACE BIBLICAL SEMINARY | MEXICO

Glaucoma is an illness that causes the gradual loss of the eye's peripheral vision, usually in an imperceptible way. When the illness is not dealt with properly, people who have the disease may come to have tunnel vision, whereby they can only see what is central to their field of view.

The people of Israel experienced something similar. Though God promised them certain blessings, they forgot them when trials came. Though God promised protection, they relied instead on the surrounding nations during crises. Though God continually provided for them, they were ever quick to look elsewhere. They focused on their circumstances while overlooking God's glorious purposes in them. They were self-inflicted with spiritual glaucoma.

Sadly, Christians today are not much different. Like the Israelites before us, we tend to focus on the trials rather than on the God who stands above us. We tend to lean on our own understanding rather than to trust in God. But God wants us to know something: His thoughts are not our thoughts. They are far better, far higher, and far more pure. Similarly, God's ways are not our ways. We will never understand everything about the trials we face, but we can trust in the God who stands above them.

Has spiritual glaucoma eroded your vision? Has your attention been consumed by your circumstances in such a way that you have forgotten the full picture? Remember that God's ways are not your ways—and be grateful for that! For who but God would have sent His only Son to die so that we might live? His ways are good. Keeping this in mind will prevent tunnel vision.

Tastes and Sights

O taste and see that the LORD *is good; how blessed is the man who takes refuge in Him!*

PSALM 34:8

KRISTIAN BRACKETT: THEOLOGICAL BIBLICAL ACADEMY | CROATIA

Croatia, like every country, has many great foods to taste and sights to see. God is good to give us sensory perception so that we can enjoy meals and vistas. But He gives us these blessings to spur us to a greater reality—to understand and know Him. The psalmist invites the worshiper to experience God and to recognize His goodness. He is good to the upright and the evil as he sends rain and sunshine upon all. He is generous with His kindness to allow those who love Him and those who hate Him to enjoy relationships and seasons of life. But His goodness is seen most of all in His sending His Son to die on the cross.

All the good things we taste and see—from pumpkin seed oil on garden-grown tomatoes and cucumbers to warm cheese strudel to the blue and green hues of the Plitvicka lakes with their connecting waterfalls to the pristine Adriatic Sea—as well as all we hear, smell, and touch—point us to the greater goodness of God, the giver of all good things.

We dare not despise His goodness and kindness. Instead we must run to God and find in Him a true refuge. He is that refuge, and all who look to Christ in faith have their lives hidden in Him. God is good for many reasons, but His greatest good is Jesus Christ who died for us.

What do you enjoy tasting and seeing? Give praise to God for them.

Declare the Whole Purpose of God

*For I did not shrink from declaring to you the whole
purpose of God.*

ACTS 20:27

CARLOS NUNEZ: EVANGELICAL MINISTRIES OF THE AMERICAS | HONDURAS

Honduras is a country full of prosperity gospel preachers and supposedly miraculous healings. An emotionally based gospel is taught and the preaching of God's word is replaced with entertainment-like Christian concerts. True exposition of the Bible is absent in most churches. It's urgent that God's people pay attention to Paul's declaration in Acts and treat it with all seriousness.

This passage defines biblical ministry for all godly men with its solemn central message. The whole purpose of God is to be declared. God's word is to be proclaimed.

The apostle Paul was committed to serving God with his whole being, even if it meant giving up his freedom and his life. Preserving his life was not of the utmost importance. Rather, his greatest concern was completing the Lord's work, of which he had been charged—spreading the good news through the power of the Holy Spirit.

Paul will later echo these same convictions in his second letter to Timothy, the last epistle he would write before he was martyred in Rome. Paul wrote it to his beloved companion and young pastor, Timothy, who needed to follow Paul's example. The mandate to preach God's word comes from God Himself, and He has commanded His shepherds to proclaim all of His word.

The responsibility of a pastor and teacher is to explain the meaning of Scripture to believers and unbelievers so that they might know and understand what God desires. Thus, shepherds are under God's watchful eye, and He looks at how we treat His word. Pray that God would raise up more faithful pastors in Honduras—and in the place where you live.

Truth or Lies

*You are of your father the devil, and you want to do the
desires of your father. He was a murderer from the beginning,
and does not stand in the truth because there is no truth in
him. Whenever he speaks a lie, he speaks from his own nature,
for he is a liar and the father of lies.*

JOHN 8:44

GIAMPAOLO NATALE: ITALIAN THEOLOGICAL ACADEMY | ITALY

Satan is the father of murder and lying. These words recall the Garden of Eden where he deceived Adam and Eve, and as result, sin and death entered the world. John Calvin said, "As soon as man was created, Satan was impelled by a wicked desire to hurt, and directed his strength to destroying him."

When Jesus said "you are of your father the devil," He was accusing the Jews of being offspring of Satan. The reason why the Jews wanted to kill Jesus was that they manifested their father's characteristics. They did not believe in the truth, and like the devil, they wanted to destroy Jesus, who is truth incarnate.

For believers today, these are challenging times. Many people get offended, like the Jews of Jesus' day, when we tell them the truth. Proclaiming that Jesus Christ is the only way to salvation will alienate and offend. This postmodern culture views truth as being relative to each individual. It insists that objective and absolute truth does not exist. These claims must be exposed as lies and the truth must be proclaimed.

What shall we do then? First, we must remember that there is absolute truth. Second, there is a clear distinction between truth and lies. Christ is the ultimate manifestation and standard of truth (John 14:6). Satan and those who reject Christ are the ultimate manifestation of lies. Third, we need to remember that the gospel of Christ is the only hope for this postmodern world. Anchor your convictions in the truth and be faithful to share it with others.

Forgiven to Forgive

Then Peter came and said to Him, "Lord, how often shall my brother sin against me and I forgive him? Up to seven times?" Jesus said to him, "I do not say to you, up to seven times, but up to seventy times seven."

MATTHEW 18:21–22

YOHANE KANTHUSI TEMBO: CENTRAL AFRICAN PREACHING ACADEMY | MALAWI

We all have offended others, and others have offended us, in one way or another. Peter's question and our Lord's answer touch on a very profound topic, one that is part of our day-to-day life. Peter wanted the Lord to approve his seemingly generous forgiveness limit of seven times. But Jesus told him that it was seventy times seven, meaning that Peter should forgive for as many times as it takes.

To truly understand forgiveness, we must start by recognizing that we all have been forgiven by God for innumerable offenses that we would never be able to settle on our own. So, refusing to forgive someone is being unjust to God, who Himself is ready to forgive.

The kingdom of God, to which we belong, is a kingdom of mercy. We have been granted grace, and we are to extend the same grace to others, even when they offend us. We must remember that all offenses are toward God, and God's mercies are new every morning.

By nature, we want to keep a record of wrongs and set limits on forgiveness. We don't want others to take advantage of us, so we reserve mercy for situations that we deem worthy of it. But this text reminds us that true forgiveness that is characteristic of God's kingdom is unending and without measure. God expects us to forgive just as He forgives us in Christ.

Hallelujah! We have received perfect forgiveness in Christ. Let us then forgive others.

The Immeasurable Love of God

See how great a love the Father has bestowed on us, that we would be called children of God; and such we are. For this reason the world does not know us, because it did not know Him.

1 JOHN 3:1

R. M.: ASIA (NAME WITHHELD FOR SECURITY)

This verse talks about the infinite and immeasurable love of God, which cannot be measured or understood by human intellect. We must humble ourselves as we enter into contemplation of this great subject.

The apostle John focuses on this divine love as expressed in the Father sending His Son, our Lord Jesus Christ. Through His Son—functioning as Messiah and Mediator, dying on the cross to pay for all our sins, and giving us new life—God has enabled us to become His children. He has poured out this amazing love upon us! He loves to call us by name, as a father calls his own children. This is a special love reserved for those whom He calls His children—a blessing greater than God's common grace to a fallen, unbelieving world.

What an encouraging truth this is for growing our faith in our great Father. It is encouraging because of who we were when we received this love. We were prodigal sons—His enemies—despising the goodness of God. Yet He drew us back to Himself with His irresistible grace, and made us not only friends but children who inherit all of heaven's blessings. It is also encouraging because of who He is to us; He is our Father, He calls us by name, and allows us to know Him. Truly what a great love we walk in as Christians!

Take a moment and marvel at this other-worldly love that God the Father has shown to you.

Living Wisely

Conduct yourselves with wisdom toward outsiders, making the most of the opportunity.
COLOSSIANS 4:5

MIGUEL APARICIO: EVANGELICAL MINISTRIES OF THE AMERICAS | HONDURAS

Modern society, as in the past, is characterized by foolish hearts and minds, which rebel against and reject God. While these influences are in our sinful natures, the gospel demands that every Christian "conduct [himself] with wisdom." In our daily lives we are to demonstrate God's wisdom by behaving righteously and lovingly toward God and others.

Conduct refers to a lifestyle and implies a permanent behavior, not one that is temporary or on occasion. What is the purpose for conducting ourselves with wisdom toward outsiders if those outsiders are foolish? It is so that they can see the effects of the gospel of Christ in us.

The second part of the verse says "making the most of the opportunity," which means taking advantage of the time that we have. This is incredible. The Scriptures here teach us that every day precious opportunities will present themselves for us to proclaim Christ and honor Him through our actions. We must take advantage of these opportunities so that with wise conduct, the world can receive a clear and effective testimony.

To make the most of the time, we are called to not lose sight of the opportunity to testify and to conduct ourselves wisely in our everyday relationships with family, at work, in school, etc. Remember, we were once the outsiders characterized by foolishness, rebellion, and rejecting God; but God, having redeemed us, grants us the capacity to display His wisdom. Make the most of today's opportunities. Let your life be the commentary that explains the message you proclaim.

Walk in Love

*Walk in love, just as Christ also loved you and gave Himself up
for us, an offering and a sacrifice to God as a fragrant aroma.*
EPHESIANS 5:2

ALEKSANDER G.: RUSSIA (FULL NAME WITHHELD FOR SECURITY)

The world and Christians define love differently. The world's definition of love is associated with feelings, often masquerading
egoism and lust. Christians look to God to define love, pictured in
the sacrifice of Christ for unworthy sinners. Why is it important to
remember the difference? Because the world is actively *selling* God's
church their faulty view of love.

How should we respond to the world's offer? We don't need a sur-
rogate! We have different standards, a different orientation. We don't
imitate the heroes of Hollywood, but the Lord Jesus Christ, who gave
His life so sinners could be reconciled to God.

Our love must be oriented on Christ. Think about how easy it is to
love theoretically and how difficult it is to show love in action. Without
the power of Christ, we could not love as God calls us to. Therefore,
we are reminded of Christ and understand that if He loved us—undeserving sinners—and sacrificed Himself for us, then we have no reason to pick and choose whom we should love, to prefer our own good
instead of pleasing God by serving our neighbor, or to disappoint
God in our daily lives by thinking of ourselves more than of others.

The sacrifice of Christ reminds us of the standard of love that God
expects from us. Dedicate some time to prayerfully meditate on the
awesome work of the Savior at Calvary and strive to be like Him in
the course of each day, since love is nothing less than imitating the
self-giving sacrifice of the Lord Jesus Christ!

Immunization from Heresy

For certain persons have crept in unnoticed, those who were
long beforehand marked out for this condemnation, ungodly
persons who turn the grace of our God into licentiousness and
deny our only Master and Lord, Jesus Christ.

JUDE 4

DANIEL CORRAL: BEREA SEMINARY | SPAIN

A good shepherd guides and defends his sheep, as David writes in Psalm 23:4: "Your rod and Your staff, they comfort me." Jude is a true pastor and writes to skillfully teach other shepherds to use the rod (defense) and the staff (guidance) to preserve their flocks from heresy.

What sparked the need to protect against heresy? Our verse has the answer: "For certain persons have crept in unnoticed." The verb *crept* is only used here in the New Testament. It has the idea of weaseled, slipped, infiltrated, or entered secretly. "Certain persons" had "crept in" like a virus in the body.

Jude provides the reader with a vaccine. He will not give the persons' names, because, like a virus, they mutate. Therefore, Jude will expose their pattern because it is not new or sophisticated, but rather old and known ("those who were long beforehand marked out for this condemnation").

First, they are godless and wicked (Titus 1:16; 2 Pet. 2:7–9). They may call themselves Christians, but they act godlessly (1 John 3:10), for their goal is not the glory of God but rather to satisfy their uncontrolled lusts (2 Tim. 3:6). Second, they "deny our only Master and Lord, Jesus Christ." To know Christ determines your salvation (John 14:6). If anyone does not acknowledge Him as Master and Lord, then they are not saved.

Jude has proven to his readers how to strengthen their immune systems to fight the infection of heresy. Now ask yourself, Is my spiritual immune system strong?

God's Gift to Your Church

*And He gave some as apostles, and some as prophets, and
some as evangelists, and some as pastors and teachers, for the
equipping of the saints for the work of service, to the building
up of the body of Christ.*

EPHESIANS 4:11–12

NICK KALENA: EUROPEAN BIBLE TRAINING CENTER | GERMANY

The Bible teaches that everything was created through Jesus (Col. 1:16). According to our passage, Jesus Himself, as gracious Lord of all, has given you and your church a special gift. And this gift has a specific purpose. His gift to your local church is pastors who tend to your soul. The text lists five offices of the gifted people granted to the church: 1) apostles, 2) prophets, 3) evangelists, 4) pastors, and 5) teachers. The church today no longer has apostles like Peter or prophets who reveal a new word from God. We do have evangelists who proclaim the one true gospel, and pastors and teachers who proclaim and apply the word of God. Biblically qualified pastors are a reflection of God's grace to the church He loves.

God puts pastors in churches for a specific purpose. He intends that through their diligent labor, you will be equipped for the work of the ministry. It is their job to get you ready to proclaim the gospel, to encourage others with the truth, to restore those caught in sin, and to give of yourself generously and graciously. To claim that you are not gifted is contradicting what God has said. We are all responsible to join in Great Commission work.

Are you feeling unequipped for the task? Seize the opportunities your church provides for you to be equipped. Seek to be discipled. As God grows you, then seek opportunities to disciple others. And pray for the missionaries who have gone out to raise up pastors and churches who will continue the model of Ephesians 4:11–12.

God Meant It for Good

As for you, you meant evil against me, but God meant it for good in order to bring about this present result, to preserve many people alive.

GENESIS 50:20

VITALIY PELIKHATYY: WORD OF GRACE BIBLE INSTITUTE | USA

Joseph said these words to his brothers, his own family who had conspired to destroy his life out of jealousy when he was still just a youth. They nearly succeeded too, as they sold him into slavery, a life worse than death. And that's not even the whole story. While in Egypt, Joseph the slave is elevated, then wrongly accused and placed in jail for a number of years. While the first injustice was the work of his brothers, Joseph could have easily blamed God for the second injustice. Those who have experienced injustice know all too well how easy it is to blame God and demand Him to justify Himself.

Yet Joseph doesn't! His contentment is not tied to his circumstances, but is deeply rooted in the character of God. What God allows, does, and how He does it can often be confusing and disorienting, yet God is always working to bring about good. Through our circumstances, God wants to bring good to us and through us to those around us.

God used the greatest human evil, the murder of His Son, to bring about our greatest good—salvation. As we look to our lives, to the injustice around us and toward us, we ought to say with the apostle, "He who did not spare His own Son, but delivered Him over for us all, how will He not also with Him freely give us all things?" (Rom. 8:32).

Worship in Spirit and Truth

But an hour is coming, and now is, when the true worshipers will worship the Father in spirit and truth; for such people the Father seeks to be His worshipers.

JOHN 4:23

DAVID MCWHITE: CZECH BIBLE INSTITUTE | CZECH REPUBLIC

Jesus' words to the woman at the well do more than discard the notion that proper worship of God is contingent upon one's physical location. Jesus makes plain to her—and to us today—that those who truly follow God do so not merely with external obedience but with internal worship, in our hearts and our minds, with our desires and our thoughts—in spirit and in truth.

Born-again Christians make up less than one percent of Czech Republic's population, so we minister amid a people who do not worship God in spirit or in truth. In fact, they do not seek to worship Him at all. Our ongoing prayer is that God would transform their hearts and minds and make them into true worshipers. We know such transformation is solely God's gift (Eph. 2:8) and that we can neither give them faith nor help them produce faith from within themselves. So, what are we to do? We are to share God's truth (John 17:17) in the power of God's Spirit (Acts 1:8) and trust the Spirit to convict and convince unbelievers of the truth, so they might become true worshipers.

And we pray that we would faithfully worship God in spirit and in truth, that God's Spirit would convince us daily of the truth of God's word and conform us to the image of God's Son (Rom. 8:29). We must share God's truth with the lost and apply God's truth to our own lives, trusting the Spirit to bring about change in both instances. Pray with us, that true worshipers of God would grow greatly here, both in number and spiritual depth.

Faith and Sight

Jesus answered and said to him, "Because I said to you that I saw you under the fig tree, do you believe? You will see greater things than these." And He said to him, "Truly, truly, I say to you, you will see the heavens opened and the angels of God ascending and descending on the Son of Man."
JOHN 1:50–51

JOSE CARLOS ANGELES FERNANDEZ: WORD OF GRACE BIBLICAL SEMINARY | MEXICO

Nathanael believed, having had only a little taste of Jesus' supernatural knowledge. While he was under the fig tree, probably praying, Jesus saw him. Had it merely been a physical sight, it would not have made any impact on Nathanael. But he knew that Jesus had seen him inwardly, and this is what made him believe.

Now, Jesus' ministry was just beginning. Much more was coming to validate His identity as the Son of God. Nathanael and the other disciples would see the power of God coming from heaven and displayed in Jesus. They would come to recognize that through Him would come all divine communications and comforts, like a ladder that messengers from God could use to bridge heaven and earth.

But Nathanael believed in Jesus before seeing any of these things. His faith was quick, unreserved, and decisive. There are many today who want to know everything about Christianity before they will believe in Jesus. They demand a college degree but refuse to go to elementary school. There are even Christians whose faith is greatly inhibited because they have not yet seen or understood certain things.

Oh, that we could learn from the faith of Nathanael, an Israelite in whom there was no deceit (John 1:47)! He was honest at heart and eager to believe the truth. And Jesus promised Him much more to come. As Augustine once said, "Faith is to believe what you do not yet see; the reward for this faith is to see what you believe." Hold fast your sincerest belief in Jesus and He will show you great and wonderful things in and through His word.

True Goodness

And Jesus said to him, "Why do you call Me good? No one is good except God alone."
MARK 10:18

RAYMOND KWAN: JAPAN BIBLE ACADEMY | JAPAN

These famous words come from Mark's account of Jesus' conversation with the man known as the rich young ruler. It's amazing how skillfully Jesus, whom the man greets as "Good Teacher" (Mark 10:17), deals with his main problem. Before responding to his question, "What shall I do to inherit eternal life?" (Mark 10:17), Jesus addresses the man's understanding of goodness.

Next, Jesus gives the man an opportunity to acknowledge his sin by asking him if he has kept several of the Ten Commandments. Foolishly, the man says that he has kept them all. This reveals how he views himself and what his standards are.

Jesus gives this man one last chance by asking him to do something that He knew he was unwilling to do—namely, sell his possessions and give the proceeds to the poor. With this question the man's true condition is revealed; his loyalty is to self, not God. Tragically, the conversation ends here; it should have been where he saw the answer to his original question.

God's standard is absolute perfection. Everything God does is good. God has never done, and cannot do, anything that is not good. In fact, as someone has said, God doesn't do things because they're good; things are good because He does them. He is the very definition of good. There isn't a higher standard of good that God abides by. He sets the standard.

When we consider who we are before God, we ought to be humbled that He would offer salvation to people who fall so short of His goodness. Praise Him for His goodness.

Acting upon Convictions

The LORD is the one who goes ahead of you; He will be with you.
He will not fail you or forsake you. Do not fear or be dismayed.
DEUTERONOMY 31:8

ANSELM STREHLKE: EUROPEAN BIBLE TRAINING CENTER | GERMANY

In this fallen world, our words often don't match our deeds. It is one thing to affirm biblical convictions, but a whole other thing to act upon those convictions when faced with a challenge. We are tempted in the moment to lay aside what we know to be true and to only see ourselves and the problem. The greater the challenge, the greater our fear of failure.

When Moses handed the baton of leadership to Joshua, there were massive challenges ahead for Joshua. He was supposed to lead a stubborn people into unknown territory and use them as an inexperienced army to fight against the mighty Canaanites. In this situation, God had some encouraging words for the new leader of Israel. He could have said, "Come on, Joshua, you can do this," in order to temporarily alleviate Joshua's fear and puff up his self-esteem. Instead, God reminded him that he was not going to be the first to cross the Jordan River—God was. God Himself had not only prescribed the way to go but was also committed to His servant and His promise to lead him to victory.

Joshua had expressed his conviction earlier that God would give Canaan into the hands of Israel. But now it was up to Joshua to not only believe what God had said, but to actually go forward in faith.

How do you react when your biblical convictions are challenged? Do you rely on God's word when the problems seem insurmountable? Our Almighty God is asking you to trust Him and stand firm on what He said, whatever comes. He is asking you to act upon your convictions.

The Ultimate Sufficiency Found in Christ

I know how to get along with humble means, and I also know
how to live in prosperity; in any and every circumstance I have
learned the secret of being filled and going hungry, both of
having abundance and suffering need.

PHILIPPIANS 4:12

MICHAEL PARK: TMAI HEADQUARTERS | LOS ANGELES, CALIFORNIA

"From this day forward, for better, for worse, for richer, for poorer, until death do us part." This is a typical vow you hear at a wedding ceremony. The bride and bridegroom stand in front of everyone looking at each other with adoring eyes and confidently say, "Yes!" However, this vow can quickly vanish when the winds of hardship blow into their lives. Suddenly, life is filled with dissatisfaction, complaints, and discomfort.

This is something that we face from time to time in our Christian walk. How can we stand strong in faith and remain content regardless of circumstances? We need to listen to the one who learned the secret of contentment.

The apostle Paul, by the Lord's appointment, was beaten, stoned, in hunger and thirst, often without food, and in cold and exposure (2 Cor. 11:25–27). Can you imagine this? This man was in prison when writing a letter to fellow believers in Philippi, yet he repeatedly exhorts them saying, "Rejoice in the Lord always; again, I will say, rejoice!" (Phil. 4:4). How can he rejoice in the Lord even in the midst of severe trial? How did he learn the secret of being filled and going hungry, both of having abundance and suffering need?

The answer? "I can do all things through Him who strengthens me" (Phil. 4:13). His unmovable contentment came from the only source of all-sufficiency, the Lord Jesus Christ. He was filled with contentment, comfort, and satisfaction in every and any circumstance because he found his ultimate sufficiency in Christ alone.

Where in your life do you need to look to Christ for all sufficiency, instead of your circumstances?

The Christian Verdict: Not Guilty

Therefore there is now no condemnation for those who are in Christ Jesus.

ROMANS 8:1

GENCI C.: ALBANIA (FULL NAME WITHHELD FOR SECURITY)

This royal pronouncement, like a trumpet blast from heaven, seizes the attention. No condemnation! This means that there is absolutely no punishment or remaining debt for us to pay. Our sins have been taken away (John 1:29), blotted out (Acts 3:19), washed away (Acts 22:16), covered (Rom. 4:7), and will never be remembered again (Heb. 8:12)! Notice for whom this applies—"for those who are in Christ Jesus." This trumpet-blast pronouncement is for believers in Christ because we have a new position in Him.

This truth should carry us forward each day in the blessed freedom of grace. God no longer has anything against us because He has already punished Christ for all of our sins—past, present, and future. He is pleased with us because we have been clothed with the perfect righteousness of His Son.

Even though we still commit sins, these do not condemn us, nor does death have any power over us. The law has been satisfied and God has been appeased in Christ. Armed with this powerful pronouncement, we are enabled to live freely in Christ as victors over sin. Grace is not license to sin—may it never be! It is the seedbed of righteousness. We know that if we abide in Christ, He is like an invincible fortress that protects us from every danger of condemnation. For those who abide in Christ, there is nothing but forgiveness and eternal love. The slanderous accusations of the devil are nothing but empty words. Jesus paid it all, and all to Him we owe.

A Compassionate Father

*Just as a father has compassion on his children, so the L*ORD
has compassion on those who fear Him.

PSALM 103:13

MARIO KUSHNER: THEOLOGICAL BIBLICAL ACADEMY | CROATIA

When I was growing up, fathers typically worked hard to provide for the family. They were often thought of as strict and distant. The emphasis was usually on correction and instruction. It wasn't uncommon to hear a mother say: "Wait till your father comes home from work!"

The Scriptures, however, reveal a fuller and more endearing portrait of God as the believer's Father. Psalm 103:13 emphasizes God's fatherly *compassion*. In the larger context of the psalm, David is preaching—to himself (vv. 1–5), then to the nation of Israel (vv. 6–18), and finally to the whole universe (vv. 19–22). He urges Israel to bless the Lord for His actions (vv. 6–7) and attributes (vv. 8–9). God's love, mercy, and forgiveness are extolled (vv. 3, 8–10, 12–13, 17).

Rather than trying to understand God as our Father by looking at human fathers, we must look to the Lord to define fatherhood. Yes, He is the King who is to be feared and obeyed (vv. 19–22). But He is also full of love, eager to forgive, and filled with tender concern for His children.

The Gospel guarantees that God will never condemn the one who comes to Him in faith. God's unique Son, Jesus, bore the penalty for our sin on the cross, and rose again—so that the Father can shower love, forgiveness, and compassion on us as His children. To those in Christ, God is not a harsh Judge, but rather a loving Father.

Psalm 113 reminds us to preach to ourselves daily the glories of the Father's everlasting love, to embrace His boundless forgiveness, and to rest humbly in His tender mercy in Christ.

June 19

Foremost of Sinners

*It is a trustworthy statement, deserving full acceptance, that
Christ Jesus came into the world to save sinners, among whom
I am foremost of all.*

1 TIMOTHY 1:15

D. K.: ASIA (NAME WITHHELD FOR SECURITY)

Most people in this world do not like to speak of themselves as
bad or sinful. Yet, in our verse there is this shocking statement,
coming from none other than the esteemed apostle Paul. He wasn't
exaggerating, because he knew his own heart well. He did not forget the pit of sin that he was drawn from, and exemplifies for us an
important reality. This reality is the breeding ground of gratefulness
(1 Tim. 1:12) and humble worship (1 Tim. 1:17). A Christian who
brags of himself or his work has forgotten that it is God's grace alone
through Christ alone that makes him who he is.

God did not save Paul simply to take him to heaven. He also did
not save him just to preach the gospel. God could have used many others to do His work. The purpose of Paul's salvation was to showcase
God's grace, power, and patience. It was also for this reason that Paul
found mercy.

We are also the chief of sinners in our time, saved only by the grace
of God in Christ. Before salvation we had a faulty view of self as good
and worthy before God and men. But this verse humbles us both in
ministry and life. When we live with self-confidence, we are useless to
God, but when our confidence is in God's strength and grace, we are
vessels fit for His service. A truly born-again Christian will confess
that he is a sinner and even the foremost!

June 20

One Message for All

He said to them, "Thus it is written, that the Christ would
suffer and rise again from the dead the third day, and that
repentance for forgiveness of sins would be proclaimed in His
name to all the nations, beginning from Jerusalem."

LUKE 24:46–47

CESARE ALBANESI: ITALIAN THEOLOGICAL ACADEMY | ITALY

In Italy, we have two proverbs that describe an attitude that is widespread in many cultures: "Town you go, habit you find," and "When in Rome, do as the Romans do." We try to accommodate the people around us. We try not to offend them, to be politically correct, to accept them for what they are, and sometimes even to avoid the truth for the sake of "peace." Now, there is nothing wrong with being accommodating or desiring not to offend people, but we should not compromise the truth about Jesus and the message of the gospel, even if it offends (1 Cor. 1:23).

The commission that Jesus gave to His disciples (and to all believers) is to proclaim Christ's death and resurrection, and to call all men to repentance. This was to be proclaimed to all the nations. Implied in Jesus' commission is the fact that this gospel is transcultural, and that no modification of content was necessary from one nation to the other.

The temptation we face in our daily lives, though, *is* to accommodate the culture we live in, by making the message more appealing or less offensive to the people around us. However, this is not what we have been commissioned to do. Our goal is to proclaim Christ crucified and that repentance in His name is necessary for the forgiveness of sins.

How are we responding to Jesus' commission? Are we being faithful to His message, or are we compromising the truth? May God grant us the courage to speak faithfully and without compromise wherever He leads.

Saved for Good Works

For we are His workmanship, created in Christ Jesus for good works, which God prepared beforehand so that we would walk in them.

EPHESIANS 2:10

JOSE SORIA: INSTITUTO DE EXPOSITORES | USA

Those who love the sixteenth-century Protestant Reformation have been strong to assert that justification is by grace alone through faith alone, and not by human works. But does this mean that works have no place in Christianity? Does this truth lead, as some claim, to immoral living?

Not according to Paul. He doesn't undermine the importance of good works. Rather, he teaches that God sovereignly predestined us not only to be adopted as His children (Eph. 1:5) but also to a life of moral excellence with good works (Eph. 2:10).

As one carefully reads Ephesians 2:8–10, it is evident that salvation is never the result of good works, but rather good works are a result of salvation. If you have been saved by God, you are then to walk in and perform good works that bring God glory. The Reformers had a saying: "We are saved by faith alone, but the faith that saves is never alone!" As Martin Luther explained, "It's not against works that we contend; it's against trust in works that we contend."

Since God has done a work in you through regeneration, walk in the works He has for you. Remind yourself regularly that God's purpose in saving you was that you might live a holy life filled with good works (Eph. 2:10; Titus 2:14). Make it your priority today to live life characterized by good works, all for the glory of His name. If you have been saved *by faith*, you have been saved *for good works*.

Our Greatest Comforter and Friend

For we do not have a high priest who cannot sympathize with our weaknesses, but One who has been tempted in all things as we are, yet without sin.

HEBREWS 4:15

KITO ESPIRITU: THE EXPOSITOR'S ACADEMY | PHILIPPINES

Being a disciple of Jesus Christ is often difficult. Though we seek to manage our lives well, trying to obey all of God's commands stretches us beyond our limits and exposes our weaknesses. It can sometimes feel like we are wet sponges with our sins being squeezed out of their concealment. This can be humiliating and disheartening and can cause us to crave sympathy.

Having a fellow believer to talk and pray with can be a great help. However, even the best friends can be limited in their understanding of how to help with our needs and limited in their ability to show compassion. This is not so with Christ, our high priest. Having lived and died as a human being like us, He can sympathize with us because He understands our weaknesses and the difficulty of living in this fallen world. Yet unlike us, He never sinned. Hebrews 4:14 reminds us that He is also the Son of God who "passed through the heavens" and is now seated at the Father's right hand. There, He lives to intercede for us (Heb. 7:25). So Christ's sympathy is *real* because He is human, it is *holy* because He never sinned, and it is *boundless* because He is God.

What a comfort! In the midst of our failures in this life, God is to be our foremost comforter and friend. This is why the writer to the Hebrews writes in the next verse, "Therefore let us draw near with confidence to the throne of grace, so that we may receive mercy and find grace to help in time of need" (Heb. 4:16).

Anchored by the Word

As a result, we are no longer to be children, tossed here and
there by waves and carried about by every wind of doctrine,
by the trickery of men, by craftiness in deceitful scheming.
EPHESIANS 4:14

ROBERT KENSINGER: EVANGELICAL MINISTRIES OF THE AMERICAS | HONDURAS

Have you ever been on a boat being tossed to and fro by fierce winds and mounting waves? If you have, you know that it's not a pleasant place to be. You feel completely out of control and victim to the whims of the wind and water as they take you wherever they wish. This is the environment described in Ephesians 4:14 for the person without sound doctrine. The blowing winds of the "trickery of men" pushes one to dangerous places, lacking proper navigation to understand the deceitfulness of the devil. And the crashing waves of "craftiness in deceitful scheming" threaten to capsize lives void of a steady anchor to ground them in the truth. This picture describes the lives of the spiritually immature "children" because they haven't been grounded in sound doctrine from the word of God.

So, how can this situation be prevented or changed? How can God's people learn to properly follow the compass of Scripture so that they can navigate the storms of life without being shipwrecked by the winds of trickery and the waves of deceitful scheming?

The answer lies in the context of the previous verses (Eph. 4:11–13). God has given gifts to the church in the form of spiritual leaders: initially apostles and prophets, followed by evangelists and pastors and teachers. Their role is to equip the saints for the work of service, resulting in the edification and maturation of the church. Such a church will then be anchored in the word and able to withstand the wind and waves of false doctrine.

Thank the Lord for your pastor today and for those who trained him in the word!

Contagious Gospel Zeal

... [we] preach the gospel even to the regions beyond you, and not to boast in what has been accomplished in the sphere of another.
2 CORINTHIANS 10:16

DMITRIY ZHEREBNENKOV: WORD OF GRACE BIBLE INSTITUTE | USA

This wonderful and encouraging passage should stir the heart of every Christian toward global mission work. The apostle Paul was a zealous and passionate promoter of what he believed in. Before his conversion, his zeal for the Law created a wave of persecution of the early church. When God turned him around on the road to Damascus, he instantaneously became passionate about spreading the gospel of Jesus Christ to the ends of the earth. But what is more exciting and encouraging is that his zeal spread like an infection to the people around him. It seems that many who interacted with Paul became zealous evangelists and missionaries.

We often get inspired for specific tasks by the zeal of others. We find the same to be true in spiritual disciplines. In 2 Corinthians 8:1–8, Paul provokes believers in Corinth to be sacrificial in their giving by the eagerness of the Macedonian believers. He invites those same believers to imitate him as he imitates Christ (1 Cor. 11:1).

The implied *we* in our passage communicates that this vision for global mission work was so contagious that there were others who had become partakers in it. So it must be with us! Take time to pray for the preaching of the gospel to all the people groups of the world. But also evaluate your own heart, and answer this simple question: Am I zealous for the gospel to be preached to the ends of the world to such a degree that people around me are catching the same vision and passion?

Pray for a Worthy Walk

… so that you will walk in a manner worthy of the Lord, to please Him in all respects, bearing fruit in every good work and increasing in the knowledge of God.

COLOSSIANS 1:10

THEO FRIESEN: EUROPEAN BIBLE TRAINING CENTER | GERMANY

How is your prayer life? This question usually humbles believers when it is asked. Our prayer is often consumed with temporal requests for health, success, and physical blessing. Are you regularly praying for spiritual growth?

Consider Paul's words about prayer and even his recorded prayers. One reason we have his prayers recorded in Scripture is so we will follow his focus and heart. Paul prayed for the Colossians that they might walk in a manner worthy of the Lord to please Him. The prayer was not about fleeting aspects of everyday life. He prayed for good works and an increasing knowledge of God!

Start to implement prayer requests of eternal things for yourself, your spouse, your children, and friends. But don't stop there—Paul gave thanks and prayed regularly for believers he himself had never even met. Pray for the people in your congregation that they might bear fruit in every good work. Pray for the people group served by a missionary you know that they might increase in the knowledge of God.

Paul often told others that he was praying for them and specifically what he was praying for. Let someone you pray for know what you are thankful for and what you prayed for, and encourage him or her by that.

Take time to pray! But also, take time to consider what to pray for. Pray that you would walk in a manner worthy of the Lord.

Humble Service

For even the Son of Man did not come to be served, but to serve, and to give His life a ransom for many.

MARK 10:45

Francisco J. Reche Luz: Berea Seminary | Spain

The Gospel of Mark presents Jesus as the suffering Servant of the Lord, employs the phrase, "Son of Man" fourteen times as a designation for our Lord Jesus. This expression is a messianic title used by the prophet in Daniel 7:13, referring to the Messiah, Christ.

In our verse, Jesus uses this same expression, Son of Man, to emphasize His humility. He had just told His disciples that He would be rejected, suffer, be killed, and rise again after three days. Immediately following that, two of the disciples asked Jesus for the preeminent place in His kingdom (Mark 10:37), thereby demonstrating no understanding of the humility that must characterize a disciple of Jesus.

In Mark 10:45, Jesus concludes His teaching with a lesson of supreme humbleness. Jesus, the sovereign Son of God, did not come to be served but to serve, and this was going to result in His death. He was voluntarily giving away His life to pay the ransom for those who believed in Him, freeing them from the slavery of sin. With His death, He was satisfying the demands of justice and the wrath of God. Jesus was training His disciples to develop a mindset of humility and service, which opens the door for effective evangelism.

In a world full of pride, arrogance, and ambition, we, as believers, must be humble servants of our Lord and Savior, proclaiming His word and serving others while we wait for His return. We have a clear example to follow in Christ. How can you express a godly humility to those around you today?

Character that Comforts

Who is like Me? Let him proclaim and declare it; yes, let him recount it to Me in order, from the time that I established the ancient nation. And let them declare to them the things that are coming and the events that are going to take place.

ISAIAH 44:7

JONATHAN MOORHEAD: CZECH BIBLE INSTITUTE | CZECH REPUBLIC

When you experience hurt, what brings you most comfort? Is it a philosophical argument on suffering, or the fact that an all-wise, all-powerful, all-loving God has ordained your trial for a specific purpose, and that He will never leave nor forsake you?

Having a high view of God and His attributes is critical in times of discouragement or uncertainty, and so it was with ancient Israel in the context of Isaiah 44. Because of their sin, the Israelites faced removal from the land God promised them (Gen. 12). With hope diminishing, many asked if God would abandon them completely.

Ensuring a God-centered focus, this verse begins with the power of a question, "Who is like Me?" As in a court of law, God challenges any rival by drawing attention to Himself. He lays the hope of Israel upon His character, and not upon her circumstances. To solidify the point, he calls any contender to "proclaim and declare it," and to "recount it to [Him] in order."

When the nature of God is considered in the book of Isaiah, it is clear that He is the only God, that He "established the ancient nation" Israel, and that He will keep His promise to them. Not only that, but being omniscient, God knows "the things that are coming and the events that are going to take place." God has a plan, He is true, and we are called to wait upon Him.

If you are suffering, think upon the character of God. It is there that you will find peace, comfort, assurance, and hope for the future. God is faithful, and His steadfast love endures forever.

Humility before Exaltation

*For this reason also, God highly exalted Him, and bestowed
on Him the name which is above every name, so that at the
name of Jesus EVERY KNEE WILL BOW, of those who are in heaven
and on earth and under the earth.*

PHILIPPIANS 2:9–10

PATRICK ELIAS TSIGA: CENTRAL AFRICAN PREACHING ACADEMY | MALAWI

God's principle of humility and then exaltation never changes. When Jesus had humbled Himself, God exalted Him highly and gave Him a name that is above every name. Many times pride and self-justification have been a hindrance to promotion. It is no wonder God resists such proud people. God gives more grace to the humble, but He resists the proud.

People often forget that God does not violate His own principles. If Jesus Christ, being God, learned to put into practice the principle of humility in order to be exalted, how much more do you and I need to do the same—we who struggle with pride, selfishness, self-justification, and self-centeredness?

May God grant us the grace to realize that humility brings many blessings. In fact, God is looking for people who can humble themselves. When you humble yourself before God, it is a sign that you totally trust in Him and acknowledge that you cannot do anything on your own. And this is what pleases God most. We need to learn how to humble ourselves before God in every situation, just as Jesus demonstrated for us.

Take a moment today and examine your heart to see if there is any element that would cause God to resist you. Then seek to be humble before Him so that in due course, He will lift you up.

The Sacrificial Shepherd

"For this reason the Father loves Me, because I lay down My life so that I may take it again. No one has taken it away from Me, but I lay it down on My own initiative. I have authority to lay it down, and I have authority to take it up again. This commandment I received from My Father."

JOHN 10:17-18

ROMAN K.: RUSSIA (FULL NAME WITHHELD FOR SECURITY)

Christ speaks of Himself here as the Good Shepherd of Israel and those saved from other nations. This imagery is often used in Scripture as a clear illustration of God's care for us. A shepherd's labor is marked by difficulty and danger. Every shepherd risks his life when he goes out to pasture his flock. Christ's mission, however, did not involve the risk of death, it included the *certainty* of death—He came knowing He would die. Death was not an undesirable outcome, but a desirable one.

Christ declares that the salvation of His flock requires not just the presence and protection of the Shepherd, but first His death in place of the sheep. This is why He came. What a reminder this is of our need for a substitute, the depth of our sin, and the necessity of Christ's death and His great love for us.

Christ also brings to light the divine plan of salvation and the amazing harmony between the Persons of the Trinity. The Father loves the Son and the Son in His ministry willingly submits to the Father and His command. The Son has the power to rise from the dead and the Father raises Him (Acts 2:24).

This passage is filled with excellent theology. Find time to meditate on the beauty of the gospel, the great love of our Lord, the awesome harmony between the Persons of the Trinity in salvation. Praise God the Father for His excellent plan of salvation and Christ Jesus for putting it into action and the Holy Spirit for applying it to us. Thank Christ for being the Good Shepherd.

June 30

Philippines

Spanish explorers first brought the Roman Catholic faith to the Philippines in the 16th century. Today, over 80 percent of the population identifies as Roman Catholic—more than any other country in Asia. Yet there are many churches eager for pastoral training. The Expositor's Academy is responding to these requests and is training men from all over this island country.

TODAY, PRAY FOR

Many among the Philippines' largely Catholic population to repent and believe the gospel.

God to raise up and send trained Filipino pastors to be missionaries in the surrounding Asia-Pacific region.

The protection of TMAI's faculty and students amid the country's growing influence of radical Islam.

Encouragement in Conflict

And I will put enmity between you and the woman, and be-
tween your seed and her seed; he shall bruise you on the head,
and you shall bruise him on the heel.

GENESIS 3:15

BRIAN KINZEL: GRACE BIBLE SEMINARY | UKRAINE

Christians in Ukraine know about spiritual conflict. The evangelical church suffered for many years, first from the oppression under the Czars, and then under the communists. Our first students at
the seminary in the 1990s were excited just to study the Bible freely
during daylight hours instead of secretly at night.

Persecuted believers are encouraged by this verse, knowing that,
though they might feel vulnerable and weak, their Lord and Savior
Jesus Christ has crushed death and provided atonement by His blood.
Our enemy, the serpent, who inflicts painful bites, is defeated.

This verse explains that the conflict that believers around the world
experience began at the very dawn of history. Despite the gloomy
context in Genesis 3 (the Fall), this verse brims with hope—it gives the
first promise in the Bible that points to Jesus' atonement. This verse
also gives hope to all believers living in conflict. Whenever we suffer
for righteousness, we know that we are on the side of God, who put
enmity between the snake and the woman. Those who suffer reproach
for the truth know that the seed of the woman promised a lethal blow
to evil; the promised Messiah is from that seed (Gal. 3:16).

Let us all remember and be encouraged that the God of peace will
soon crush Satan underneath our feet (Rom. 16:20)!

Only a Footnote

Many false prophets will arise and will mislead many. Because
lawlessness is increased, most people's love will grow cold.
MATTHEW 24:11-12

SAMUEL HEREDIA CANOVACA: BEREA SEMINARY | SPAIN

In this passage, Jesus is telling His disciples about the signs before the end, warning them that in the last days many false prophets will arise. Their only goal will be to distort the gospel's message, and thereby bring eternal consequences in people's lives.

False teachers hate God, and try to hide Him from the eyes of their followers. They put in His place false, worldly, and empty inventions. For them, Jesus is only a footnote to their godless purposes. They use His name to fool those who pursue Him. False teachers claim to come from God. They appear as sheep, but inwardly they are ravenous wolves.

The church will only be relevant when it transmits all of God's message in the way God intended it. No other message, no matter how important it may be or seem to be, can occupy the place of the message of God. Just as Paul wrote to the Galatians, "If any man is preaching to you a gospel contrary to what you received, he is to be accursed!" (Gal. 1:9).

We must be aware of this. As Christians who embrace the gospel, we must rely on the sufficiency of Scripture. We must listen to, love, and proclaim the truth. Are you daily feasting on God's word, living a life of joyful obedience? That will help you discern and avoid error, and keep your love from growing cold.

The Joy of a Humble Heart

And Mary said: "My soul exalts the Lord, and my spirit has rejoiced in God my Savior, for He has had regard for the humble state of His bondslave. For behold, from this time on all generations will count me blessed."

LUKE 1:46–48

DMITRIY ZHEREBNENKOV: WORD OF GRACE BIBLE INSTITUTE | USA

Everyone pursues happiness and joy in life. The world runs after temporary substitutes that never satisfy. Believers know the better way, but sadly often search for joy in the wrong places. Hear then the invitation of this passage; look at Mary's true joy. It is the joy of a humble heart!

When Mary says, "For He has had regard for the humble state of His bondslave," she identifies herself as a lowly servant. Only humility can bring you to the point of magnifying and exalting the Lord the way Mary did. And this is the link between joy and humility. Humility recognizes the need in salvation ("God my Savior"), but also is able to see the majesty and the glory of God, which brings true joy.

Why is this important? Since the Fall, the human heart is under the bondage of pride. It is pride that eventually keeps people from magnifying and rejoicing in the Lord. Because of pride, worship can become dull and dry. Because of pride, a ministry can lose its passion and focus on the God of the Bible.

Take some time to look into your own heart and prayerfully ask God to reveal to you if there is any pride that has been hindering you from fully rejoicing in the God of your salvation. Confess and turn away from any pride, and embrace God in purified and renewed worship that magnifies the Lord. Then, you will know the joy of the humble heart!

Reckon Yourself Dead to Sin

For the death that He died, He died to sin once for all; but the life that He lives, He lives to God.

ROMANS 6:10

SERGEY K.: RUSSIA (FULL NAME WITHHELD FOR SECURITY)

The problem of so-called *cheap grace* arises in any Christian culture, anywhere around the world. At its core, this doctrine says much about grace and less (or nothing) about practical holiness and sanctification. At a practical level, cheap grace shows itself through dissipation and disregard for living a God-centered life, even though there may be much Christian talk.

How should preachers and people in the pews respond to this? The solution is complex, but one answer is found in Paul's response to this problem in Romans 6. Here we discover that the problem of cheap grace is partly the problem of not understanding what it means to be united to Christ. In Romans 5, Paul argues that the only way we can be completely set free from death and obtain eternal life is being united to Christ through faith. If this is where forgiveness and grace are found, the natural question arises: "Doesn't this encourage Christians to disregard striving for godliness?" (Rom. 6:1, 15). "Absolutely not" is Paul's answer. You obtain life only in Christ's death and life (Rom. 6:3–5). And He died to sin once for all. And He lives to God. Such is true of those united to Him.

Have you been united to Christ through faith and do you possess eternal life in Him? Live out this transfer from death to life through a God-centered life which demonstrates that your union with Christ is a reality. Then reckon yourself dead to sin and alive to God in Christ Jesus (Rom. 6:11).

Chosen and Equipped

*You did not choose Me but I chose you, and appointed you
that you would go and bear fruit, and that your fruit would
remain, so that whatever you ask of the Father in My name
He may give to you.*

JOHN 15:16

MARIO ALVAREZ RIVERO: WORD OF GRACE BIBLICAL SEMINARY | MEXICO

There are things in this life that we can choose. Friends, for example, usually choose one another due to common interests or shared values. But God's choice is not determined by any good that He sees in us. It is only through the unconditional and sovereign character of Christ's eternal love that God could choose sinners to become His friends.

Christ's followers *are* His friends, and as such, He enables us to share in His work. He appoints us and puts the treasure of the gospel in our hands so that we may bear fruit. But branches only bear fruit if they abide in the vine. We are dependent on Christ for every good fruit. And the primary directive as ambassadors of Christ is the sublime task of proclaiming His gospel, the good news of forgiveness and eternal life in Christ Jesus!

We have the privilege of proclaiming this gospel to every man, woman, and child. From the pulpit to children's Sunday School to outreach ministries, the church has the opportunity to bear fruit that *remains*. Not only does Jesus choose us to serve Him, but He also promises us that the Father will answer our prayers. In doing so, He guarantees that we will be equipped to produce the promised fruit.

In light of God's choosing us to be a part of His kingdom, we should be actively involved in producing fruit for the kingdom through prayer and our actions. Let us never forget that we were chosen and equipped to produce *eternal* fruit!

Money or the Master

*No one can serve two masters; for either he will hate the one
and love the other, or he will be devoted to one and despise the
other. You cannot serve God and wealth.*

MATTHEW 6:24

TAKUYA KAJIHARA: JAPAN BIBLE ACADEMY | JAPAN

Money is important for us to live. However, we should not live for
money. We should live for God. A life of serving God is the life
of a child of God.

In my life, there are many times when I try to live for my own glory.
What I am doing is seeking to live a life where I am king. I want to
be respected; I want to be praised. However, God's word teaches that
we are to serve Him, not ourselves or money or anything else. When
I remember this, I think about whom my life is for. If my life were
my own, I would serve money and treat myself as king, as countless
people do. But my only king is Christ and I am just a servant of Christ
my king. A servant should faithfully serve his king. To serve anything
else is to serve a rival to the true king, Christ.

How important it is, then, to believe that Christ is our king. There
are many things in this world that seek to keep us and blind us from
following Christ, the true king. It could be money, pleasure—even
ourselves. But when we turn to Christ's word, we can know His will
for us, and we must follow it instead of our own will or the will of
wealth.

Examine your heart. Are there any rivals to Christ's kingship over
it? Then, consider Jesus' words—you cannot serve two masters. Serve
the true king with your whole heart.

July 7

Seek and Taste

And without faith it is impossible to please Him, for he who comes to God must believe that He is and that He is a rewarder of those who seek Him.

HEBREWS 11:6

L. J.: ASIA (NAME WITHHELD FOR SECURITY)

People in the world can try to please God in a variety of ways, but this verse claims that God can be pleased only through faith. The context of this verse, which carries the list of heroes of the Bible, proves that men and women gained approval from God through faith. This contradicts the popular saying, "seeing is believing."

We must be reminded that our entry into the family of God took place through believing in God, who saves by grace. Thereafter, as children of God, we are called to walk by faith in Him. What a privilege it is to hold His hand and walk, trusting Him, in the wilderness of our sojourning on earth!

God's unchanging, eternal existence and His ongoing providential care for you are questioned when you doubt Him at any point in your life. Your unbelief can hinder God's gracious care when He intervenes in your situation. But seeking God instead by faith through prayer no matter the difficulties—in times of sickness, financial difficulties, strained relationships, and obstacles in ministry—brings Him delight.

When my plans for planting a church were recently shattered by events beyond my control, I was confronted by this verse to trust in God and move forward by faith. It is a solemn warning that shrinking back in faith would displease God. Unbelief can cause only additional pain to the misery, whereas your faith in God in the situation will be surely rewarded. How sweet it is to seek God always and taste His gracious provisions!

Spiritual Cannibalism

But if you bite and devour one another, take care that you are not consumed by one another.

GALATIANS 5:15

MELVIN ZELAYA: EVANGELICAL MINISTRIES OF THE AMERICAS | HONDURAS

One seemingly calm afternoon in 1969, I was preparing to eat dinner when roaring jets suddenly came from the east and bombed our nearby airport. Immediately we lost power, and in an instant everything changed. This attack set in motion many long-term, negative consequences that have been felt ever since in my country (and our neighboring country, as well). A land lawsuit and political issues ensued, as military clashes led to casualties, which disrupted many families within a matter of days. Sadly, many trained soldiers and defenseless civilians died.

Since then, almost fifty years have passed, during which I have observed similar episodes between other countries on almost every continent. Why do we do this to ourselves? Where does it come from? Fighting arises from the human heart and its selfish desires (James 4:1–2).

Perhaps you have not been involved in a war, but on a smaller scale we all are inclined to bite and devour one another, whether defending our opinions, fighting for our personal rights, taking advantage of others, or discriminating against those who are not like us. These sinful attitudes crop up every day in familiar settings, such as the workplace, home, and even church.

But Scripture calls those of us who have been saved by grace to do the opposite. In the previous verses (Gal. 5:13–14), Paul explains that we haven't been saved to harm one another; rather, we've been saved to love one another! So, fight every urge to bite or devour, which only leaves a mess of spiritual carnage in its wake. Instead, love your neighbor as yourself, thereby fulfilling the law of Christ.

Cutting It Straight

*Be diligent to present yourself approved to God as a workman
who does not need to be ashamed, accurately handling the
word of truth.*

2 TIMOTHY 2:15

MIKE ABENDROTH: EUROPEAN BIBLE TRAINING CENTER | GERMANY

Paul charges Timothy, his young apprentice, to put forth every effort into the proper study of God's word. No short cuts. No excuses for a casual or lazy approach. God and His word demand excellence and precision. Timothy, and by extension all who handle God's word, are called to be "workmen." "Cutting straight" is the goal.

It is one thing to be shamed by the world, a parent, or a teacher, but receiving shame from a thrice-holy Savior is something that must not be underestimated. The reverse is also true: when Scripture is accurately handled, there is commendation from the Lord.

Roads or paths are cut through a forest to help travelers in reaching their destinations with ease. The same principle is true for handling God's word. The teaching of the word must remain faithful to the author's intent so that every reader gets to the right destination (the meaning of the text) easily and accurately. There must be no additions to Scripture, no subtractions, no mutilations, no perversions, and no changes to the word. Exactness is the goal of the teacher. He is to be in stark opposition to Elymas the magician, who made "crooked the straight ways of the Lord" (Acts 13:8–10).

If you teach the Bible, or study it, you have the wonderful responsibility to follow in the steps of Timothy.

To Whom Are You Devoted?

You shall have no other gods before Me. You shall not make for yourself an idol, or any likeness of what is in heaven above or on the earth beneath or in the water under the earth.

EXODUS 20:3–4

JOSUE PINEDA DALE: INSTITUTO DE EXPOSITORES | USA

The people of Israel were to be wholly devoted to God. He had redeemed them from Egypt, and as the only true God He demanded exclusive worship. The surrounding nations had many gods, and they worshiped everything but the true God. They made themselves gods according to their own desires and passions. Despite the seriousness of the command for exclusive worship, Israel kept following the examples of those around them. They disobeyed, worshiping other gods and making idols—which was blatant sin against God.

Today we are also tempted to worship idols, but in a subtler way. We compromise our worship. We sacrifice our faithfulness to Him. We cherish things that are worthless. We can be prone to follow idols—whether in pew or pulpit.

In ministry, God-centered worship can be a challenge. We may serve the Lord and yet secretly serve ourselves. What happens when the song you are playing or singing on any given Sunday does not turn out the way you intended? If you become frustrated, is it because God did not receive your best, or because it made you look bad? What about the lesson that you prepared so hard to teach but did not deliver very well? Do you truly feel bad for the glory of God or for yourself? Have you made an idol of yourself, of your own image and reputation?

Paul, in Colossians 3:5, commands us to put to death anything "which amounts to idolatry."

Be vigilant. Guard your heart. Beware the risks of not ascribing full devotion to God. He alone is God; turn your eyes toward Him today!

Defense against Temptation

And do not lead us to temptation, but deliver us from evil.
MATTHEW 6:13

FREDDY RICK LAVEGA: THE EXPOSITOR'S ACADEMY | PHILIPPINES

In our long list of prayers, we often emphasize asking God to meet our daily needs, such as food, water, shelter, and clothing. Sometimes we ask God for personal success in life or to excel in the groups we are involved with. While our perceived needs tend to focus on the physical and emotional, we often forget our need for the spiritual.

When we pray, we must understand that we are living in a fallen world with a lot of corruption and strong temptations to sin. Man can easily be tempted and, without protection, it is easy for us to fall into Satan's traps.

In John 17:15, Jesus prayed to the Father that we be kept from the evil one and that we be sanctified. While our physical and emotional needs are important, Jesus' prayer shows how important it is for us to depend upon God to win our daily spiritual battles against the temptations of the enemy.

This is a fight that we cannot afford to lose, and we can only win through prayer and the working of the Spirit.

I have found myself crying out to God in frustration many times after falling for the enemy's schemes. My failures have shown me my need to pray and ask God for deliverance from temptation and the evil one. As poor and needy people, we are in constant need of God's help and our only hope to avoid enticement to sin, evil, and temptations is to cling to God in prayer.

Obey Your Leaders

*Obey your leaders and submit to them, for they keep watch
over your souls as those who will give an account. Let
them do this with joy and not with grief, for this would be
unprofitable for you.*

HEBREWS 13:17

STANFORD KAPANDA: CENTRAL AFRICAN PREACHING ACADEMY | MALAWI

One of the leaders in a church here resigned because the members mistreated him in various ways. It was a tragedy to see such a lack of submission within the body of Christ. We need to remember that local church leadership is ordained by God's Spirit (Acts 20:28). If we are to be spiritual people, we should submit to God's ordained leaders. These leaders serve the church on behalf of Christ.

Hebrews 13:17 instructs believers both to obey and to submit to their leaders. This submission speaks of entrusting ourselves into their care. Why? For they watch over our souls, and they will give an account to God.

We should, therefore, treat them well and support the job they do, allowing them room to do their work with joy and not with groaning, for that would be of no advantage to us. Rather than cause difficulty for leadership, the church ought to help its leaders do their work with satisfaction and delight (1 Thess. 5:12–13).

As a church leader myself, I have experienced the blessing of a good flock. A congregation that follows the biblical mandate of Hebrews 13:17 brings joy to a pastor, but a congregation that refuses is a cause of much grief. It is difficult enough to lead without disobedience and defiance within the church. May each of us consider carefully whether or not we tend to bring joy or grief to our pastors, and let us seek to do what is most profitable for the body of Christ.

Friend or Foe?

You adulteresses, do you not know that friendship with the world is hostility toward God? Therefore whoever wishes to be a friend of the world makes himself an enemy of God.

JAMES 4:4

WESLEY ROBINSON: CZECH BIBLE INSTITUTE | CZECH REPUBLIC

How committed are we to our friendships? There are some friends that we would do anything for, while with others we just enjoy their company. The more time we spend with a friend, the more influence he or she will have on us. What type of influence have your friends had on you recently?

James is direct and serious with his readers. Adultery is a very strong accusation and should not be taken lightly. Although adultery is defined as cheating (sexually) on your spouse, James speaks of a different kind of adultery that is also serious. This adultery occurs when we desire the world and what it offers more than desiring God. James uses the imagery of friendship to describe our relationship with the world. We are not to be friends with the world; for if we are, we make ourselves enemies of God. We must fight against the desire to be friends with the world. When we are tempted to enjoy and desire what the world offers, when we desire to be accepted by the world, we must fight. Because we were bought with a price (1 Cor. 6:20), we are to live in such a way that reflects who we are in Christ; we are to reflect God's glory.

When we find ourselves becoming friends with the world, we must repent. We are no longer slaves to sin, but sin hinders our relationship with God. Rather than being friends with the world, we must love God with all our heart, with all our soul, and with all our might. Remember— if you are the world's friend, you are God's foe.

Predestined for Adoption

In love He predestined us to adoption as sons through Jesus Christ to Himself, according to the kind intention of His will, to the praise of the glory of His grace, which He freely bestowed on us in the Beloved.

EPHESIANS 1:4c–6

CAMERON HEATHMAN: CHRIST SEMINARY | SOUTH AFRICA

Before the waters of the Indian Ocean licked Durban's beach shores. Before the Drakensberg Mountains stood guard, like a barrier of spears, on the borders of KwaZulu Natal. Before the lion roared at the red sun setting over the thorny Acacia trees, and before the elephant traversed the vast savannahs. Before the stars shone bright in the seemingly endless depths of African skies, and before the hyena cackled in the night. Yes, before all of creation, before the foundations of the earth were laid, and before planets were hung on nothing.

There, dear friend, in the very depths of eternity past, God almighty, the sovereign Ancient of Days, thought of us (the church). His thoughts were fixed on one particular plan. That plan being to adopt you and me, as sons and daughters, to become His children, and He did this out of His own love for us.

It was His will that we would become His adopted children, bringing Him glory, showing His grace towards us, and presenting a gift that was freely given only to His beloved children. Adoption was God's gift. Adoption is still His gift. Adoption for us, His beloved chosen church, has been carried out through the grand work of the king, our only Lord, Jesus Christ. Therefore, that plan of God has indeed come to pass, and we are the recipients of that plan and desire God had.

Does this not fill you with wonder, my brother, my sister? Consider that you have a Father who desires to have a real relationship with you, whereby He calls you "child," and you call Him "Father." Amen.

Think Eternally

Then Jesus said to His disciples, "If anyone wishes to come after Me, he must deny himself, and take up his cross and follow Me. For whoever wishes to save his life will lose it; but whoever loses his life for My sake will find it."

MATTHEW 16:24–25

JORDAN STANDRIDGE: ITALIAN THEOLOGICAL ACADEMY | ITALY

Jesus wants you to think eternally.

Every day that you wake thinking about Jesus, you are instantly led to think about eternity. Though it is easy to waste days, and even months and years, chasing after worldly pleasures, Jesus calls each believer to deny himself and his hopes and dreams and to put his hope and dreams in eternity.

Recently, one of the college students in my ministry put a note on the door of our house, informing us that she would not be following Christ anymore. Sadly, she counted the cost of being a disciple of Christ and she chose to follow the world instead. She recognized the difficulty of being a Christ-follower and did not want to give up what the world could offer.

Some pastors train their young people to say a prayer for salvation. Others promise comfort, wealth, and worldly peace. But Jesus Himself promised hardship, self-denial, and even death for those who would follow Him. Jesus had His eyes set on something much greater than this life, an eternal life with God in heaven. This is the gospel we must preach to those around us.

Every morning we wake up, we must fix our eyes on eternity and must live every moment with this truth in our minds. Only then will we be able to, with the help of the Holy Spirit, pick up our cross and follow our Savior. Only then will we be able to lose our lives. And only then will we store up treasure for the life to come.

The Greatest Mission

*Go therefore and make disciples of all the nations, baptizing
them in the name of the Father and the Son and the Holy Spirit.*
MATTHEW 28:19

KRISTIAN BRACKETT: THEOLOGICAL BIBLICAL ACADEMY | CROATIA

Jesus' final words to the disciples outline a task that requires
faithful service, substantial sacrifice, and supernatural help. The
whole church inherits this project and must take it seriously. We may
think the goal is only that the gospel would spread to all nations.
But Jesus is specific. He commands His followers to make disciples,
helping them to grow in Christlikeness and then encouraging them
to take on this task themselves.

Jesus outlines the means to "make disciples." This requires baptizing them or calling them to identify with Christ and his followers in
a public way upon hearing and believing the gospel with repentance
from sin. It also requires "teaching" (Matt. 28:20). Jesus expects the
church to undertake a comprehensive course of instruction that includes all Jesus has commanded. The formation of disciples in all
nations requires a serious investment of time, energy, and resources
from every member of his church. The goal is regeneration, obedience, and training of each new follower of Christ to participate in
this task.

This project depends on both God's saving work and the believer's faithful service. It is far from over. Many cities throughout
Europe, Asia, Africa, the Americas, and the Middle East lack an
adequate number of Bible-believing churches. Many towns and villages throughout China, Honduras, Russia, Mexico, India, Spain,
Malawi, Croatia, and the rest of the world are unreached with the
gospel. What is your role? Will you commit to form disciples in your
household and workplace? Will you go to the unreached? Will you
invest in others to be trained to lead the church in this great task
given by our risen and glorious Lord?

Chosen for Salvation

He chose us in Him before the foundation of the world, that
we would be holy and blameless before Him.

EPHESIANS 1:4

A. H.: MIDDLE EAST (NAME WITHHELD FOR SECURITY)

Looking at this verse, we learn who makes the determinative choice in salvation. Man is not the one making the decision, but God. While this can be hard to swallow, it is what the word of God says—we must submit to its teaching. Remember that man cannot choose God because man is dead in his sin (Eph. 2:1). He also does not seek God (Rom. 3:11). Instead, he uses his will to sin against this holy God. But God, being rich in mercy, shines the light of the gospel into the hearts of His chosen ones and saves those whom He has chosen.

Consider the conversions of Lydia and Paul. Speaking of Lydia, Acts 16:14 states, "The Lord opened her heart to respond to the things spoken by Paul." Lydia did not respond to an altar call or invite Jesus into her heart, but rather responded because God had chosen her and opened her heart. Concerning Paul, Jesus declared that "he is a chosen instrument of mine" (Acts 9:15). Paul was not looking for Jesus; on the contrary, he was going to persecute Jesus' church. Christ showed Paul grace without him asking for it. God chose Paul for His glory, and then redeemed him, even though Paul was actively attacking His people.

Recognize, then, the sovereignty of God in salvation. Your salvation is secure not because you chose God, but because He chose you. Rejoice in and be humbled by His kindness toward you.

A High Calling

But you are A CHOSEN RACE, A *royal* PRIESTHOOD, A HOLY NATION,
A PEOPLE FOR GOD'S OWN POSSESSION, *so that you may proclaim*
the excellencies of Him who has called you out of darkness
into His marvelous light.

1 PETER 2:9

ALEKSEY K.: RUSSIA (FULL NAME WITHHELD FOR SECURITY)

There was a period in my life when I studied under a master violin maker. In order to better understand my business and create good instruments, I needed more knowledge of the violin, so I began to study. I learned that you can have perfect pitch, use a good violin, but still play it out of tune. "You can't hold it like you hold a guitar," I was told. I held it properly and agonized until a musician showed me the proper hand placement. When placed correctly, your fingers come down on the strings right where they should be, and then it's not difficult to follow the intonation.

Something similar happens in the spiritual world. We can be so concentrated on what we must do and what our behavior should be like. We then remember our shortcomings and grow weary. We grow tired and feel like we are overwhelmed by sin—even though Christ is our Lord and we love the Savior. We can think we are just believing *sinners.*

However, Peter gives a comforting word that answers the question, "Who are you?" The answer helps to correct our thoughts: "You are A CHOSEN RACE, A royal PRIESTHOOD, A HOLY NATION, A PEOPLE FOR GOD'S OWN POSSESSION." If you have true faith in Jesus Christ, these four descriptions answer the question of your calling and special position. God chose you and He made you a priest, someone who knows Him and represents Him to others. By His grace, you are holy and God took you into His realm as His possession.

Christian, remember your high calling! Go therefore and proclaim God's excellencies.

July 19

A New Dawn in Albania

So then you are no longer strangers and aliens, but you are fellow citizens with the saints, and are of God's household...
Christ Jesus Himself being the corner stone, in whom the whole building, being fitted together, is growing into a holy temple in the Lord, in whom you also are being built together into a dwelling of God in the Spirit.
EPHESIANS 2:19–22

ASTRIT A.: ALBANIA (NAME WITHHELD FOR SECURITY)

These great truths that the apostle Paul wrote to believers in Ephesus apply very concretely and poignantly to us believers in Albania. Not very long ago we were strangers, without God, without a witness for Him. This was because faith in God was strictly forbidden. Openly declaring your faith would have landed you in prison. The word of God was outlawed and so we lived in total spiritual darkness. But then at last the saving grace of God came to our country. The light began to shine in this dark land and God's word, which once was forbidden, is now available to all.

Now that we are "fellow citizens with the saints, and are of God's household," this should motivate us to be built up and to build up each other upon the strong and sound foundation. Just because we now have the freedom to believe in Christ doesn't mean that we are automatically protected from false teaching. The challenge before true Albanian believers is for the church to be built up upon sound teaching. We need the word of God to light our path. Only then will the church continue to declare God's truth, be a solid witness before the unsaved, and give glory to God. The foundation of the apostles and prophets is the Bible. Only the Scriptures are given to dictate what we should believe and how we should live.

Thank you, God, that we now have Your wonderful word here in Albania, and the freedom to worship You and to proclaim Your truth!

July 20

Submission as a Way of Life

*You younger men, likewise, be subject to your elders; and
all of you, clothe yourselves with humility toward one
another, for God is opposed to the proud, but gives grace
to the humble.*

1 PETER 5:5

BRYAN DAVID: TMAI HEADQUARTERS | LOS ANGELES, CALIFORNIA

In America today, submission to authority is seen as naïve, weak, and cowardly. Sadly, this same negative view has made its way into the American church, where the concept of submission to church leaders is rejected by many as antiquated and undemocratic. Peter reminds us, however, that beginning with younger people, we are all to submit to our church leaders. Submission is not only biblical, it is a blessing—both for you and for your leaders (Heb. 13:17).

But submission to authority is more than just a mandate for life in the church. The Bible is clear that, unless you're being told to sin, subjecting yourself to God-ordained authority should be the norm in *all* of life. Children are to submit to their parents (Eph. 6:1), slaves to their masters (1 Pet. 2:18), citizens to their government (1 Pet. 2:13), wives to their husbands (1 Pet. 3:1), and husbands to Christ—just as the church itself is subject to Christ her Lord (Eph. 5:23–24).

As today's verse shows, submission to authority is inseparably linked to humility, and the extent that we are humble is the extent that we will receive God's grace. The concept is simple: if we oppose our authorities, God will oppose us. If, on the other hand, we humble ourselves in subjection to our leaders, God will give us grace and exalt us (1 Pet. 5:6).

Dear believer, I am certain that you do not want God's almighty hand opposing you today. So humble yourself. Remind yourself of God's call to submission. Subject yourself to your authorities in church, government, work, and family, and see God's grace exalt you at the proper time.

The Father's Pleasure

But the LORD *was pleased to crush Him, putting Him to grief;*
if He would render Himself as a guilt offering, He will see His
offspring, He will prolong His days, and the good pleasure of
the LORD *will prosper in His hand.*

ISAIAH 53:10

ROBERT KENSINGER: EVANGELICAL MINISTRIES OF THE AMERICAS | HONDURAS

It's hard to imagine a father being "pleased" to crush his son, but that's exactly what Isaiah 53:10 tells us happened when Jesus was crucified on the cross. Here we are given a glimpse into the very heart of God the Father as he "caused the iniquity of us all to fall on [His Son]" (Isa. 53:6). Nowhere else in Scripture do we see God *pleased* about punishing men for their sin. He is pleased to bless Israel (Num. 24:1) and to make them His people (1 Sam. 12:22). He is pleased with "a broken and a contrite heart" (Psa. 51:16–17). He is pleased with proper worship in the Jewish temple (Hag 1:8), as well as with the sacrifices of praise through "doing good and sharing" (Heb. 13:16). However, we never see God pleased in the chastisement of a man for sin except for here in Isaiah 53:10.

The question, then, is: Why? Why would God the Father be pleased to crush His own Son, putting Him to grief? It is because the Son has made Himself a substitutionary offering for sin so that the grace of God may be eternally revealed in all its fullness and the glory of His love may be put on display for all to see. Through His sacrifice, the Son is blessed with His spiritual posterity (believers, both Jew and Gentile), the eternal enjoyment of the fruits of His labor, and the personal pleasure of having all things placed beneath His feet.

Glory be to God for His perfect and *pleasing* act of redemption!

The Song of Simeon

Now Lord, You are releasing Your bond-servant to depart in peace, according to Your word; for my eyes have seen Your salvation, which You have prepared in the presence of all peoples, A LIGHT OF REVELATION TO THE GENTILES, and the glory of Your people Israel.

LUKE 2:29–32

JONATHAN MOORHEAD: CZECH BIBLE INSTITUTE | CZECH REPUBLIC

One of the grand masterpieces of art is Rembrandt's "The Song of Simeon." In this portrait, the elderly Simeon gazes upon the face of Christ in his arms, with Mary shaded in the background. As beautiful as this piece of art is, it cannot communicate the theology expressed in these verses, which show God's faithfulness to fulfill His promises.

Apparently God revealed to Simeon that he would see the Messiah prior to his death. We do not know if Simeon waited days or decades for it. Rejoicing in the fulfillment of this personal promise, Simeon glories in the fulfillment of the ancient promises of God concerning this Messiah.

First, Jesus, whose name means "salvation," is identified as "Your salvation." Simeon understood that this child would be God's agent of spiritual deliverance. Second, this salvation would be offered to all people, to the world, to Jew and Gentile. Hearkening back to the Abrahamic covenant of Genesis 12:3, through Abraham's seed all of the families of the earth would be blessed. Forty-two generations later (Matt. 1:17), that promise was fulfilled in Jesus: a light of revelation to the Gentiles, and the glory of God's people Israel.

Are you in a season of waiting on the Lord? Rest in the faithfulness of God. Wait on Him, and remember the words of Isaiah 40:31: "Yet those who wait for the Lord will gain new strength; they will mount up with wings like eagles, they will run and not get tired, they will walk and not become weary." God is good, and He *will* fulfill his promises.

Marking Out Apostates

To the pure, all things are pure; but to those who are defiled and unbelieving, nothing is pure, but both their mind and their conscience are defiled.

TITUS 1:15

S. W.: ASIA (NAME WITHHELD FOR SECURITY)

Paul has been warning Titus about the characteristics of false teachers and apostates beginning in verse 10 of Titus 1. Here he focuses on the crucial issue—the corruption of their hearts. In this context, the phrase "to the pure, all things are pure," describes the opposite of apostates. True believers have a life of productivity in holiness. In other words, they are not thinking about what is evil, but are setting their minds on that which is God-centered and useful.

On the other hand, false teachers are impure of heart and without faith in Christ. Because of this they see nothing as pure, but are legalistic and condemn even the practice of good and pure things. In context, Paul is thinking about the Judaizers who follow "Jewish myths and commandments of men" (Titus 1:14).

A mark of false teaching is an overemphasis on rules and legalistic regulations. False teachers are often marked not by *what they are for*, but *what they are against*. The ultimate reason Paul gives for this is that their minds and consciences are defiled. They have hidden sin in their thinking and hearts, and their legalism is often a smokescreen to cover and perpetuate their sin.

Let us then be on guard, and avoid letting our minds and consciences become defiled. Our lives should not be marked primarily by the lists of things we are avoiding, but instead by our singular devotion to and following after Christ.

The Dangers of Dead Religion

When you did not know God, you were slaves to those which by nature are no gods. But now that you have come to know God... how is it that you turn back again to the weak and worthless elemental things, to which you desire to be enslaved all over again? ...I fear for you, that perhaps I have labored over you in vain.

GALATIANS 4:8–11

MYKOLA LELIOVSKYI: GRACE BIBLE SEMINARY | UKRAINE

Over 85 percent of Ukrainians identify with Eastern Orthodoxy. Only around one percent are Evangelical. So in our context, Paul's warning about dead religion seems to jump right off the page. He identifies three dangers that everyone should beware of. First, dead religion is slavery to idolatry. Just as the early Gentiles worshiped the gods of the Greco-Roman pantheon, many in the Eastern Orthodox Church are caught up in the unbiblical veneration of saints and images, including even at times divination and ancestral worship.

The second danger of dead religion is that it is weak and worthless. It neither saves nor sanctifies. Man-made religion may have the appearance of wisdom, but it is of no value in fighting the flesh (Col. 2:23). It nullifies the power of the gospel and the grace of Jesus Christ. Those who turn to the self-reliant religions of this world are left with nothing but their own meager efforts and merits.

The last danger is that dead religion demands a preoccupation with rituals. When there is no inner life, all that is left are the external trappings. Rituals provide a sense of routine and religious accomplishment, but offer nothing in terms of a relationship enabled by the work of Christ alone. Lacking true fellowship with God, followers of man-made religion content themselves with outward observances.

Only the gospel of Jesus Christ, which Paul defends throughout Galatians, can save and liberate a soul from dead religion. Rejoice that God has not left it up to us to save ourselves! He sent His Son to accomplish *everything* on our behalf, so that we who believe might live through Him!

Foundations for Faithfulness

And one called out to another and said, "Holy, Holy, Holy, is the LORD *of hosts, the whole earth is full of His glory." ... Then I heard the voice of the Lord, saying, "Whom shall I send, and who will go for Us?" Then I said, "Here am I. Send me!"*

ISAIAH 6:3, 8

ALLAN LUCIANO: THE EXPOSITOR'S ACADEMY | PHILIPPINES

God commissioned Isaiah into a very challenging ministry. He was to call God's people to repent as they were drifting further and further away from the Lord. He was to address an audience whom God already said would hear but not understand, would see but not perceive (Isa. 6:9). Isaiah was to deliver a message to a people who were both unteachable and uninterested in what he had to say.

The story of Isaiah's life shows that he remained faithful to his commission, having served through the reign of four Judean kings (Isa. 1:1). He ministered as a prophet for about sixty years in total.

How did he remain faithful throughout all those years against all the challenges that he faced? Isaiah's faithfulness to his commission was grounded on a clear and compelling conviction about God's character. Witnessing the seraphim sing "Holy, holy, holy" to each other left a strong impression on Isaiah. "Holy One of Israel" was one of his favorite ways to refer to God, using it a total of 26 times in his book. What he knew of God propelled him to a life and ministry of faithfulness, regardless of the circumstances that faced him.

Like Isaiah, you too have a Great Commission from the Lord. How well do you know the God who commissioned you? A clear conviction about God's character is the foundation for a lifelong ministry of faithfulness to the Lord. Only as you share in Isaiah's awe of God's holiness will you share in Isaiah's faithfulness in saying, "Here am I. Send me!"

Christ, Our True Source of Life

I am the true vine, and My Father is the vinedresser.
JOHN 15:1

D. G.: ASIA (NAME WITHHELD FOR SECURITY)

The main focus of this passage is the vine, Jesus Christ. He is the true vine and His Father is the vinedresser who cares for the vine. God the Father helps the branches—which abide in the vine—bear fruit by pruning them. And He removes any fruitless branches. This imagery was also used of Israel in her relationship with Yahweh; sadly, she failed to bear fruit (Psa. 80).

People are created for the glory of God and yet we fail to glorify God. Christians, though, by abiding in Christ Jesus, can glorify God (John 15:8). Christ's work on the cross made this abiding possible. Jesus, as the true vine, gives us eternal life and nourishes us so that we can bear fruit for Him. We are wholly dependent on Him for life and fruitfulness. A major fruit that Christians will bear is sacrificial love for Christ and His people (John 15:17). This is radically different than what the world holds in high esteem—like gaining riches, being successful, having self esteem.

Are you abiding in the vine—Jesus Christ, and His words? If so, you will bear fruit for God. If you are bearing fruit, expect God's pruning work in your life—this may be painful yet He intends it to produce more fruit, so humbly accept His loving discipline (Heb. 12:6–11). Or, are you merely religious, without love for other believers in the church? If that is the case, be careful. Jesus promises that His Father, the vinedresser, will remove fruitless branches.

Strength in an Unstable World

Only be strong and very courageous; be careful to do according to all the law which Moses My servant commanded you; do not turn from it to the right or to the left, so that you may have success wherever you go.

JOSHUA 1:7

ALEKSEY K.: RUSSIA (FULL NAME WITHHELD FOR SECURITY)

Today many people talk of strength and courage, but in practice strength becomes cruelty and courage becomes brutality. As incorrect as these notions are, we need to orient ourselves to the Bible and what it says strength and courage are.

After Moses' death, Joshua was to lead the people of Israel. Here God commanded him to be strong and courageous. This command was given three times in the first chapter alone. How interesting when we remember that Joshua was not one of the ten fearful spies, and that he faced death on more than one occasion; however, God considered it necessary to give him this command. A great task stood before Joshua that demanded greater strength and courage.

Where was this strength and courage to be found? From God's word. Joshua was to carefully keep the commandments, without turning to the right or the left. If a man has this kind of relationship to the Scripture, he will find strength from God and courage to face whatever circumstances or trials come.

Truth is, it's not easy to be courageous while overcoming temptations and experiencing pain. It's difficult to find strength to hold to your beliefs, to be tender in your relationships with other people, and to endure hurtful behaviors while being willing to forgive. Hear the Lord's appeal from the pages of the book of Joshua—be strong and courageous.

Reacting to Wretched News

*He said, "Naked I came from my mother's womb, and naked
I shall return there. The LORD gave and the LORD has taken
away. Blessed be the name of the LORD."*

JOB 1:21

UWE SEIDEL: EUROPEAN BIBLE TRAINING CENTER | GERMANY

In March 2016, I was diagnosed with colon-rectal cancer. Barely a
month later my beloved spouse was diagnosed with a brain tumor.
Death was always a reality for us, but it was "out there." Now the
"shadow of death" had broken into our home.

We were not the first in this dire condition. Many years ago, a man
named Job, a righteous and wealthy man of outstanding piety, was
hit with the bad news of losing all his wealth to enemy forces, culmi-
nating in hearing all his children were killed in a furious storm. How
did he react?

First, Job was silent. As the bad news sank into his mind and soul,
it left him numb and struck by deep grief. By no means a stoic, we see
him rising, tearing his robe and shaving his head, silent expressions
of his extreme grief and deep mourning. Stripped-down to his bare
mettle, his core beliefs were about to be revealed.

Second, Job spoke. In godly piety, he realized that "we have brought
nothing into the world, so we cannot take anything out of it either"
(1 Tim. 6:7). Being a believer, Job says, "The LORD gave and the LORD
has taken away." Faith gives us eyes to see God is present and active in
every situation, good or bad or ugly, and lets us run into His presence.

Third, Job worshiped. Instead of cursing God, as Satan had predicted, Job blesses God. Amid severe, hurting loss, the believer experiences God in deep ways and his soul is lifted from shallow faith to
heights unknown.

Love, honor, and trust God as Job did, and rest assured that God
will be with you in your deep valleys!

A Liberating and Purifying Gospel

For if, after they have escaped the defilements of the world by the knowledge of the Lord and Savior Jesus Christ, they are again entangled in them and are overcome, the last state has become worse for them than the first.

2 PETER 2:20

DMITRIY ZHEREBNENKOV: WORD OF GRACE BIBLE INSTITUTE | USA

This passage was not written for the purpose of creating theological arguments and debates, but rather to serve the church. Look at this passage as an instrument in God's hands that can help any believer.

There are two lessons that can be taken from this passage. The first lesson is the purity of the gospel. It is dangerous to come so close to the gospel and yet not submit to it in perseverance. The sad reality is that counterfeit Christianity often functions in this way—close enough to the gospel to be welcomed and accepted, yet still lacking the saving and transforming power of it.

The second lesson is that the gospel must liberate people from the bondage of sin (Rom. 6:22). When a person truly believes the gospel, and puts his trust in the Lord, the truth liberates such a person (John 8:32) to be able to say no to sin.

Take time to evaluate your own understanding of the gospel (1 Tim. 4:16). Thank God if what you believe is rooted in truth as it is presented in the Bible. This is one of the ways God will preserve you for eternity. Also, if you find yourself struggling with sin, may this passage alert you and encourage you to remember that the true believer has all the necessary power to overcome sin, and that he must do so. Pray specifically for people who are held captive by any false gospel, that they might find freedom from the bondage to any half-truth and sin.

The Broad Way and the Narrow Way

*For the gate is small and the way is narrow that leads to life,
and there are few who find it.*
MATTHEW 7:14

HEBER TORRES: BEREA SEMINARY | SPAIN

I'm sure you've heard many times the saying, "All roads lead to Rome." Many have been seduced by the succulent proposal behind this statement and have applied it to all spheres of life, even to the final destiny of souls. With the hope of having a clear conscience, some believe that any decision they make in terms of "being right with God" is equally legitimate, yet believing that is no guarantee. In the same way that all roads do not lead to Rome, not all paths lead to eternal life.

In the middle of His speech about the kingdom, Jesus does not even consider the countless alternative routes. He narrows it down to only two options: the broad way and the narrow way.

He who presents Himself as that narrow way—*the* way—warns His audience against the dangers of taking the broad way. Many fall prey to it, and it leads to destruction. Jesus also tells His listeners that the narrow way is hard to find. Indeed, few find it.

It should sadden our hearts to think of the many people who walk in the broad way, whose only destination is destruction. Likewise, it should compel us to proclaim the only and sufficient Savior to those around us. Pray that in this era of religious pluralism and moral relativism, the gospel's message will resound stronger than ever. Indeed, "to whom shall we go? You have words of eternal life" (John 6:68).

Spain

Berea Seminary

Spain has long been a stronghold of the Roman Catholic Church and it wasn't until 1980, following the death of dictator Francisco Franco, that Spaniards had religious freedom. Today, a culture of nominal Catholicism pervades Spain with over 68% of the population identifying as Catholic. Berea Seminary is strengthening evangelical churches and training more men to faithfully preach the true gospel across Spain.

TODAY, PRAY FOR

The gospel of salvation by faith alone to penetrate through the errant Catholic religion of works.

Berea Seminary as it seeks to expand its teaching sites to meet the growing desire for training.

Local churches across Spain, that their members would be faithful to live out and preach the gospel.

The Greatest Transfer

He made Him who knew no sin to be sin on our behalf, so that
we might become the righteousness of God in Him.
2 CORINTHIANS 5:21

SAMSON CHOLOKOTO: CENTRAL AFRICAN PREACHING ACADEMY | MALAWI

Picture a courtroom setting. One individual is guilty, having committed multiple heinous crimes. A second individual is innocent, having committed no crime. It would be shocking and scandalous to see these two individuals' judicial standing switched, the guilty pronounced innocent and the innocent pronounced guilty—and punished accordingly. Indeed, it is unfathomable and incomprehensible. Yet, that's a picture of the gospel.

Guilty sinners are treated as if they are innocent and righteous. Jesus Christ, however, was treated on the cross as if He sinned, though He never did. A great transfer occurs—God transferred our sins upon Christ as our sin-bearer, and Christ's righteousness is conferred upon us. This is the greatest exchange!

While this scenario is shocking, in God's wisdom it perfectly upholds His standard of justice. Sin is completely punished as God's wrath was poured out on Christ. God then graciously treats saved sinners as if they lived the perfect life of Christ, all because Christ's righteousness is transferred to them when they place their faith in Christ.

This wonderful and glorious transfer and exchange is captured in the word imputation. Our sin was imputed to Christ. The righteousness of Christ is imputed to us. This is what Paul means when he writes 2 Corinthians 5:21.

This gift of Christ's righteousness only comes to those who have trusted in Christ for salvation. Have you placed your faith wholly and exclusively on Him? If so, rejoice today with Jeremiah and praise "the LORD our righteousness" (Jer. 23:6).

True Love for Christ

Jesus answered and said to him, "If anyone loves Me, he will keep My word; and My Father will love him, and We will come to him and make Our abode with him."

JOHN 14:23

FILIP PINTARIC: THEOLOGICAL BIBLICAL ACADEMY | CROATIA

Modern Christian culture is often stubbornly anti-intellectual. It insists that we abandon doctrine and simply love Jesus. "We should stop focusing on doctrine and start just loving Jesus and others instead," is a common complaint. But, contrary to this contemporary view, true love for Christ cannot be separated from love for His truth. Those who love Christ will keep His word. The word "to keep" means to guard or watch over protectively. Jesus expects His believers to guard His word as our treasure, as something very valuable to us. Those who love God delight in His word; they take pleasure in His gospel. The words of Jesus Christ are like riches to them.

Today, many profess to love God while being indifferent to Scripture and its truth. How can we say that we cherish Christ and at the same be apathetic toward His words? How can we profess to love Christ and not be determined to understand and live by the teaching He left us? Our love toward God is not measured by our warm feelings or ecstatic experiences, but by our attitude and affection for His truth.

Do you delight in God's word? Do you seek to understand and live in the light of the gospel of Jesus Christ? Make God's word your treasure. And take heart, for those who delight in the word of God are given a great promise—they will be loved by the Father. The Father loves those whose hearts delight in the Son and His word.

Do You Love Your Wife?

*Husbands, love your wives, just as Christ also loved the church
and gave Himself up for her.*
EPHESIANS 5:25

DUAN DU TOIT: CHRIST SEMINARY | SOUTH AFRICA

The essence of true love is giving. Christ "loved the church and gave Himself up for her." Or to put it in the words of the apostle John: "For God so loved the world, that He *gave* His only begotten Son" (John 3:16).

At this point the love of Christ astounds us. Christ loved the church so much that He gave *Himself* up for her. There is nothing more valuable than God Himself. At the same time, there is no one more underserving of God's love than a rebellious sinner. Yet, the second Person of the Trinity chose to *give Himself* up for His bride, the church, by dying on a cross. In doing so He covered her shame, bore her disgraces, and mended her wounds. He paid the full price of her sins in His own body on the cross. If Jesus Christ's main ministry was to love His bride to such a lavish extent, how, then, are husbands to live that out with their wives? Herein lies the wondrous mystery revealed—that a man's love for his wife displays the love of Christ for His church.

Husband, is your love for your wife conditional? Since when did the church deserve such a loving Savior? Never. Are you humbly loving your wife? Do you hold your love till it is earned or deserved? Consider the extent of humility that Christ had when He gave Himself up for His bride.

The task is indeed too great for us to accomplish on our own. Praise God for His forgiveness and enablement. Learn how to love your wife by observing the Savior's love for you, in spite of your failures to obey this command.

The Devious Delight of Sin

When the woman saw that the tree was good for food, and
that it was a delight to the eyes, and that the tree was desirable
to make one wise, she took from its fruit and ate; and she gave
also to her husband with her, and he ate.

GENESIS 3:6

ANGEL CARDOZA: INSTITUTO DE EXPOSITORES | USA

In the beginning, God blessed Adam and Eve with precious, unblemished gifts. They had flawless companionship with God, who was their Creator, Sustainer, and Friend. Despite their perfect condition, they chose to sin against God. Their experience gives some transcendent truths about the devious delights of sin.

Sin appears more pleasing than obedience. Despite the blessings Adam and Eve enjoyed in the garden, they were lured toward sin by the one thing they could not experience—the tree of the knowledge of good and evil. In their foolishness, they looked away from the beauty, provision, and greatness of God. This is the same strategy Satan uses on believers today. He tries to deceive us so that we look away from our great God.

Sin appears more fruitful than obedience. While desiring wisdom is commendable, seeking it apart from God is not. In their covetousness, Adam and Eve pursued the way of evil to obtain something that can only be acquired by fearing and obeying God. Believers must remember that although the way of sin might appear beneficial, it only leads to destruction (Prov. 13:15).

Sin is a choice, just as obedience is a choice. Adam and Eve were faced with a decision: trust in Satan's lies or obey the Creator. Sadly, they followed the devious scheme of the evil one, bringing the consequences of their actions upon all mankind (Rom. 5:12). Thankfully, through our Lord and Savior Jesus Christ, God has granted the power and means to overcome Satan's schemes of temptation and sin (James 4:7).

As you treasure the Savior today, guard yourself against these devious delights of sin.

How Do You Bring Joy to the Lord?

The LORD *favors those who fear Him, those who wait for His lovingkindness.*

PSALM 147:11

SERGEY M.: RUSSIA (FULL NAME WITHHELD FOR SECURITY)

What brings you joy? A good deal? A great vacation? A delicious meal? Your favorite team winning? Each of us finds joy in something. But have you wondered, what brings God joy? In what does He find satisfaction? The psalmist tells us.

God favors and finds joy in the person who demonstrates two qualities. First, the person fears God. The Lord rejoices in people who stand in awe before Him and humbly bow before His majesty and holiness (Isa. 8:13), hate sin (Prov. 8:13), and strive to be obedient in all things (Prov. 14:2).

Second, God finds joy in the person who waits for His lovingkindness. God is pleased when the only hope a person possesses is in His mercy. That person understands what he truly deserves (punishment in hell) and is thankful for God's mercy. He knows that God loves to show mercy (Mic. 7:18). He understands that God's mercy is based on the sacrifice of Jesus Christ. And thus, he will patiently wait upon God and trust in His perfect, wise timing.

Would the people who know you testify that you are someone who fears the Lord? Would they say you exhibit confident and patient trust in God? Are you someone whose only hope is in God's steadfast love and mercy? Bow before the Lord today. Ask Him to make you a person who fears Him and trusts in His mercy. This is how you can bring God joy.

August 6

The Wisdom of Silence

*O that you would be completely silent, and that it would
become your wisdom!*

JOB 13:5

CORNELIUS RIVERA: EVANGELICAL MINISTRIES OF THE AMERICAS | HONDURAS

In Spanish-speaking countries we say, "Habla hasta por los codos,"
when referring to someone who talks too much. The literal translation is: "He even talks through his elbows." In English, one might
say, "He talks his head off." Do you know such a person? Some just
make a nuisance of themselves, rambling on about one thing or another. Others, by constantly directing their words against another,
place their relationship with that person in danger. I knew a woman
who continually derided, criticized, and contradicted her husband in
whatever he said or did. She did this within the hearing of others,
letting everyone know that in private she was no different. Another
lady had the habit of giving unsolicited advice to just about everyone
she met.

One's words often betray the absence of wisdom. Hearing inces-
sant speech, criticism, or advice not requested incites people to respond just as Job did to his unwelcome counselors: "O that you would
be completely silent!"

Job wished that their silence would become their wisdom, for their
words revealed the opposite. Their uninvited counsel revealed a lack
of wisdom and an absence of understanding. Their tongue revealed
their ignorance regarding God's work in Job's life. As the proverb
goes, "When there are many words, transgression is unavoidable"
(Prov. 10:19); but, "He who restrains his words has knowledge" (Prov.
17:27).

Restraining our lips—instead of expressing opinions and speculations—lets others know that we understand that God is at work,
even though we might not know exactly what He is doing or why.
What do your words reveal about you? Have you learned the wisdom
of silence?

We Have a Father

For this reason I bow my knees before the Father, from whom
every family in heaven and on earth derives its name.
EPHESIANS 3:14–15

MYKOLA LELIOVSKYI: GRACE BIBLE SEMINARY | UKRAINE

Moved by God's glorious grace, Paul bows his knees before the Father to pray. His bowed knees express humility, and his reference to God as Father expresses familiarity. In Paul's letters, the fatherhood of God is seen in three ways. He is the Father of Jesus; He is the Father of all creation; but most frequently, He is described as the loving Father of believers, a relationship established through Christ.

Scripture portrays God as the ideal Father, the Father par excellence. Whatever good that can be said of earthly fatherhood is rooted in the fatherhood of God. Like a good father, God is far more willing to give than His children are willing to ask (Eph. 3:20). As any good father, God the Father is aware of His children's needs. Unlike earthly fathers, however, He has the ability and wisdom to provide exactly what is necessary in every situation.

The family unit in Ukraine has been devastated by alcoholism, with many children growing up without fathers. Although my earthly father was never there for me, I have found great comfort in knowing that in Christ I am God's child, adopted into the spiritual family of my loving, heavenly Father. We may trust that our Father will provide for our needs, protect us from harm, and prepare us to inherit His kingdom. As John writes, "See how great a love the Father has bestowed on us, that we should be called children of God; and such we are" (1 John 3:1).

Modeling Servitude

*For He grew up before Him like a tender shoot, and like a
root out of parched ground; He has no stately form or majesty that we should look upon Him, nor appearance that we
should be attracted to Him. He was despised and forsaken of
men, a man of sorrows and acquainted with grief; and like
one from whom men hide their face He was despised, and we
did not esteem Him.*

ISAIAH 53:2–3

L. J.: ASIA (NAME WITHHELD FOR SECURITY)

We live in an era when serving the church as a full-time minister
is generally considered an honorable, and even enviable, voca-
tion. Some people enter the ministry with wrong motives, and are later disappointed after chasing the deceitfulness of personal glory. But
Jesus Christ our Master is set forth as the Suffering Servant of Isaiah
53. He stands in sharp contrast to the self-gratifying ministry we too
often see in ministry "professionals."

Take note of a few key aspects of the suffering nature of His service. The picture of a "tender shoot" and "parched ground" speaks
about the humble circumstances in which Jesus grew up. There was
nothing special in His external appearance that would capture the attention of others. Moreover, those He came to serve did not approve
of or give respect to Him. He was an obedient servant who fully ex-
pended Himself to the ministry handed Him by the Father.

The true call for Christians is to become like Jesus in His serving.
Suffering and serving go together in Christian ministry. If you seek
after glory, you will be disappointed. Expect that suffering will come
along the way when serving the church—do not be surprised. It is the
call and experience of Christians worldwide.

Let us walk in the footsteps of the Master-Servant, and serve the
people in His church. Take comfort when you suffer, because you are
modeling Christ in your serving.

Love Suffers Long

Love is patient.

1 CORINTHIANS 13:4A

ALEKSEY P.: RUSSIA (FULL NAME WITHHELD FOR SECURITY)

In the New Testament, several words are used to communicate the idea of bearing up under difficulties. The word Paul uses here is one of those. When he begins his description of true love and says it is patient, he means more than most of us realize.

More than the simple idea of patience, Paul uses a word that means to suffer long—hence, the idea of bearing with and bearing up under difficulties. The word also means slow to anger. This word then describes the ability to refrain from getting angry over the shortcomings and blunders of those around you.

What does this look like in practice? "First, a patient person has an *open heart* that doesn't nitpick and is not annoyed by people's shortcomings. This is someone who is large-hearted with people, who makes relationships easy and pleasant. Second, this looks like a *readiness to endure an injury suffered*. You endure and bear with whatever wrong has been suffered, and certainly do not respond in retaliation.

In view of understanding patience, stop and reflect on your life and actions. Are you patient only when everything is going according to plan and when relationships are easy? What happens when you suffer a wrong? What is your first response? Would those close to you consider you open-hearted, someone who is slow to get angry? If not, take a moment and reflect on the Lord Jesus Christ and the many times in the Gospels He perfectly exemplified that love is patient. Ask Him for grace to be patient in the same way.

Love Does Good Deeds

Love is kind.

1 CORINTHIANS 13:4B

ALEKSEY P.: RUSSIA (FULL NAME WITHHELD FOR SECURITY)

What is kindness? Many understand it to mean being good, benevolent, and generous. But few realize it also involves *doing* good deeds to others. In other words, kindness is exhibiting goodness and benevolence in attitude and action. And this kindness, according to Paul, is a product of love.

Considering this aspect of love, it is right to ask, how can kindness be shown? What do deeds of love look like in practice? First, kindness is shown by a *self-denying relationship* to people around you. Love takes up the position of a servant and sets aside personal interests for the interest and needs of others. It genuinely prefers the good of others to your own.

Second, kindness is shown in *effective help*. A loving person is prepared to help people practically. When we see a person in need, we can respond by either opening or closing our hearts to the person. We can act according to the principle: out of sight, out of mind. We allow ourselves to forget about the problem and, more importantly, the person. Or, in opening our hearts, we can demonstrate love in deed and truth. This means we don't forget the need or the person, and we try to help. If we ourselves cannot solve the problem, then we do our best to help find a solution. These are some ways kindness is shown.

Take stock today of your kindness. Is it only in attitude, but rarely in action? Do you exhibit a self-denying relationship to others? Do you demonstrate effective help? The answer can reveal if you are showing love.

No Room for Envy

Love ... is not jealous.
1 CORINTHIANS 13:4C

ALEKSEY P.: RUSSIA (FULL NAME WITHHELD FOR SECURITY)

Envy is the experience of being annoyed by the realization that other people enjoy some kind of superiority or advantage that you don't have. When we see someone is enjoying an advantage we do not possess and we are annoyed and bothered, this is a sign that we have succumbed to the sin of envy.

Envy can show itself in several ways. There can be the desire to have what someone else possesses. Or, we can desire to *be* in the place or position of another. Or, envy can surface in the desire to be *better* than someone else or that they would be *worse off* than us.

What feeds envy? The underlying source of any form of envy is pride. The thought pattern operating in the heart of an envious person is often: "I deserve to have what the other person has more than he; or, at minimum, I am *no less* deserving."

How do we respond when we sense we are envious? We must deal with the problem of pride. If we genuinely realize that we deserve nothing more than hell, then we will thankfully accept any manifestation (even the smallest) of grace in our life and then avoid the weariness of desiring to receive something better. A humble heart is not envious. We then must give and show love. Love is the opposite of envy—where there is love, there is no room for envy. Indeed, love delivers us from envy.

Do you struggle with envy? Then reflect on what you deserve, ask God for help, and show love to those in your life. Leave no room for envy.

Not Wrapped Up in Itself

Love does not brag and is not arrogant.
1 CORINTHIANS 13:4D

ALEKSEY P.: RUSSIA (FULL NAME WITHHELD FOR SECURITY)

Have you ever wondered what the difference is between bragging and arrogance? Bragging is outward self-exaltation and arrogance is inward pride. Bragging is noticeable to others, while arrogance can pass unnoticed as it nestles in the heart. Bragging reveals itself in self-praise, emphasizing personal merit, or attracting attention for the praise of others. Arrogance is internal self-exaltation. If bragging is when a person *signals* that he deserves praise, then arrogance is when he *feels* he deserves praise. Arrogance can even exist with a form of outward humility. C. S. Lewis expressed it aptly: "We are especially arrogant when we enjoy being humble."

Yet true love is the opposite—it does not brag and is not arrogant. How then can you begin to battle these twin sins and cultivate true love and humility?

Don't get wrapped up in yourself. Instead think about Christ! Meditate on His majesty. Be enthralled with His beauty and character as revealed in the Gospels.

Don't get wrapped up in yourself. Think about the good qualities of others. Notice their virtues. Think about what you can learn from them. Take note of how God is working in their lives and what kind of fruit He is producing in them.

Don't get wrapped up in yourself. Think about those who are needy and take interest in their lives. Find out what their needs are. Don't hide from their problems.

Finally, *don't get wrapped up in yourself.* Intercede for others in prayer. Pray for the pastors and leaders in your church. Pray for brothers and sisters in Christ. Pray for unsaved relatives and acquaintances. Pray for the leaders of your country, state, and city.

The Greatest Need

Therefore the Jews were grumbling about Him, because He said, "I am the bread that came down out of heaven."
JOHN 6:41

EDWIN ZELAYA: EVANGELICAL MINISTRIES OF THE AMERICAS | HONDURAS

Honduras has one of the highest percentages of hunger in Latin America. Just by walking along the city streets you can clearly see that hunger ravages our country. As believers, however, we recognize that there exists an even greater need in our country, a need that Christ articulated to a different generation nearly two thousand years ago.

The people in Christ's day, as in every generation, had a desperate need for a Savior—one who could give life to their dead and dying souls. What they didn't understand, and what today's generation doesn't understand, is that our greatest need is not physical but spiritual food, food that is capable of creating and sustaining eternal life!

During Christ's public ministry, many followed Him simply to have their bellies filled or to see what kind of miracle He would do next. Why do you follow Christ? Are you simply seeking for temporal blessings to feed the desires of your physical body, or do you seek the spiritual nourishment that only He can give?

When Christ said, "I am the bread that came down out of heaven," He was declaring His deity, His superiority, His unique prerogative to create and sustain life. The greatest need in the world today is not physical bread but Christ, the bread of eternal life. No matter the country, the need is the same. Let us proclaim the only hope to a spiritually starving world: that God has sent bread from heaven, Jesus Christ, through whom man can be sustained eternally.

God's Perfect Word

God, after He spoke long ago to the fathers in the prophets in
many portions and in many ways, in these last days has spoken
to us in His Son.
HEBREWS 1:1–2

ASTRIT A.: ALBANIA (FULL NAME WITHHELD FOR SECURITY)

Many understand that God spoke in the past but have questions about whether He continues to speak today.

In the past, God spoke in many ways, such as in dreams and visions. He would often speak in such ways to prophets, who would in return communicate what they had heard or seen. "Thus says the Lord" is a familiar refrain in the prophetic writings. But in these last days, God has done something even greater. He has spoken to us by His Son! A stark contrast is made between speech *by prophets* and speech *by God's Son*, who is Himself the exact representation of God's nature (Heb. 1:3). Jesus reveals God not merely as a prophet who *speaks* God's word, but as the Son who *is* God's Word. There is no clearer or more personal "speech" to mankind than the Word who was made flesh!

The Bible is God's inspired record of that message. It is the finished revelation of God in Christ Jesus. There is no water of revelation clearer than the crystal springs of Holy Scripture. By His Spirit, God will speak to us every day as we read His word, study it, meditate upon it, and apply it to our lives in specific and concrete ways.

Many want God to show Himself in some other way—some angelic voice, prophetic vision, or heavenly sign—but as Jesus said to Philip, "He who has seen Me has seen the Father; how can you say, 'Show us the Father'?" (John 14:9). If you want to hear from God, just open your Bible and listen, for He has spoken to us in His Son!

Prayer and Peace

Be anxious for nothing, but in everything by prayer and supplication with thanksgiving let your requests be made known to God. And the peace of God, which surpasses all comprehension, will guard your hearts and your minds in Christ Jesus.

PHILIPPIANS 4:6–7

HEBER TORRES: BEREA SEMINARY | SPAIN

It has been said that the busier Martin Luther was, the more time he spent in prayer. This is remarkable, especially for us living in this frenetic world, overwhelmed by so many tasks and duties. Humanly speaking, we desire to check things off our lists by all means and as soon as possible. However, this is not the biblical exhortation.

In these verses, the apostle encourages his readers to present their requests—with an attitude of thanksgiving—to God, instead of being anxious about them. Paul emphasizes that there is no place for worries or despair, not because we won't face troubles and pain, but because, as children of God, we will not succumb to them.

When we encounter the anxiety that accompanies hardship, God promises to pour His peace over us as we seek Him. This is a supernatural peace beyond comparison, beyond understanding. It is a peace that rests in the precious and perfect work of the Lord Jesus Christ, and protects the hearts of those who belong to Him. It is a personal peace because it guards our hearts, and it is an objective peace because it protects our thoughts.

And that peace comes through prayer. John Calvin once said, "It is through prayer that we will be able to obtain the riches we have in God." Reader, give yourself to prayer today and give your anxieties to God today.

Our Foundation: Creation

For thus says the Lord, who created the heavens (He is the
God who formed the earth and made it, He established it and
did not create it a waste place, but formed it to be inhabited),
"I am the Lord, and there is none else."

ISAIAH 45:18

JOHANNES PFLAUM: EUROPEAN BIBLE TRAINING CENTER | GERMANY

I once passed a house rendered uninhabitable due to visible cracks.
Prior to construction, nobody had noticed how unstable the ground
was. So, after a few years the house was only fit for demolition.

In this verse, Isaiah points to the reliable foundation of God's
word. These words are spoken by the almighty Creator, God Himself.
Some Christians may not see the need for a literal interpretation of
the account of creation in Genesis 1 and 2, but Isaiah clearly states
the opposite.

A few verses earlier, God promises to bring back the captives of
Israel by the hand of Cyrus, at a time long before Cyrus was even
born! But what seemed unthinkable at the time was fulfilled word-for-
word one hundred and seventy years later. Isaiah also refers to Israel's
future deliverance. Both promises are substantiated by the fact that
God, the Creator, formed and established the earth to be inhabited.

Only when we place unconditional trust in the creation account
can we take all other biblical accounts at face value. Because God is
the almighty Creator, He will do everything as promised.

But if we question the credibility of the creation account, we will
be like that derelict house. We won't have a firm foundation and it's
only a matter of time before the credibility of God's word will crack
in other parts. "I am the Lord, and there is none else"!

Waiting for the Hope

*For we through the Spirit, by faith, are waiting for the
hope of righteousness.*
GALATIANS 5:5

NEHEMIAH KANZANTHU: CENTRAL AFRICAN PREACHING ACADEMY | MALAWI

No amount of work, discipline, or moral behavior can save us. If a person intends to find favor or be right with God by following some of the law, such as by being circumcised, he would have to obey the rest of God's law, as well. This only leads to failure. Trying to save ourselves by keeping all God's laws, therefore, only separates us from God. Do this, warns Paul, and "Christ will be of no benefit to you" (Gal. 5:2).

In contrast to those who would work in order to be justified, Paul says that we (Christians) are eagerly waiting for the hope of righteousness. We have this hope *by faith* in Christ Jesus, not *by works*. We do not need to work for salvation; we who believe in Christ already possess a right standing before God. We may therefore rightly anticipate the day in which we are to be perfected in righteousness.

It is natural for children to trust their parents, even though parents sometimes fail to keep their promises. Our heavenly Father, however, never makes promises He will not keep. Though His plan may not go as we expect, we should place our confidence and faith in God's goodness and wisdom. Just as the first pieces of fruit to appear on a tree provide hope of a future harvest, the fruit that the Spirit produces in us now, by faith, provides hope that we will one day be like Christ in perfect righteousness.

Genuine Hope

For in hope we have been saved, but hope that is seen is not
hope; for who hopes for what he already sees? But if we hope
for what we do not see, with perseverance we wait eagerly for it.
ROMANS 8:24–25

DMITRIY ZHEREBNENKOV: WORD OF GRACE BIBLE INSTITUTE | USA

At the very moment of salvation, every believer is given hope. The hope every Christian has is as sure as their salvation. It's part of the glorious experience of being born again. How, in God's providence and provision, do we obtain this hope from day one of our salvation? By faith we embrace the *present* aspect of our salvation; by hope we embrace the *future* aspect of our salvation.

In the present time, hope helps us fix our eyes not on present sufferings, but on future glory. Hope is something that gives us meaning and strength for the next step in life. If there is no gospel hope, then there is nothing to hold on to. Evaluate your own heart. What do you hope in? Do you have hope that ties you to future glory?

The end result of this hope is patient waiting. The attitude of eagerness and endurance is the fruit of this hope. When with spiritual eyes we see future glory, our soul gains excitement and strength to wait with perseverance. We have to admit that we often fail at "waiting" in our lives, and we fall short in "persevering." Genuine hope is the remedy.

Take a moment to think about your hope. When was the last time this hope changed your reactions, actions, and attitudes in life? Does the hope of your salvation make you eager for the life to come and endure things in life without grumbling?

Shining Lights for the Glory of God

*Let your light shine before men in such a way that they may
see your good works, and glorify your Father who is in heaven.*
MATTHEW 5:16

RAFFAELE SPITALE: ITALIAN THEOLOGICAL ACADEMY | ITALY

Those who are saved by the grace of God are described by Jesus
as the "light of the world" (Matt. 5:14). This is who we are as
a result of the saving work of God in our lives. It has nothing to do
with the culture of a particular nation. The believers are light *in the
Lord* (Eph. 5:8).

Jesus not only describes believers as the light of the world, but He
also exhorts them to let their light shine before men. In a similar way,
the apostle Paul exhorts the Ephesians to walk as children of light
(Eph. 5:8). In other words, we are saved in order to let the world see
the light of Christ, just as a lamp is placed on the lampstand in order
to give light in the house (Matt. 5:15).

Our Christian life is not something private; rather, it is to be a public demonstration of God's powerful and glorious saving work. Each
believer is called to live a godly life that will attract people to God,
not to us. But why is this? Because the ultimate aim of our salvation is
the glory of God. The point of letting the world see our good works
is that they may glorify God and worship Him alone.

In this passage, we are reminded of a crucial biblical truth. No
matter where we live or in which time, our godly lives need to shine
before men. We are called to let the world see Christ through the way
we live, in order to bring glory to God.

Joy That Fails and Faith That Lasts

Those on the rocky soil are those who, when they hear, receive the word with joy; and these have no firm root; they believe for a while, and in time of temptation fall away.

LUKE 8:13

HECTOR GERARDO ROMO GARCÍA: WORD OF GRACE BIBLICAL SEMINARY | MEXICO

In 1988, my church organized a Christmas concert, so I invited an unbelieving friend. When the singing ended, the pastor preached about Jesus' birth and invited the attendees to surrender their lives to the Messiah. With great surprise, I saw this friend gladly raising his hand! As he later said, the music and the lyrics had so excited him that he responded to the pastor's invitation. Today, however, more than 29 years later, this friend regrettably lives far from Christ, saying he will not obey His word.

In this passage, we see the futility of superficially receiving God's word with emotion rather than with conviction, without faith and repentance—excitement to get the gospel's blessings without considering the cost. An emotional experience with the gospel is not a guarantee of salvation; it fails in the face of trials. Only faith that continues and grows to bear fruit is evidence of a genuine conversion. Sadly, in my friend's case, God's word was received with joy but no root.

Emotion is not conviction, and a joyful reaction to the gospel is not necessarily saving faith. Only abiding in Christ and obeying God's word evidences the fruit of a heart transformed by the Creator's grace. Ask yourself this question: When fierce temptation comes, do I still seek to obey and cling to Christ?

Do not be satisfied by mere emotional responses. Seek from God a heart that produces good works and perseveres in times of trouble. Seek from God a faith that lasts.

Grace and Peace

Grace to you and peace from God our Father and the Lord Jesus Christ.
EPHESIANS 1:2

EDUARDO L. PAMPLONA JR.: THE EXPOSITOR'S ACADEMY | PHILIPPINES

Two words we often use in the church are *grace* and *peace*. In the apostle Paul's letter to the Ephesians, he wished grace and peace upon the saints in the church. It is true that Paul was simply greeting them; however, this common Christian greeting is rich in meaning and expresses so much more than, "How are you? I hope you are doing well."

The apostle Paul knew full well how essential grace is for all Christians. This can be seen as he considered God's grace in his own life when he wrote, "But by the grace of God I am what I am" (1 Cor. 15:10). When Paul pronounced grace upon the Ephesian believers, he was expressing his desire for God to show them favor and to give them the ability to live in ways that showed the world their gratitude for God's work of salvation and sanctification in their lives through Jesus Christ.

Paul not only conferred grace upon the Ephesian believers, but also peace. God wants His people to be at peace with all men (Rom. 12:18). That is, He wants us to be on good terms with everyone. However, what is most important (even imperative) is for all men to be at peace with God. Without this peace, which can only be found in Christ, no one will be saved, nor will they experience true peace.

God wants His church to experience His grace and peace. Pray for God to give both abundantly. Pray for those who are strangers to this grace and peace, that they would trust in Christ and receive these blessings from God our Father.

Great Commission, Great Comfort

Go therefore and make disciples of all the nations, baptizing them in the name of the Father and the Son and the Holy Spirit, teaching them to observe all that I have commanded you; and lo, I am with you always, even to the end of the age.

MATTHEW 28:19–20

JONATHAN MOORHEAD: CZECH BIBLE INSTITUTE | CZECH REPUBLIC

What is the mission of the church, and by extension, what is your God-given mission in life? Some say it involves digging wells, building hospitals, fighting poverty, and protecting the environment. But Matthew 28:19–20 contains two imperatives that hold the answer: evangelize the lost and nurture the saints.

While verse 19 emphasizes making disciples, or evangelism, verse 20 stresses the need for teaching the saints all that Jesus commands. It is important to note that discipleship is not to be restricted to pastors (2 Tim. 2:2), but is for *every* Christian. As Paul wrote, "We proclaim Him, admonishing *every* man and teaching *every* man with all wisdom, so that we may present *every* man complete in Christ" (Col. 1:28). Consequently, to be a Christian is to be a disciple, an intentional evangelist, and a deliberate discipler. There are not two classes of Christian; to be a disciple is to be a disciple-maker.

Considering all Christians have this high calling of evangelistic and discipleship ministry, Jesus' final words in our verse give encouragement to persevere and provide a weight of accountability. Remember, when Moses faced the might of Egypt, God said, "I will be with you" (Exod. 3:12). When Joshua faced battle, God said, "I will be with you" (Josh. 1:5). When Zerubbabel was faced with rebuilding the Temple, God said, "I am with you" (Hag. 2:4). Now to us, faced with a faithful life of evangelism and discipleship, Jesus says, "I am with you always, even to the end of the age."

Take a few moments to evaluate your faithfulness to the mission of the church and make a plan to reform your life where it is needed.

Let Them See the True Door

I am the door; if anyone enters through Me, he will be saved,
and will go in and out and find pasture.
JOHN 10:9

DAISUKE OKADA: JAPAN BIBLE ACADEMY | JAPAN

Here we find one of the great "I am" sayings of Christ. Christ is the door that provides salvation and fullness of life. This is the fundamental and essential truth claim of Christianity. It is the exclusive claim of the gospel of Jesus Christ. There is no other door that people can enter through to have eternal life. Christ alone is *"the way, and the truth, and the life"* (John 14:6).

Unfortunately, this kind of exclusive claim is unpopular and unwelcomed by the world we live in, and Japan is no exception. In fact, not only is the concept of exclusive truth unpopular in Japan, the very notion of an exclusive truth with regard to faith and salvation is a foreign concept to most Japanese people. Throughout the entire history of Japan, the people of Japan have been taught and believed that there are, and have always been, many ways to salvation. For the common Japanese person, who or what you believe in for salvation is not at all important. Since there are many paths for salvation and fulfillment in life, what matters is simply that you have faith in *something*.

Christ's words confront this worldview and demand submission to Him as the only door through which salvation is provided. No matter how people may argue or how hardened their hearts may be, our task is to tell the world that Christ is *the only door*. Just as Christ challenged the Jews of His time to come to Him and Him alone, may we be found faithful in proclaiming to the world that He alone is the only way for salvation.

Heavenly Wisdom

But the wisdom from above is first pure, then peaceable,
gentle, reasonable, full of mercy and good fruits, unwavering,
without hypocrisy.

JAMES 3:17

BRANIMIR PLAVSIC: THEOLOGICAL BIBLICAL ACADEMY | CROATIA

There are two, and only two, kinds of wisdom: earthly wisdom and heavenly wisdom. They have great differences. As James describes them, he desires his readers to examine which one they possess.

Earthly wisdom is evil, self-centered, filled with bitter jealousy, selfish in ambition, and arrogant. This is the wisdom that characterizes the lives of unbelievers. Sadly, sometimes Christians can even fall back into this wisdom. This wisdom does not produce fruit that pleases God.

On the other hand, God loves to give believers heavenly wisdom when they ask for it (James 1:5). This wisdom is essential to live a life for God's glory, and for pursuing righteousness and honor. It enables believers to successfully pass through the trials of life and to have discernment to recognize what is good and evil.

What is this heavenly wisdom? It is first pure, especially in its motives. Pure motives are sincere and moral. It is peaceable—it promotes and loves peace, and turns someone into a peacemaker. It is gentle, demonstrating itself in restraint, meekness, patience, and tenderness. Wisdom from above is also reasonable. This describes someone who understands others, who is kind-hearted, teachable, and approachable. This wisdom is also full of mercy. It cares for people who suffer and is always ready to forgive just like God. It is also full of good fruits and stable in relationships. Finally, it is without hypocrisy, meaning it produces honesty and sincerity.

As you gaze into the mirror of the word, which wisdom do you see in your reflection? Ask God today for ever-increasing heavenly wisdom from that word—and apply it in your thinking and living.

The Uniqueness of our Savior

In the beginning was the Word, and the Word was with God,
and the Word was God. He was in the beginning with God.
All things came into being through Him, and apart from Him
nothing came into being that has come into being.

JOHN 1:1–3

L. J.: ASIA (NAME WITHHELD FOR SECURITY)

"Jesus is one among the gods" is a popular misconception among my people. But John begins his gospel by presenting the uniqueness of Jesus Christ. The matchlessness of Jesus Christ makes the gospel of God unique and powerful. Any effort to dilute the nature of Jesus Christ makes the gospel incomplete and ineffective.

As described in this text, Jesus is eternal and co-equal with the Father. The divine essence of His being unequivocally proves His deity. Amazingly, He took on the form of a human two thousand years ago, yet His years are everlasting. Moreover, His power as God has been displayed through creation as He is the cause of every creation—all things came into being through Him.

We are humbled then to learn that Jesus, in the exalted position of God, stooped down to become a substitute for unworthy sinners like you and me. He suffered the wrath of God and died for His people, and rose again victoriously. Because Jesus is God and without sin, it qualified Him to take the eternal punishment for our sins. No one else has done or could do this. Christ's death and resurrection demands that we fall at His feet, in complete surrender for the rest of our lives.

Jesus cannot be equated with anyone, because He is unique. Boldly proclaim the gospel of this Jesus and make sure to tell others of the deity of the Savior. The gospel is rightly presented when the Savior is correctly presented.

The Shepherd in the Shadows

Even though I walk through the valley of the shadow of death,
I fear no evil, for You are with me; Your rod and Your staff,
they comfort me.

PSALM 23:4

RUBEN VIDEIRA SOENGAS: BEREA SEMINARY | SPAIN

There are times in life when dark shadows loom over us, when gloomy foes sap our joy and make us grow weary. There are times when we are left clueless and hopeless, and the shadow of death becomes an adversary that we do not understand. So, how do we fight such an enemy? How do we contend with a shadow? We might draw the sword and charge against it, but again and again, after endless blows, darkness holds its ground.

And yet, there is no need to fear this dark road where evil hides, because the Good Shepherd is the very reason we are on it. He led us there. Not by accident, but by the exercise of His sovereign will. This seemingly bottomless pit is the path that leads us to the sheepfold where our strength is renewed.

In the meantime, while following the Shepherd through the valley of the shadow of death, we find comfort in the powerful protection of His rod, and the infinitely wise guidance of His staff. But, most importantly, His rod and staff remind us that He is with us. He, who overpowers darkness, He, who is the Light, shines with everlasting splendor in our gloomiest nights. The shadow of death vanishes forever under the dazzling radiance of the Shepherd.

Therefore, what ought we to do? We do not need to seek to understand that which overwhelms us, or to conquer the shadows. We simply must trust and follow the Shepherd, and let His loving and faithful presence comfort our hearts, because He is with us always, even to the end of the age.

Made Alive with Christ

But God, being rich in mercy, because of His great love
with which He loved us, even when we were dead in our
transgressions, made us alive together with Christ.

EPHESIANS 2:4–5

MYKOLA LELIOVSKYI: GRACE BIBLE SEMINARY | UKRAINE

We would be hard pressed to imagine a greater contrast than the one between life and death. It is precisely in that radical contrast that the Scriptures portray the condition of the human race. The Bible teaches that through one man sin and death entered into the world (Rom. 5:12). All who are in Adam are enslaved to sin, living out the sinful desires of the flesh in rebellion to God according to the will of Satan.

If it were not for the mercy of God, our end would be wrath and punishment. But because of His great love, when we were yet still His enemies, He sent His Son to die on the cross for our sins and raised Him for our justification, in order that—by grace through faith—we might be made alive in Christ!

In this passage, we see that the locus of our new life with God is Christ. He is both the source and means of our new life through the empowering presence of His Holy Spirit. Because the Father has blessed us with every spiritual blessing in Christ (Eph. 1:3–14), our newfound significance is not based on what we can do for God, but on what Christ can do through us.

What are we to do with this life in Christ? Shall we return evil for it? Shall we continue in sin? Shall we pursue the things of this dying world? May it never be! This life has been given to us so that we might live to the praise of the glory of God's grace.

Hope in Resurrection

But regarding the fact that the dead rise again, have you not read in the book of Moses, in the passage about the burning bush, how God spoke to him, saying, 'I AM THE GOD OF ABRAHAM, AND THE GOD OF ISAAC, AND THE GOD OF JACOB'?

MARK 12:26

SIXTO DORMI: INSTITUTO DE EXPOSITORES | USA

Eternity is written within us as human beings. Within our hearts we carry the knowledge that life as we know it is not all that there is. There is life after death. Even pagan religions offer credence to this understanding by the way they bury their dead.

Jesus spoke about the afterlife as He answered a tricky question from the Sadducees, who rejected the resurrection of the dead. Jesus recited what the Lord had said to Moses, "I AM THE GOD OF ABRAHAM, AND THE GOD OF ISAAC, AND THE GOD OF JACOB." God declared that He was still the God of these men, although they had died hundreds of years before. This proved Jesus' point: there is a resurrection.

Jesus resurrected Lazarus. He Himself resurrected from the dead. After this, many saints resurrected. He also promised His disciples that He would raise them from the dead to His heavenly home. The resurrection of Christ is our great hope!

Sadly, not everybody dies with this hope. I recently witnessed what is actually a common practice in Catholic countries. When they bury their dead, there is an absolute lack of certainty about the destiny of the individual. No mention of resurrection. No joy. No peace.

The resurrection, however, gives meaning to our lives and comfort in death. It tells us that there is reward after death; therefore, the present matters. What a consolation to know that we can face death with certainty, joy, and peace; for it is through Christ and the resurrection that this weak, earthly life will become an eternal and celestial perfect life. Give thanks today for the hope of Christ's resurrection.

I Will Uphold You

Do not fear, for I am with you; do not anxiously look about you, for I am your God. I will strengthen you, surely I will help you, surely I will uphold you with My righteous right hand.

ISAIAH 41:10

Astrit A.: Albania (full name withheld for security)

In this verse, God encourages Israel not to be afraid of a very daunting situation. The nation was surrounded by many enemies that were more than ready to destroy it. While it applies to Israel specifically, this is an encouragement and exhortation that can benefit all of God's people in every time and every place because God's character does not change. Simply because we are God's people, we will always have enemies and be in danger from various attacks, yet our God cares for and upholds His own.

What an encouragement it is to know that God, the Creator of everything, is with you even in difficult situations. He desires that His people not be afraid of challenging circumstances or people, but instead hold fast to the character of God as described in this verse. God Himself will strengthen everyone who takes refuge in Him. He Himself will help and uphold such ones with His righteous power.

When difficult situations happen in our lives, it is hard to see beyond the trial. In these moments our perspective shrinks and we begin to see such obstacles as almost insurmountable. Especially at these times, our need is to remember the promises of God and the character of God, and to remember that even in the most difficult of circumstances, God has ordained that our faith grow and be strengthened. In these moments let us glorify God by believing in Him completely and trusting in Him with all our heart.

Supreme Love

AND YOU SHALL LOVE THE LORD YOUR GOD WITH ALL YOUR HEART,
AND WITH ALL YOUR SOUL, AND WITH ALL YOUR MIND, AND WITH
ALL YOUR STRENGTH.

MARK 12:30

VASILIY TKACHEV: WORD OF GRACE BIBLE INSTITUTE | USA

Love should be the chief disposition of our souls toward God. Our God seeks to occupy the highest place in our thinking and to be the apex of our affections and desires. Thus, we must love Him supremely. It is this supreme love for God that will shape and color everything else that we do or say. This supreme love will cleanse and purify.

Yet, sometimes our love for God can wane, and consequently our work for God can be done without the love of God. There can be motives that take highest place in our thinking and desires. For example, a sense of duty is a noble thing, but unless the love of God is supreme in your heart and soul, that duty will miss the mark. All attempts to obey God without first loving him are like attempting to fly a kite without any breeze.

This issue must be important because so much of the New Testament is spent on telling us about God's love in general, and for us in particular. Love begets love. The love of God in Christ Jesus, greater far than tongue or pen can ever tell, effects and creates a response of love in us. We love because He first loved us (1 John 4:19). So let us then daily renew our love for God, and with our heart, soul, mind, and strength love Him supremely.

Japan

JAPAN BIBLE ACADEMY

This country of over 125 million people is considered one of the largest unreached people groups. With only .6% evangelicals, the needs for gospel witness in Japan are staggering. Strong Buddhist and Shinto tradition, along with one of the highest working rates in the world, make Japan a very difficult mission field. Praise God for the work of Japan Bible Academy (JBA) to equip a generation of pastors to preach the gospel and lead the church.

TODAY, PRAY FOR

Young men to be trained to replace the aging population of Japanese pastors. A Christian newspaper reported that 89% of pastors are over 50.

Open doors for the gospel among the people of Japan who desperately lack hope. Japan's suicide rate is one of the highest in the world.

JBA's ongoing efforts to train pastors. Pray that God would call many men to minister in the churches of Japan.

A Gift of His Grace

For all have sinned and fall short of the glory of God, being justified as a gift by His grace through the redemption which is in Christ Jesus.

ROMANS 3:23–24

MATTHIAS FROHLICH: EUROPEAN BIBLE TRAINING CENTER | GERMANY

The term justification comes from the judicial system. It requires that there is a law by which the defendant is examined: either he meets the requirements of the law or he conflicts with the law.

In our case, the law by which we are judged is the fulfillment of the glory of God. We are supposed to live according the glory we were created for; in summary, loving the Lord with all our heart, soul, strength, mind, and loving our neighbor as ourselves (Luke 10:27). Now every day we fail. We regularly fall short of this glory and we sin. This lack of righteousness cannot be filled up with good works; therefore, we deserve the lawful punishment and wrath of God.

The liberating message of the gospel proclaims that the only way our sin can be forgiven and the required righteousness can be accomplished is through the redemption that is in Christ Jesus. This will be granted to sinners not by merit but by the abundant grace of God: "justified as a gift by His grace." Indeed, this is a slap in the face of human merit.

Salvation by grace alone is the foundation our salvation rests on. We can neither earn our salvation nor can we pay it off. Our obligation is no more than to confirm our salvation (2 Pet. 1:10). We need to calibrate the compass of our mind every day with this truth because it exalts God and humbles the sinner.

Our salvation manifests the immeasurable grace of God. Rejoice in this grace. Praise God, for He is worthy to receive glory, honor, and power.

Grace upon Grace

For of His fullness we have all received, and grace upon grace.
JOHN 1:16

MEDSON LIMA: CENTRAL AFRICAN PREACHING ACADEMY | MALAWI

Grace can be defined as unmerited favor. We do not work for it or deserve it. Our salvation is by grace. Everyone needs grace from God because of our sin and inability to do good deeds. We talk of grace in our salvation because we know it is out of reach without grace; no one finds salvation through good works. We need grace upon grace for us to receive salvation.

Where do we get this grace? John 1:16 tells us where to get this grace—through Christ and Christ alone. Through Jesus Christ, God gives believers abundant grace. This immeasurable grace includes forgiveness of sins, redemption, and salvation. Jesus is full and rich in everything. Praise be to God, one cannot lack anything regarding salvation when Jesus is his Lord and Savior.

A simple question to consider is, have you received this grace from Christ for salvation? If the answer is yes, then rejoice in God's provision and enjoy His blessing. Abundant grace is yours. Nothing can separate you from Christ.

If you recognize you are not a Christian and know nothing of this grace, then turn from your sin and trust in Him today. Look away from any of your works, deeds, or performance, and look entirely to Christ for His grace and salvation.

Blood Must Be Shed

Without shedding of blood there is no forgiveness.
HEBREWS 9:22

MARCO BOVINO: TMAI HEADQUARTERS | LOS ANGELES, CALIFORNIA

This verse lays before us the oldest and the most significant need for all people. The greatest need that is always relevant can be stated in a question, "How can I be forgiven by God?" Long ago Job expressed this need when he fell to the ground and exclaimed, "How can a man be in the right before God?" (Job 9:2).

I spent a good portion of my life seeking to be approved by our Savior. I did not want to be just another Christian—I wanted to do great things for the Lord. I tried hard, I spent myself, and if I could sacrifice my life in the jungle, I would have done it—*yet Christ was not mine.*

Friend, maybe you're trying to do the same. Maybe you're trying to reach heaven in your own strength, but as much as you serve and strive, you cannot save yourself. Hear the message of our verse today: "Without shedding of blood there is no forgiveness." Yet hope is found in the One who shed His blood so sinners could be forgiven, the Lord Jesus Christ. Oh, how sweet it is to ponder upon such a great gospel. It does not matter how vile and frail you are; if you have trusted in Christ, He has forgiven you your sin! Stop now and consider the following words from a beloved hymn—may they stir your heart to praise the Lamb of God, our Savior Jesus.

A guilty, weak, and helpless worm, on thy kind arms I fall;
Be thou my strength and righteousness, my Jesus, my all.

Our Duty to Earthly Governments

Remind them to be subject to rulers, to authorities, to be
obedient, to be ready for every good deed, to malign no one, to
be peaceable, gentle, showing every consideration for all men.
TITUS 3:1–2

EDWIN T. MOLLASGO: THE EXPOSITOR'S ACADEMY | PHILIPPINES

This passage reminds us how we should conduct our lives in the midst of a fallen world. We are reminded of our responsibilities toward God's ordained rulers and authorities. We are to be subject to them, obedient, and always ready to do good. Christians must consider these things *especially* when government is imperfect. Being keepers of law and order will help to promote good government and aid their work as governmental officials.

Being faithful to keep those duties can be difficult because earthly rulers are often corrupt, unjust, failing to accomplish God's purpose for government. This makes it easy for Christians to fall into the pattern of the world and respond by maligning, complaining, and acting in rebellion against the government.

Many people use the shortcomings of the government to make excuses and seek ways to get around obeying the government's authority or fulfilling their civic duties. As Christians, this should not be. God calls us to be the salt and light of the world, so we should function as law-abiding citizens and good neighbors. Our good deeds may keep them from maligning the gospel and might even serve to attract them to Christ.

Rather than slandering anyone, we must be peaceable and gentle, showing wholehearted courtesy to all people. It is right to hate the sin, to be angry at the sinfulness that undermines the fabric of our society, but it is wrong for us to express indignation in ways that reveal hatred against people.

The Right Way

Jesus said to him, "I am the way, and the truth, and the life; no one comes to the Father but through Me."

JOHN 14:6

EDWIN ZELAYA: EVANGELICAL MINISTRIES OF THE AMERICAS | HONDURAS

Living in Honduras, I've realized that we're lacking something, and I wish it could be better. Though we are a country with many natural resources, we have a glaring deficiency. We lack actual addresses in most if not all our cities; there are no street names or mailboxes! When pressed to give exact directions, we can't, because the houses are not numbered and the streets are frequently unnamed. Instead, we are forced to use vague descriptions from known landmarks, like the grocery store or a gas station, as general points of reference in order to specify the location.

On a spiritual level, the same phenomenon occurs when we try to give an exact response to the following question: "How can man be right with God?" Due to a lack of serious and adequate training, even our churches produce various answers with vague spiritual generalities, which cause much confusion.

But Christ has said that *He* is the only way to the Father. The only right approach to God is through Him; the only saving path is that which follows Christ through His life, death, and resurrection. The directions are very clear. There are not multiple ways or vague guidelines. There's only one way to have a relationship with the Father, and it's through Christ Jesus.

In John 14, Jesus was encouraging His disciples not to let their hearts be troubled by worry and uncertainty. If they would follow Him, they would never be lost. Make sure that you are on the right path and that you proclaim it with clarity, for Christ is not merely one reference point among many—He is the only way!

Stimulate One Another

Let us consider how to stimulate one another to love and good deeds.

HEBREWS 10:24

HEINZ FLUETSCH: EUROPEAN BIBLE TRAINING CENTER | GERMANY

A Christian's life is marvelous because of what God has done through Jesus Christ. He has freed us from our sins and set us in perfect relationship with Himself, God Almighty. There is a new purity of conscience (Heb. 10:22), which also initiates a new perspective, one which is widely unknown to the unredeemed, selfish person. We are called to no longer live for ourselves, but for God and the family of God—the church. This transfer from self-focus to corporate focus is what God has decided for us!

We are continually called, in practice, to "consider how to stimulate one another to love and good deeds" (Heb. 10:24). The phrase "consider how to stimulate" means to play an active role and to think, constantly, how to exhort and encourage brothers and sisters to live according to God's intentions. At times this proves to be a real challenge because it puts ourselves at risk of being misunderstood and expelled. Or worse, we can think like Cain in Genesis 4:9—"Am I my brother's keeper?"—and withdraw from our responsibility.

Most local churches in Switzerland are quite small. In small communities with about 20–150 members you cannot escape continual assessment from your fellow-Christians. This means you better decide to open up and sacrifice most of your privacy before you enter the fellowship. But once you have decided this and are part of God's church, you soon will discover that the benefits of mutual encouragement far exceed your expectation.

Is your focus on self or your church family? Consider how to stimulate believers in your church to love and good deeds.

Do You Like Surprises?

Preach the word; be ready in season and out of season.
2 TIMOTHY 4:2

BRUCE ALVORD: GRACE BIBLE SEMINARY | UKRAINE

As a culture that generally prefers to plan things in detail, we aren't always good at presenting God's truth when the opportunity is sudden and unexpected.

Our Ukrainian brothers and sisters are much better at this than I am. Many times I've seen them rise quickly to the occasion, jumping in to fill the gap with an impromptu sermon from the word or an invitation to a home-cooked meal without advanced notice. Upon inquiry, Ukrainians have told me their motivation for such actions was this verse.

Instead of being worried about myself (and my preparation and presentation), Ukrainians have taught me to dive right in and evangelize, to preach extemporaneously at church, and even sing a solo with no preparation or warning! One of our funniest memories of our first year in Ukraine was traveling to a village church in the hot summer month of July. The pastor announced that they had guests who would sing for the congregation. The only song I could think of in five seconds to which I *might* have known most of the words was "O Holy Night." Attempting to appear sufficiently reverent, I proceeded to bluff my way through the song to the great delight of the Ukrainians, who knew it was a Christmas carol.

The Ukrainian people are humble enough not to be too concerned that they are not one hundred percent prepared, the most talented, or can guarantee that they won't embarrass themselves. Perhaps we should take a cue from them, who themselves have taken a cue from the apostle Paul's instruction to Timothy to "be ready in season and out."

Your First Love

But I have this against you, that you have left your first love.
REVELATION 2:4

GUS PIDAL: BEREA SEMINARY | SPAIN

The first time I visited Edinburgh, Scotland, I was astonished by the history of that city. From castles to churches, I was amazed by it all. However, what struck me in my conversations with residents of the city was how they had become accustomed to the sights and history that surrounded them. No one stopped to ponder the beauty that surrounded them where they were living.

In Revelation 2 and 3, John is writing a letter to seven churches, the first of which was in Ephesus. This was a church that had a great pedigree; good founders and theology. Yet there was a problem: they had abandoned their first love.

Sadly, that love was a person—the person of our Lord Jesus Christ. This church was rich; it had a great heritage, but it was missing one thing, the most important thing: love for Christ. They had misplaced their affection for and devotion to Christ.

As we train other men, we too can be like the church in Ephesus. Even though we should be thankful for our orthodoxy, it must never become like a lifeless relic. We do not worship books, or doctrines; we worship a person, the God made flesh, the One who ransomed us from the dead, Jesus Christ.

Examine and ask yourself, am I loving Christ the same way I did when I was first saved? If the answer is no, the antidote is simple: repent and believe, remembering who you were before you were saved. And let your love for Christ be borne out of an appreciation for what He has done for you on the cross.

True Disciples

So Jesus was saying to those Jews who had believed Him, "If you continue in My word, then you are truly disciples of mine."
JOHN 8:31

M. T.: ASIA (NAME WITHHELD FOR SECURITY)

Jesus, after giving the gospel to the crowds of Jews around Him, calls them to discipleship. Many who heard Him had believed in Him, and now were going to hear what it really meant to be a disciple of Christ.

According to Jesus, true disciples are not those who simply acknowledge the truth of who He is. They were also those who submitted to His lordship in obedience. How different this message is than what is often taught today, when people are told they only need to believe in Jesus as Savior. To be a true disciple, you must follow Him as Lord. This is genuine faith and will be accompanied by repentance.

Faith is essential, and it must be a faith that is centered on Christ. To be a true disciple, you must know that Christ is the God-man, your mediator, the One who lived a righteous life for you, died a substitutionary death for you, and was raised from the dead for you. These truths must be believed for salvation. But the inseparable companion to true faith must be repentance from that which He died for and saved you from—sin! Therefore, a lack of repentance from sin or obedience to Christ as Lord could reveal you are not a true disciple.

Gospel presentations that lack the call to both faith and repentance will not encourage true conversion (Mark 1:15). Some emphasize repentance only, which results in works-based pride. Others emphasize faith only, which produces easy-believism. May we follow the wisdom of Christ in presenting the gospel as He did, so that He can make true disciples!

The Best Recognition

You are those who have stood by Me in My trials.
LUKE 22:28

EDUARDO NERIO: EVANGELICAL MINISTRIES OF THE AMERICAS | HONDURAS

It is said that a certain Roman soldier served his country for 40 years, fought in 120 battles, and was seriously injured 45 times. As spoils of war, he kept 83 gold coins, 70 bracelets, 18 gold spears, and 23 harnesses, all as bounty from his battles.

During His three-and-a-half years of ministry, Jesus experienced many trials. His brothers did not believe in Him, His adversaries called Him the seed of Beelzebub, and He was ridiculed even by those who benefited from His miracles. There was a group of men, however, that remained faithful to Him. No matter the persecution or how hard the battle, they fought through the trials, hardships, and suffering. They held firm to the call of their Lord, and when it came time to be recognized, they heard these words: "You are those who have stood by Me in My trials." What recognition to be part of Jesus' testimony!

So I ask you, in the circumstances where you have been called to be faithful, will you be like that ancient Roman soldier, who gathered only the riches of this world, or like that group of faithful disciples, who gave up everything and stayed with Jesus through His trials? May God grant you the ability to stand firm to the end, and to be faithful to your Savior—for heavenly riches will be yours, both here and in eternity (Luke 22:29–30).

The Helper Who Reminds

*But the Helper, the Holy Spirit, whom the Father will send
in My name, He will teach you all things, and bring to your
remembrance all that I said to you.*

JOHN 14:26

MARCUS DENNY: CZECH BIBLE INSTITUTE | CZECH REPUBLIC

The saint is often ignorant of what he should already know and forgetful of what he has already learned. Unlike a sponge, eager to absorb the riches of God's word, his mind becomes impervious to truth and oblivious to the riches in the Scriptures.

For this reason Christ has given us the Holy Spirit. The word translated as *helper* was used by the Greeks to describe an adviser or representative, one who assisted others in doing what they could not do for themselves. Jesus makes clear in His promise that the Holy Spirit helps us in two ways: *teaching* and *reminding* us of all that Christ has said.

Four years ago, Jaroslava contracted Lyme disease. She has suffered much and has every reason to focus on her disease. Yet, the Holy Spirit has continually reminded her of the great price Jesus paid to redeem her and the great debt from which He delivered her. Though she is tempted to dread the pain, become anxious, or look for excuses to neglect others, Jaroslava has exemplified the opposite. The teaching and reminding ministry of the Holy Spirit through the word of God has graced her with the fuel to live for Christ, serve others, and experience inexplicable joy.

In what areas do you need the Spirit's assistance? What truths have you become ignorant or forgetful of? Pray for His ministry in your life today. Pray for a tender heart. Be taught and reminded by Him of who Christ is and all He has done for you. Find your heart refueled to live this day for Him who bled and died for you.

Faith and Works

But someone may well say, "You have faith and I have works;
show me your faith without the works, and I will show you my
faith by my works."
JAMES 2:18

VENIAMIN PORTANSKY: WORD OF GRACE BIBLE INSTITUTE | USA

Imagine this scenario. One person speaks of salvation by faith in the substitutionary sacrifice of Christ, but shows negligence in matters of practical sanctification, seeing obedience to God's word as an attempt to convert him to legalism. Another person focuses all her attention on external behavior as proof of salvation, minimizing the importance of faith. What a contrast! Sadly, this is all too common.

Saving faith cannot exist without good works of righteousness, and works cannot be righteous without faith. God does not accept our works if they do not come from true faith. Without faith, man cannot please God!

James says that saving faith cannot be separated from the fruit of righteousness. If faith does not manifest itself in spiritual growth, then that faith is dead. Indeed, faith is a state of mind and it can be seen and evaluated only on the basis of how it affects a person's thinking and behavior. Just as breathing testifies to the presence of life in the body, so does the fruit of righteousness to living faith within a person.

We are "created in Christ Jesus for good works" (Eph. 2:10). Does your faith display itself in a godly life, or do you continue to live an unfruitful, unholy life? Do not justify an unfruitful life by the fact that you are born again but have not yet committed yourself to Christ. That is not an option. The only proof of genuine faith is practical obedience to the truth of Scripture.

Are You Sanctified in Truth?

*For their sakes I sanctify Myself, that they themselves also may
be sanctified in truth.*

JOHN 17:19

RUAN STANDER: CHRIST SEMINARY | SOUTH AFRICA

Jesus makes it clear that He sanctified Himself, and that He did this so that His disciples might be sanctified also. Unlike Jesus, they could not sanctify themselves, but needed to be sanctified by the Father, and the Father sanctifies in truth. In John 17:17, Jesus indeed asked the Father to sanctify them in this truth, which is God's word. Jesus called Himself the way, the truth, and the life (John 14:6); truth saturates His being. Man, on the other hand, has exchanged the truth for a lie (Rom. 1:25).

We live in a pluralistic, postmodern society that views truth as subjective, where countless call upon some or other god, while few call on the living God, Yahweh. Scripture tells us that Yahweh is near to all who call upon Him, but only those who call upon Him in truth (Psa. 145:18). This truth is Jesus Christ, who is God incarnate (Col. 2:9), and man's only Savior (Acts 4:12). This truth is objective and exclusive (1 John 2:21; John 3:36).

The passage is therefore concerned with our sanctification. And not only that of the disciples, but all who would come to believe in Jesus "through their word" (John 17:20). The purpose of our sanctification is bearing witness to the truth that Jesus is from the Father. Through our words and sanctified lives, the world will know that Jesus undeniably is: the way, the truth, and the life.

Man is a creature of habit; thus, we should strive to be sanctified in the truth by cultivating habits that are conducive to our sanctification. Are you saturated with God's truth daily?

Love Your Enemies

But I say to you who hear, love your enemies, do good to those who hate you.

LUKE 6:27

McJoster Mwalweni: Central African Preaching Academy | Malawi

Human beings are born with the tendency to seek vengeance. We do good to those who do good to us, and we do evil to those who do evil against us. But ask yourself this question: Does God deal with *me* in the same way I deal with *others*?

When Jesus was on the cross, He said, "Father, forgive them; for they do not know what they are doing" (Luke 23:34). And Stephen, when being stoned, cried out, "Lord, do not hold this sin against them!" (Acts 7:60).

In our verse today, Jesus exercised His divine authority as He said, "But I say to you …" This means that these words were coming from Him directly, and that we are to obey them. Jesus is contrasting His teaching with the traditional teaching of the scribes and Pharisees. These leaders misused Leviticus 24:20 ("eye for eye, tooth for tooth") as justification for hating their enemies. They took this verse as more than a statement about punishment fitting the crime; they extended it to teach that we should exercise vengeance on our enemies.

Jesus rejected the hateful teaching of the scribes and Pharisees and gave several ways to demonstrate love to our enemies instead. He speaks of doing good to those who hate us (Luke 6:27), blessing and praying for them (Luke 6:28), not doing harm to them (Luke 6:29), giving to them what they ask from us (Luke 6:30), and doing to them whatever we would want them to do to us (Luke 6:31).

Brothers and sisters, let us not seek hateful vengeance on our enemies. Instead, let us love them even as Christ has loved us.

September 15

Waging War Against Self-Importance

Do nothing from selfishness or empty conceit, but with humility of mind regard one another as more important than yourselves.

PHILIPPIANS 2:3

MATTHEW JOHNSTON: ITALIAN THEOLOGICAL ACADEMY | ITALY

The autopilot of our hearts is self—self-concern, self-pity, self-righteousness, and self-preservation. Our thoughts drift rather instinctively to the way *we* hope to be used, the significance of *our* contributions, and the way others will appreciate *us*. Truth be told, we'd really like others to treat *us* as more important than themselves. Sadly, our selfish ambition even seeps into our attempts at sacrificial service. To consider others as more important than ourselves is to put to death our self-importance.

Christ's example is the weapon Paul gives us to deal self-importance its death blow (Phil. 2:5). Christ's humility exposes our pride, shatters our attempts to justify self-seeking, and then models the way forward toward selfless, others-centered service. His every step on this earth, from His incarnation to His exaltation (Phil. 2:6–11), was wrought in sacrifice and self-denial. The one who was indeed more important than all others considered us as more important than Himself.

Christ's attitude must become our own. He gladly laid aside His glory, taking the form of a servant (Phil. 2:6–7). Are you prone to give things up to serve others, or to tightly grasp and guard your perceived rights? Christ's humility knew no bounds: He was "obedient to the point of death, even death on a cross" (Phil. 2:8). What limits do you set on the way you will serve? For Christ, exaltation came after a life of humiliation (Phil. 2:9–11). Do you expect exaltation and ease now in this life?

Don't believe the lie that you can let self-importance live in your heart and still selflessly serve others. May our earthly ministry be like our Savior's.

274

Freedom to Love

For you were called to freedom, brethren;
only do not turn your freedom into an opportunity for the
flesh, but through love serve one another.

GALATIANS 5:13

THOMAS BUSCH: EUROPEAN BIBLE TRAINING CENTER | GERMANY

Who doesn't love the idea of being really free? Free of all responsibilities, appointments, and oversights. When young people live alone for the first time after school and studies they feel this supposed freedom. No parents watching over them. No explicit standards for classroom attendance. Everything is more or less free. So they think. How often do they get on the wrong track so quickly in this great freedom and lock themselves up without notice. They become captives of their own selfish needs and desires. Everything is about their fun and their fulfillment in their lives. Unfortunately, they often notice too late that such a selfish life is not real freedom and they end up in emptiness. This temptation is not just experienced by young people; it is a snare in every stage of life.

But there is good news—God offers true freedom, in Christ.

Jesus Christ saved us utterly from slavery to sin and the law. He caused us to be born again through His death at the cross on Golgotha and His resurrection from the dead. In saving us, He has given us freedom. We may enjoy this freedom and use it for a glorious purpose. We may love one another and glorify the Lord Jesus. We truly are freed to love. How wonderful is it to meet other people with this God-given love and bless one another? The love that leaves all boundaries behind and reaches out to those people who are not sympathetic toward us—this love is not human; it is divine. Yes, this is real freedom. Use your freedom to serve one another through love.

God-Centered Salvation

I, even I, am the one who wipes out your transgressions for My own sake, and I will not remember your sins.
ISAIAH 43:25

MIROSLAV BALINT-FEUDVARSKI: THEOLOGICAL BIBLICAL ACADEMY | CROATIA

Yahweh is unlike all would-be or imagined gods. None fashioned by human imagination could ever abound with such glory and grace. Yahweh alone is the true God. Yet Isaiah reminds us that He is a redeeming God who once saved His people from Egypt and even now has undertaken an incomparably greater redemptive plan. In both instances of salvation—past and present—it comes to ungrateful and insubordinate people, who always fall short of His standard.

When measured against God and His standard, the contrast is great! On one side there are sinners, corrupted to the core and totally incapable of seeing beyond their selfishness. On the other, behold Him! Isaiah repeats twice in God's proclamation that attention and focus is to be on Him. Both in creation and in salvation, the orbit is theocentric—God is the focus and God receives the glory.

What wonder! For His own name's sake He will wipe out our transgressions. His glory drives our salvation. His glory is displayed in the richness of His unmerited love and mercy as He determines to not remember our sins. And indeed, this is all possible because in the greatest manifestation of His glory, Yahweh came in the flesh in the person of Jesus to bear the iniquity and punishment for His people.

If God is about His glory, and His salvation magnifies His glory, then the gospel we proclaim must also be God-centered. A self-centered and self-indulgent world must be pointed to the One who alone is worthy of worship. Consider what you say to lost sinners. Does your gospel proclamation *begin* and *end* with God?

Trusting in the Faithful Savior

And he was saying, "Jesus, remember me when You come in Your kingdom!" And He said to him, "Truly I say to you, today you shall be with Me in Paradise."

LUKE 23:42–43

T. P.: ASIA (NAME WITHHELD FOR SECURITY)

Crucifixion is perhaps the most humiliating and painful form of execution. Yet, our Lord did not resist it and showed no resentment. He even prayed for those responsible for His death. Nevertheless, it was the fulfilment of prophecy (Isa. 53:12). The thief's statements reveal he had heard and probably seen Jesus' kingdom activities (Luke 23:35, 38, 41). Jesus in His compassion offered salvation to the penitent sinner.

The confidence of the dying thief in the dying Savior is very touching and striking. He believed the rejected Lord will one day appear again as king in His glory. He asks no special place in that kingdom, rather he only asks that the king not forget him. In a painful situation in the face of death, he surrendered his life to the Lord. This gives us hope to continue to witness to even the worst of sinners about Christ, so that God in His time may draw them to salvation.

The thief was saved wholly by grace; it was the gift of God (Eph. 2:8–9). The thief did not deserve salvation and he could not earn it. His salvation was secure and guaranteed by the word of Christ. Jesus forgave him that very day, and he died and went with Jesus to Paradise. Glory to God!

These verses challenge us to bow down in worship before our Savior for His abounding mercy to save sinners like us. Each day He is preparing us as His servants. What an undeserving privilege to trust in and serve this faithful Savior and Master!

Faith, Works, and Dead Bodies

For just as the body without the spirit is dead, so also faith
without works is dead.

JAMES 2:26

ASTRIT A.: ALBANIA (FULL NAME WITHHELD FOR SECURITY)

Have you ever seen a dead body? Because the soul has departed, the body is lifeless, unable to rise or do the things that it used to do. Without the soul, the body is purposeless, destined to decompose and be destroyed.

In this verse, James tells us that such is faith without works. In other words, this kind of "faith"—faith that produces no fruit—is like a dead body, lifeless and decomposing, suitable only for disposal and destruction. It is utterly useless. A person who claims to have faith but has no accompanying works is a walking contradiction, like a moving corpse. He is still spiritually dead, and his faith, therefore, is of no value, since it leaves him lifeless. It will not save him (James 2:14).

Works cannot save sinners. Works are not a condition for salvation. But works are a demonstration of true faith. Just as movement and intelligent action reveal that a body is alive, so works reveal that a person's faith is living. Good works are prepared beforehand by God for believers to walk in them (Eph. 2:10). They are the inevitable fruit of a saving faith and will manifest in every believer's life.

It is good and right to strive for good works. We don't do this to earn God's favor but in response to it! So make every effort to supplement your faith with good works today, for they assure your heart that your faith is alive and keep you from being an ineffective servant of Christ Jesus (2 Pet. 1:5–8).

Persecution for the Sake of Righteousness

Blessed are those who have been persecuted for the sake of righteousness, for theirs is the kingdom of heaven.
MATTHEW 5:10

MELVIN ZELAYA: EVANGELICAL MINISTRIES OF THE AMERICAS | HONDURAS

I live in one of the most dangerous cities in the world. Every day I witness different forms of persecution toward those who mention God's name, confess Jesus as Lord, or simply carry a Bible. Some of the more serious forms of this persecution include domestic violence, assault, kidnapping, violent theft, and even murder. In addition, church services have recently been the object of attacks by crooked people who don't want to know anything about the kingdom of heaven. These circumstances weigh heavily on the church, making it challenging to be God's message-bearers of salvation and hope.

Throughout history, many have been persecuted for the sake of righteousness, losing material goods, families, and even their own lives. Today, as well, many have decided to follow and honor Christ in spite of the consequences. The church keeps opening its doors, the Bible continues to be taught, and the preaching of the gospel is reaching farther than ever. If you're willing to live a godly life or valiantly share the gospel, at some point you will likely be persecuted (2 Tim. 3:12).

And, if you suffer persecution as a result, our Lord Jesus Christ wants us all to know that this brings great blessing. In fact, the very kingdom of heaven awaits such as these. If you are persecuted for the sake of righteousness, let your heart be encouraged, for yours is the kingdom of heaven.

The Power of Weakness

And He has said to me, "My grace is sufficient for you, for power is perfected in weakness." Most gladly, therefore, I will rather boast about my weaknesses, so that the power of Christ may dwell in me.

2 CORINTHIANS 12:9

IGOR BODUN: GRACE BIBLE SEMINARY | UKRAINE

How do weakness and power work together? At first glance, this might seem like a ridiculous question. Doesn't weakness sap one's strength until there is nothing left?

However, one the most successful and influential ministers of the church learned that weakness and power work together in a significant way. At a moment of great weakness, Paul prayed three times for the Lord to remove the source of his weakness (2 Cor. 12:8). Paul mentioned that he suffered from "a thorn in the flesh" (2 Cor. 12:7). Despite his prayers, God did not remove this thorn, but rather gave him a right understanding of weakness as a tool in the hand of a sovereign God.

Through his weakness, Paul learned about God's power. He learned about God's power to protect him from pride (2 Cor. 12:7); His power revealed God's sufficient grace (2 Cor. 12:9a); and His power was shown through Christ who dwells in him (2 Cor. 12:9b).

Looking at the contemporary evangelical churches in Ukraine, there are many who do not understand God's sovereign power and, as a result, do not respond correctly when they encounter various kinds of weakness. Whether it be poor health, low wages, lack of education, opposition to the church, or some other weakness or struggle, they do not respond like Paul.

But like Paul, we need to recognize that the Lord brings struggles and weakness into our lives so that we will learn about His power. Let us always remember: God shows His strength the most by taking the weak and making them strong.

A Warning About Empty Words

Many will say to Me on that day, "Lord, Lord, did we not prophesy in Your name, and in Your name cast out demons, and in Your name perform many miracles?" And then I will declare to them, "I never knew you; DEPART FROM ME, YOU WHO PRACTICE LAWLESSNESS."

MATTHEW 7:22–23

RAMON COVARRUBIAS: TMAI HEADQUARTERS | LOS ANGELES, CALIFORNIA

In these verses, we find a very serious warning. Jesus expresses that many will approach Him "on that day" with full confidence of their right to enter into the kingdom of God. However, many will face a frightful and unexpected reality—being rejected by the Lord.

Jesus wants to make His hearers aware of the danger of *empty words*. Among those who listened to His sermons were many who *invoked* His name without any intention of obeying him. They *professed* Him with their mouths, but their deeds denied Him. Surely, they *claimed* to perform works "in His name" (prophesying, casting out demons, and working miracles). But, to these false followers, Jesus will declare that He never knew them, and He will order them to depart from His presence as true evildoers.

In my thirteen years of pastoral ministry, I have come across countless people who *claim* to have fellowship with the Lord, yet deny Him with their deeds. These people place unwarranted trust in their own works, their use of the Lord's name, and their involvement in church activities. Their *words* are empty, however, as they live in blatant disobedience to the Lord.

Dear reader, live your life in light of this great warning! Be certain that your confidence is not in empty words, as those whom Jesus confronted. Only those who genuinely know the Lord and follow Him in humble obedience can be confident that Jesus will allow them to enter into His kingdom "on that day."

All Go Astray

All of us like sheep have gone astray, each of us has turned to his own way; but the LORD has caused the iniquity of us all to fall on Him.

ISAIAH 53:6

MAYAMIKO KUTHYOLA: CENTRAL AFRICAN PREACHING ACADEMY | MALAWI

This text paints a remarkable picture of mankind's love of sin and the Savior's love for mankind. Jesus entered into humanity as our righteous king. He did not deserve any kind of suffering due to sin, but He proved His great love by dying a shameful death on the cross so that mankind could be reconciled to God.

God is our Creator. He does not want to see His creatures living in sin, yet it is true that all of us like sheep have gone astray. Every man has turned his face away from God to seek his own desires. This text reminds us that man naturally turns away from the things of God. This is what sin has done to man; it causes him to wander from God's will like a sheep going astray without direction.

But God laid the punishment of these sins upon His own Son. Though He deserved all glory, the Savior humbled Himself to bear the sins of man. He was even named "a man of sorrows" (Isa. 53:3) due to the consequences of sin that He bore. This sober picture of God's willingness to lay our sins upon His Son should motivate us. Let the sufferings that our Savior went through as He bore our sins help you to live your life in a way that brings honor and glory to His name. We no longer need to wander as sheep that have gone astray, because now we have a Good Shepherd.

Trusting God Through the Gospel

He who did not spare His own Son, but delivered Him over for us all, how will He not also with Him freely give us all things?
ROMANS 8:32

MIKE LEISTER: EUROPEAN BIBLE TRAINING CENTER | GERMANY

If Romans has been referred to as "the cathedral of the gospel," then Romans 8:32 is one of the magnificent steeples of this cathedral. Here Paul powerfully demonstrates the connection between the gospel and God's character.

With his question, Paul wants us to think rightly about God's character. If God, in His grace, was indeed willing to sacrifice His own Son for us sinners, then yes, how will He not, now that we are His children, also freely give us all things that will work for our good and glorify him!?

In Romans 8, Paul explains that believers, just like the rest of creation, are not exempt from suffering. Believers experience illness, persecution, trials, and suffering. And how quickly do we then waver and question God's character and doubt His goodness. In Romans 8:32, Paul uses the whole weight of the gospel to dispel all doubts about God's goodness. If God was indeed willing to give His greatest treasure for us in the gospel, how can we, as His children, raise doubts about His good intentions for us in hard times?

All too often the gospel is reduced to being merely a "ticket to heaven." But it's way more than that! It's God's most powerful means to reveal His character and His glory! It will take the believer a lifetime of studying the gospel to get a proper view of God's character through the lens of the cross. This view will give us the strength we need to trust the Lord, especially during difficult times. Don't doubt God's intentions—He spared not His Son. Trust His character; He will freely give us all things.

How Much Does He Love Us?

But God demonstrates His own love toward us, in that while we were yet sinners, Christ died for us.
ROMANS 5:8

ERWIN QUIMBOY: THE EXPOSITOR'S ACADEMY | PHILIPPINES

Twenty-five years ago someone shared the gospel with me. I listened politely as he read John 3:16. Then he encouraged me to replace the word "world" with my name. "For God so loved Erwin." Those words melted my heart.

But for someone who was born in a country where patriotism is premiere, where heroes die for country and countrymen, I am rather acquainted with the thought of dying for other people. God gave His Son to die in my stead, but how was His death so different from the deaths of the many heroes that died for my nation? This thought nagged at me during my early years as a Christian, that is, until I read Paul's letter to the Romans. His gospel presentation was powerful, showing the beauty of redemption and the ugliness of sin. As I turned my Bible to Romans 5, reading verse after verse, it hit me. While I was still weak and His enemy, Christ died for me. He showed His love by dying for me while I was still a sinner.

A famous line from one of our heroes goes, "The Filipinos are worth dying for." In Jesus' case, however, He did not wait for me to become worthy, for I never could. He died to pay the penalty of my sins, for one who is not worthy of such grace, for one who was His enemy by nature. This is a powerful demonstration of true love, in that while we were yet sinners, Christ died for us. This is how much He loves you and me.

The Only Anchor for Life's Storms

If Your law had not been my delight, then I would have perished in my affliction.

PSALM 119:92

DAVIDE BARBIERI: ITALIAN THEOLOGICAL ACADEMY | ITALY

There are multiple ways to die. Clinical death occurs when our heart stops beating. But there is another kind of death that comes even while all of our vital functions may be normal. There is a death to the soul that happens when all hope ceases to exist. It can afflict a person through any of life's adversities, such as disease, tragedy, and loss. It oppresses when the hope of a better tomorrow grows dim. It strikes when our transient and fleeting plans suddenly shipwreck and everything seems lost.

How do you face moments like that? In what do you place your hope and where do you find your comfort? How do you heal?

Just as there are multiple ways to die, there are multiple ways to heal. There is a temporary healing, in which the pain is slowly dulled through new goals in life or through pharmaceutical remedies. This is only effective until the next affliction comes, and then the darkness falls again. But there is another kind of healing, too, which is deeper, internal, more effective, and lasting. This healing is found in the word of God. It is based on the solutions that God gives to the problems we face. The psalmist here recognizes that his only hope is anchored in the joy and comfort of God's word. If the word had not been his delight, his soul would have plunged into despair. But the word has power to give life to those who place their delight and hope in it. Are you preparing for life's storms by delighting in God's word?

The Truth About Unity

*Now I urge you, brethren, keep your eye on those who cause
dissensions and hindrances contrary to the teaching which you
learned, and turn away from them.*

ROMANS 16:17

VENIAMIN PORTANSKY: WORD OF GRACE BIBLE INSTITUTE | USA

This text reveals Paul's passionate care and love for people in
the church. He loves these people and is concerned about unity
among them. He knows that unity is in danger from false teachers
who creep into churches, teach contrary to the apostles, and cause
division and confusion.

Sound doctrine is foundational for true unity in the church. Without submitting to the authority of the word of God, there is no
foundation other than personal preferences and majority opinion.
A church built on the traditions and opinions of people will elevate
these things above Scripture—and it will be marked by dissensions
and factions. Therefore, Paul warns his brethren to have nothing to
do with false teachers who preach a different gospel. In such cases,
isolation preserves unity.

In the contemporary Christian world, there are two polar opposite
positions: valuing truth above all, even at the expense of relationships;
and valuing relationships above all, even at the expense of truth. The
former is ready to take a firm stand in the struggle for the purity of
truth, while the latter argues that love and acceptance is more important than doctrine, twisting the meaning of Scripture to suit its
interests.

God's love is grounded in truth. What the world calls love is fickle
and self-serving. We must reject any claim of love that is contrary to
the truth—especially if it leads us to disobey the truth. Remember,
only the gospel of Jesus Christ creates true unity. Therefore, love people and seek to unify them in the sound doctrine of the gospel.

Slaves in the Fortress

For the wages of sin is death, but the free gift of God is eternal
life in Christ Jesus our Lord.
ROMANS 6:23

TAN MOLINA: BEREA SEMINARY | SPAIN

When I was ten years old, the first long book I read was *Ciudad Dorada* (*The Golden City*). This book is a modern gospel allegory where Itor and Yasir live in the fortress of Endor, ignoring that they are slaves. Life is normal to them, but one day they start to wonder about the outside world. To keep them from leaving the city, the chief of the guards grants them some extra privileges. As they both hear the call from the king and his son from the Golden City, they make the dangerous decision to leave Endor and start walking to freedom.

It should be a no brainer, shouldn't it? We tell people the bad news: they are slaves of sin; they come and go minding their own business without even considering God; the wages of their sin are "privileges" that lead to death. At the same time, we tell them the good news: Christ has earned their freedom on the cross and offers them the free gift of eternal life, a true life that starts now.

Who could be so foolish to reject such an offer? But they do. Even so, be encouraged and do not despair! As you proclaim the gospel and labor for the cause of Christ, remember that you also rejected Christ for a while. But, in His infinite love and patience He made you die to sin and be united to Him.

The gospel is the power of God for salvation! Proclaim it to those enslaved in the fortresses of this world, and by faith believe that God will call them to Himself and they will start walking to freedom!

Quintessential Knowledge

... that I may know Him and the power of His resurrection and
the fellowship of His sufferings, being conformed to His death;
in order that I may attain to the resurrection from the dead.
PHILIPPIANS 3:10–11

ROGELIO ESPINOSA HUERTA: WORD OF GRACE BIBLICAL SEMINARY | MEXICO

Paul wanted to know Christ. His identification with Christ's *death* involved a costly obedience that was not always easy, but his identification with Christ's *resurrection* assured him that it would all be worth it in the end. Our union with Christ is no different. It brings new desires that control us and drive us to higher aspirations. We learn to know Christ and identify with Him even when our obedience, like His, leads to suffering.

During our Christian life of service, we will have victories and failures, joys and griefs. But we should never forget that the best part is ahead. We must continue with our eyes set on Christ, longing to know Him, always remembering that obedient conformity to Christ (even unto death) brings great reward. It brings eternal life!

How is it possible for a Christian to be more and more like Christ? The only way is to know Him more. Make it a goal today to spend more time with Him, to read more of His word, and to seek obedience even when it is difficult, and even if it leads to suffering. When we suffer according to God's plan, we are simply following in the footsteps of our Savior, first to the cross, then to the grave, and finally to the sky above. May we lay everything aside in order to know Christ and the power of His resurrection!

Latin America

WORD OF GRACE BIBLICAL SEMINARY | MEXICO
EVANGELICAL MINISTRIES OF THE AMERICAS | HONDURAS

While the majority of Latin America has historically been Catholic, Christian leaders in the region have recently observed what has been called a "quiet Reformation." Many are turning from Catholicism to the gospel and the great need today is for trained men to establish Christ's church on the authority of God's word. TMAI anticipates its greatest near-term growth in this region.

TODAY, PRAY FOR

God to call many qualified men into pastoral ministry to meet the demand for leaders in the growing Latin American church.

Strategic partnership and coordination opportunities among TMAI's growing number of Spanish-speaking training centers.

The truth of the gospel to prevail over the widespread and deceptive prosperity gospel.

Beware Defeatism or Syncretism!

Do you not know that when you present yourselves to someone as slaves for obedience, you are slaves of the one whom you obey, either of sin resulting in death, or of obedience resulting in righteousness?

ROMANS 6:16

MARK TATLOCK: PRESIDENT, TMAI HEADQUARTERS | LOS ANGELES, CALIFORNIA

Do you find yourself thinking that you have no choice but to yield to sin's temptation? Perhaps a repeated pattern of lust, envy, gossip, or anger has caused you to feel defeated, and to think that you have no choice but to sin? Our verse today is a reminder that a defeatist mentality is not biblical, nor will it position you to experience the freedom from sin that God promises us here and now.

Paul makes a bold assertion that we have a choice as to whether we "present" ourselves to sin or to righteousness. Prior to our salvation, we were slaves to our sinful lusts, and we could not choose otherwise. But now, in Christ, we are no longer slaves to sin (Rom. 6:6) and we have freedom to choose to do what is righteous (Rom. 12:1–2; Gal. 5:13).

In cultures dominated by Islam, Buddhism, or other major false religions, when someone comes to faith in Christ, the choice has very clear consequences, including rejection by family and society. For Westerners, however, the subtle integration of the world's values clouds their ability to see the distinct difference between choosing righteousness or sin. Trying to serve the world *and* Christ results in a functional syncretism (the blending of one's religious values and beliefs with those of another faith system—in this case, the world's).

Consider today whether you have resigned yourself to this way of thinking. Ask God to point out to you where your attitude is either one of defeatism or of syncretism. Rejoice in the promise that you are free to choose, through the Spirit's power, to live as a slave to Christ.

Waiting on the Lord

I wait for the LORD, my soul does wait, and in His word do I hope.
PSALM 130:5

ROGELIO ESPINOSA HUERTA: WORD OF GRACE BIBLICAL SEMINARY | MEXICO

Frequently, due to circumstances in our lives or sins we commit, we fall away from the straight path in life. When we wander and go astray from God and His perfect will, we feel lost, sad, and even anguished in heart.

In times like these, God's children come to the throne of grace with fervent and insistent pleas. When there is no exit on the horizon, we cry out to God from the innermost part of our soul, and God *always* hears our prayer. Sometimes His answer comes immediately. At other times, He teaches us to wait. When this happens, we learn to persevere in faith, hoping in the promises we know, even though God appears to be silent.

Let us always remember that God is true and His promises are sure. Were it not for the certainty of His promises, our soul would not only be downcast, but our heart would also despair to the point of breaking. We would be without the hope of God's soothing and strengthening presence, without the hope of a sure and eternal future in heaven.

But God is true, and His word never fails! In this we do hope. Just as sentinels wait for the dawn, we wait out the night, hoping to see new mercies in the morning. And we trust that the Lord will, sooner or later, bring light and hope to our troubled souls.

Innate Knowledge

*For the wrath of God is revealed from heaven against all
ungodliness and unrighteousness of men who suppress the
truth in unrighteousness, because that which is known about
God is evident within them; for God made it evident to them.*

ROMANS 1:18–19

VENIAMIN PORTANSKY: WORD OF GRACE BIBLE INSTITUTE | USA

The word of God uncovers the depth of human depravity. Every person has an innate knowledge of God, which God Himself has placed within them. This knowledge is not easily ignored, nor silenced. No one can justify themselves before God by saying that they have no knowledge of Him.

Yet, in opposition to this knowledge, people consciously rebel against God. In their unrighteousness, they reject God for one simple reason—that they may live in a way that seems right to them. And so the world is filled with idol worship. The essence of idol worship has remained unchanged: observing rituals and sacrifices to receive something for yourself—protection, provision, benevolence, or personal righteousness.

Such pagan approaches to God are even found in the church. Many people come to God for selfish reasons. They base their relationship with God on what they have and how they feel. They even work hard to win God's favor, to receive from Him what they desire. The goal of this approach is personal gain, not God's glory.

People even try to use God's word merely for personal benefit. They know the truth, yet consciously reject it to go their own way. In word they may have the right theology, but in practice they reject that theology. Against such sin, God's wrath will be revealed.

In light of this truth, we should always check our hearts to see whether any desire of ours has taken priority over the desire to please God. Our knowledge of God should lead to right worship of God.

Compelled by the Gospel

So then, while we have opportunity, let us do good to all people, and especially to those who are of the household of the faith.

GALATIANS 6:10

SEAN RANSOM: THE EXPOSITOR'S ACADEMY | PHILIPPINES

Throughout our lives, God graciously gives us *opportunities* to help people spiritually and physically. Mature followers of Christ recognize these times and seek to do good to those in need, especially to believers. Paul wrote, "Do not merely look out for your own personal interests, but also for the interests of others" (Phil. 2:4). To do this, God has made us stewards of spiritual gifts and material resources so that we can edify and help others.

Opportunities to "do good" in the spiritual lives of God's people in the Philippines are plentiful. The relatively young age of the Filipino church and thousands of untrained pastors creates the need for sound teaching, leadership development, and application of the word.

Additionally, opportunities abound to help with physical needs in the Philippines' urban centers. With poverty woven throughout the fabric of its massive population, there are many chances to be the hands and feet of God by showing love to the poor, the needy, widows, and orphans. It is estimated that more than 1.2 million children live on the streets throughout the Philippines, 70,000 of whom live in Manila.

The gospel should *compel* followers of Jesus to "do good to all people" by living for God instead of self (2 Cor. 5:15). Pray for the compassion, motivation, and ability to sacrificially meet the needs of believers and unbelievers in the Philippines and other contexts where great suffering exists. And pray to seize upon these opportunities as God presents them to all of us.

Who Carries Your Burdens?

Come to Me, all who are weary and heavy-laden, and I will give you rest.
MATTHEW 11:28

EVIS CARBALLOSA: EVANGELICAL MINISTRIES OF THE AMERICAS | HONDURAS

Christ directed this offer to the people who were overwhelmed by the religious leaders at the time. The religious leaders tied up heavy burdens and laid them on men's shoulders, but they themselves were unwilling to help—even a little—those on whom they had placed the load (Matt. 23:4).

These loads came in the form of worldly commands, traditions, and religious rituals that were worthless for satisfying God's demands. Jesus the Messiah, the eternal Son of God, however, came into the world to *relieve* sinners of the weight of sin—"For the wages of sin is death, but the free gift of God is eternal life in Christ Jesus our Lord" (Rom. 6:23).

Jesus' call is urgent, but at the same time it is a loving and compassionate invitation, as is expressed by the phrase, "Come to Me." Jesus' listeners were "overwhelmed," that is, in a state of exhaustion because they had been "heavy-laden" with impossible-to-carry loads by the religious leaders of their day. The Lord Jesus told them to lay their loads on Him so that they could find spiritual rest.

Maybe you, too, feel overwhelmed by the heavy load of your sin or by the burdens of everyday life; or maybe you are distraught by the burdens imposed by men or the religion that you have been practicing. Jesus compassionately invites you to come to Him so that you might find true rest for your soul. If you do, you will find immediate rest and solace.

Wherein Is Your Refuge?

Cease striving and know that I am God; I will be exalted among the nations, I will be exalted in the earth.

PSALM 46:10

THOMAS HOCHSTETTER: EUROPEAN BIBLE TRAINING CENTER | GERMANY

We are in a war, a raging battle fought against our souls! Day in and day out we are bombarded with lies, temptations, disappointments, and the seemingly arbitrary hardships of life. We then are faced with the issue of where we seek refuge.

It is encouraging to learn that David knew about this battle against his soul. He was often attacked from his enemies and had to deal with his own sinful choices. And yet, we observe throughout the entire Psalter that he always found his fortress and present peace in the One who is mightier than anything in all creation!

You see, in our Western world, we are tempted to make quick fixes our refuge. Whether it be the fleeting rush of materialism, the bittersweet allure of immoral thoughts and deeds, or the cul-de-sac of self-pity, there is a plethora of alternative fortresses for you to try and hide in.

But none will give peace. None will hold firm. None will last. None but this one: "Be still, and know that I am God." David calls all people to lay down their weapons, to stop attacking and blaming God, to stop worrying about things outside of their reach. And instead to know the One who "makes wars to cease to the end of the earth" (Psa. 46:9).

Where do you hide when you are being attacked? What brings you peace and satisfaction? What is your sure escape?

Be still. Know that God is God! It is not what you feel or perceive at the moment. It is about knowing. Know God! Make Him your sure refuge!

Bear and Forgive

Bearing with one another, and forgiving each other, whoever
has a complaint against anyone; just as the Lord forgave you,
so also should you.

COLOSSIANS 3:13

SAMUEL GARCIA: BEREA SEMINARY | SPAIN

The ability to bear with and forgive others is almost extinct in our society. Pride and personal vainglory float just like oil in water. What is really alarming is that this lifestyle is influencing the church, and many believers are not seeing and following Christ as the supreme example of humbleness and forgiveness.

The main essence of Christianity is the forgiveness of our sins, as Christ bore the punishment for them on the cross. Paul exhorts us to exemplify this forgiveness in our attitude toward others. "Bearing with" and "forgiving" are two different actions that must mark the life of the believer, who according to Colossians 3:12 has "put on a heart of compassion, kindness, humility, gentleness and patience." Therefore, Paul doesn't make forgiving optional. He says that we must have Christ's supreme example always in mind in our fellowship with our brethren in Christ. In other words, only a regenerated believer, clothed in Christ, is able to bear and forgive in the manner of Christ.

Consider your ability to bear and forgive. Don't embrace the selfish influence of this Christless world. The unavoidable question is: How did Christ forgive you? He forgave all your sins, sins that made reconciliation with God impossible, and He did it in the most humiliating way: the just dying for the unjust, to make you a child of God.

If Christ forgave you, what will you then do with your brethren in Christ?

Forgive Like Your Heavenly Father

For if you forgive others for their transgressions, your heavenly Father will also forgive you. But if you do not forgive others, then your Father will not forgive your transgressions.
MATTHEW 6:14–15

DMITRY S.: RUSSIA (FULL NAME WITHHELD FOR SECURITY)

To call God Father is a great privilege. To be in God's family means having access to many blessings and the special fatherly care of the Creator of heaven and earth. At the same time, it's also an immense responsibility. To be a part of God's family means we should resemble our Father—reflecting Him and His actions in the way we live.

Jesus speaks of this reality in His familiar words from the Sermon on the Mount, yet to our ears these words are startling. Since God forgives, His children should—indeed, must—forgive. How can someone truly call Him Father, having experienced His forgiveness, and not extend forgiveness to others? To Jesus, this is unthinkable. As someone once said, "Forgiveness is the most God-like action a Christian can do." Believers must forgive!

If someone harbors an unforgiving spirit, they may come under the loving but firm hand of God's parental discipline and correction (Heb. 12:4–11), or worse, they may not truly know God as Father. A lack of showing forgiveness can demonstrate a hypocritical life; for, how can someone pray to God, asking for forgiveness, and then refuse to forgive others? If this is the case, we have no right to expect God's forgiveness but only His corrective intervention in our lives.

Christian, you must be attentive in your walk of faith. You must be quick to forgive others, as God in Christ has forgiven you. If you find yourself struggling to forgive, consider the wrong done to you and measure that to the wrongs you committed against God. Let that move your soul to forgive like your heavenly Father.

Blessing in Suffering

Blessed are you when people insult you and persecute you, and falsely say all kinds of evil against you because of Me. Rejoice and be glad, for your reward in heaven is great; for in the same way they persecuted the prophets who were before you.
MATTHEW 5:11–12

V. S.: ASIA (NAME WITHHELD FOR SECURITY)

Normally, people think that a man who is blessed is one who has property, cars, and other luxuries of life. But here Jesus gives a counter-cultural perspective of blessedness, or joy, being found in suffering for the sake of our faith in Christ. This challenges our human understanding, but it is scriptural and true.

Consider that this world hates Jesus, and so it will hate us as well (John 15:20). When we suffer for following Jesus, and not for our own sinful foolishness, we are blessed as our faith and endurance grows stronger (James 1:3). When people attack and revile us as we seek to do kingdom work, we will have greater intimacy with God through the Spirit (1 Pet. 4:14). When people persecute us, revile us, or even take our lives for Christ's sake, we are blessed. It defies the world's definition of blessing, but from a biblical viewpoint, God does great things in His people's hearts and lives through suffering.

We should rejoice always and be glad because Jesus commands us to. This means great joy and peace should guard our hearts. We may lose much in this life, but spiritually our loss is gain now and in the future. Notice the motivation Jesus gives. First, our reward in heaven is great. Second, we are not alone—we can look to the models of suffering in the prophets who were martyred for faithfulness.

Dear Christian, remember and know that you are blessed when you are suffering *for Jesus*. Be glad by looking at your spiritual blessings in Christ. Encourage other brothers and sisters to grasp on to the unshakeable joy of Christ.

Good Mourning

Blessed are those who mourn, for they shall be comforted.
MATTHEW 5:4

MARTIN THOM: CENTRAL AFRICAN PREACHING ACADEMY | MALAWI

The Beatitudes of Matthew 5 are memorable for their teaching, yet sadly they are regularly misunderstood. Far from giving nice principles to live by, Jesus is declaring the necessary evidence of the kind of person who will be part of His kingdom. It is a portrait of a true kingdom citizen.

In the second Beatitude, there are three words that are important to understand. The first word is the first word of the verse, *blessed*. This describes someone who has received divine favor, someone who is blessed spiritually. In other words, it is describing someone who has been saved by God and has His favor on them.

The second important word helps narrow who is the person who will receive divine favor. It is the person who *mourns* and does so over their sinful state. It is a person who mourns that they are spiritually bankrupt because they have recognized they are poor in spirit. This mourning is at the heart level, as there is sorrow over sin that has been committed against God.

The third important word is *comforted*. Jesus promises that the person who truly mourns over his sin and looks to God for salvation will find forgiveness, and in finding forgiveness will be comforted. This means that there will be relief and freedom spiritually.

Bringing all the words together, it means that the person who is heartbroken and expresses sorrow for his sin before the Lord will receive freedom from God's wrath, and comfort in finding salvation.

When was the last time you mourned over your sin? Go to the Lord today and, through Christ, receive His comfort.

The Sorrow That Leads to Happiness

For the sorrow that is according to the will of God produces a
repentance without regret, leading to salvation, but the sorrow
of the world produces death.

2 CORINTHIANS 7:10

IGOR BODUN: GRACE BIBLE SEMINARY | UKRAINE

Russia is engaged in an "unofficial" military conflict with Ukraine. Over the last four years, over 10,000 have died in the east of Ukraine, and another 25,000 have been seriously injured. Thousands of Ukrainians live with a continual sorrow and grief because of their losses. Many who have been injured in the fighting do not see any point or hope in the future. Some have even become so sorrowful and depressed that they have committed suicide. These desperate acts cause even more pain and grief in families that were already suffering.

According to Paul, there is another kind of sorrow—a sorrow that actually leads to repentance without any regrets, and which ultimately moves toward salvation in Christ (2 Cor. 7:8–13). This "sorrow" has some very important features: it continues "only for a while" (2 Cor. 7:8b); it brings joy and comfort (2 Cor. 7:9, 13); it leads to true repentance before God (2 Cor. 7:9–10); and it is manifested in godly attitudes (2 Cor. 7:11). Furthermore, there is no cause for "regret" because this happens according to the perfect will of our sovereign God (2 Cor. 7:10), who "causes all things to work together for good to those ... who are called according to His purpose" (Rom. 8:28).

Let us think correctly about the sorrows that are around us. We must guard our hearts against those sorrowful thoughts that would lead to death, and instead have a tender heart, open to the conviction of the Holy Spirit, which leads to life and renewal (2 Cor. 4:16; Col. 3:10).

Let All Nations Call Him Blessed

May his name endure forever; may his name increase as long as the sun shines; and let men bless themselves by him; let all nations call him blessed. Blessed be the LORD God, the God of Israel, who alone works wonders. And blessed be His glorious name forever; and may the whole earth be filled with His glory. Amen, and Amen.

PSALM 72:17-19

PATRICK GALASSO: ITALIAN THEOLOGICAL ACADEMY | ITALY

Italy defines itself historically and culturally as Christian. God and Jesus Christ are held in consideration, but they remain suppressed by traditions, superstition, and by Mary, along with a considerable number of other saints, whom they call upon to intercede for them. As a result, the very heart of Christianity is lost, which is a true relationship with God and with Christ, marked by a deep hope in God and a desire to bless Him alone.

This is exactly the point that the psalmist desired to emphasize with these words in Psalm 72:17–19. The psalmist reflects on the coming king, the descendant of David, who would reign forever. The direct consequence of a government whose goal is the glory of God is that the people will experience joy and happiness as they enjoy His blessings and express their gratitude forever.

This Psalm implies that all hope that man places outside of God is empty, since He alone can intervene in time, in history, in space, and in the destiny of men. Therefore, it is proper that every inhabitant of the earth bless God's name, as the one who is above everyone and everything.

In Italy, where the ultimate aim for many is not to glorify God, but rather to seek one's earthly comfort, hoping to somehow make it through judgment, I, as a disciple of the king, have the responsibility to demonstrate to my fellow countrymen that true Christianity is based on a relationship marked by a loving desire to see Him blessed.

Is it your goal to lead people in your nation to bless God?

Christian Love in the Face of Death

But I say to you, love your enemies and pray for those who persecute you.
MATTHEW 5:44

JOSE CARLOS ANGELES FERNANDEZ: WORD OF GRACE BIBLICAL SEMINARY | MEXICO

In 1952, Jim Elliot, with great expectations, set out as a missionary to the Indians in Ecuador. A year and a half later he married his bride, Elisabeth. About two years after the wedding, Jim and four other missionaries were speared to death by the Indians they were trying to evangelize. In an amazing display of Christian love, Jim's widow, Elisabeth, decided to stay in Ecuador with her baby daughter to continue the work her husband had begun. She sought salvation in Christ for the very people who killed Jim. Elisabeth and a sister (Rachel Saint) of another of the martyred missionaries served faithfully in the work of evangelism. Over time, God used their efforts to bring to saving faith some of the Indians who had participated in the massacre.

What kind of love does one need to do something like that? What prompted these women to speak of salvation to those who had killed their beloved family members? It is only Christ who can do something like that in the hearts of people. It is the desire to please God, no matter the cost, that makes it possible to obey the command to love our enemies, look for their welfare, pray for their salvation, and even renounce our own personal comfort and safety to take the gospel to those who persecute us.

How unbelievable are God's ways! Our natural reaction would be to seek revenge. God's way is to convert a former enemy into a dear friend. We try to destroy. Our Lord wants to build. We would retaliate instead of evangelizing, but God wants to save.

O Lord, help us see things from Your perspective!

The Pinnacle of Prayer

Be exalted, O God, above the heavens, and Your glory above all the earth.

PSALM 108:5

MARCUS DENNY: CZECH BIBLE INSTITUTE | CZECH REPUBLIC

What is the greatest thing you have ever prayed for, could ever pray for, and should be praying for? What comes to mind? Consider the answer that lies in this singular verse. David's plea is the very pinnacle of prayer for it encapsulates the principal plan of Scripture, the passion of the church, the maxim of missions, and the chief end of God—that God would be glorified.

Yet how idolatrous is much of our praying! How easily we turn the ultimate purpose of prayer on its head and turn it into an idolatrous event where our wants, our desires, and our will become supreme!

Let us do away with praying that speaks of God's glory in attempt to manipulate Him to do our will. Such praying is not the pinnacle of prayer but the putrescence of it.

Read David's plea again and ask yourself, "Do I really know how to pray? Is this verse the cry of *my* heart? Is God's glory *my* chief end? Is the goal of my praying truly *His* exaltation?"

Confess to the Lord the times you have made prayer an idolatrous ceremony. Ask Him to purge your heart of the love of all *lesser* glories. And cry out with great urgency that by the power of the Holy Spirit the cry of the psalmist would become the cry of your own heart—that David's prayer would encapsulate the essence of your own prayer. Let us learn to pray with him: *Be exalted, O God, above the heavens, and Your glory above all the earth.*

Reflecting on God through Joy and Unity

*Therefore if there is any encouragement in Christ, if there is
any consolation of love, if there is any fellowship of the Spirit,
if any affection and compassion, make my joy complete by
being of the same mind, maintaining the same love, united in
spirit, intent on one purpose.*

PHILIPPIANS 2:1–2

CARLOS AGUILAR: EVANGELICAL MINISTRIES OF THE AMERICAS | HONDURAS

One day a believer came up to me and asked, "What aspects of the church should stand out to show the world that we believe in Christ?" I paused for a moment and remembered what Paul, as a pastor, desired to see in the Philippian church, and this passage came to mind.

Paul wanted the church to understand that the rich blessedness of the Christian life ought to unite us with one mind, one love, one spirit, and one purpose. Have you received encouragement from Christ? Have you been consoled by His love? Do you have fellowship now with the Spirit of God? Have you come to understand the affection and compassion of God in Christ Jesus? If so, these things should establish bonds between you and others in God's family. And if so, these things should be reflected in our relationships with one another.

As those who have received affection and compassion from Christ, believers must respond with unity of mind, love, spirit, and purpose. This requires a willing response on our part, which is pleasing to God. Specifically, Christ's church must keep a single focus of mind by being faithful and obedient to His word. They must maintain a consistent and enduring love for one another; they must remain united in spirit and in harmony with one another; and they must be dedicated to the same purpose of exalting Christ.

These are the things that make believers stand out to the unbelieving world, as "children of God above reproach in the midst of a crooked and perverse generation, among whom [they] appear as lights in the world" (Phil. 2:15).

The Future in the Present

Blessed is a man who perseveres under trial; for once he has been approved, he will receive the crown of life which the Lord has promised to those who love Him.

JAMES 1:12

DMITRY S.: RUSSIA (FULL NAME WITHHELD FOR SECURITY)

The past influences the present. Few would argue with this statement. Lay a good foundation in the beginning and it will help you avoid problems today. Make a mess of things in your youth, and you may hobble through the rest of your life. The principle of reaping what you sow is well-founded and illustrated in Scripture.

However, there is another principle in Scripture: *the future influences the present.* The Bible has many times parted the curtains of the future in order to influence people living in the present. The foundation of what God promises to His children in the future profoundly influences their lives in the present. Scripture is filled with verses revealing the tremendous blessing of heaven in the future for those who love God in the present.

James writes of a promised blessing for those who endure difficulties in the present, because in the future they will be rewarded with the crown of life. We need to love this promise and rely on it every day as we walk by faith. This truth helps us get through the difficulties of the present by relying on God's promises. They help us see beyond the problems, the anxieties, and the pain.

Let's be attentive to Scripture and persevere under trial in order to receive the crown of life and escape the chains of death. Let's remember in the present God's promises about the future. May they fortify your faith and fan the flame of your love for Him.

Unity: A Present Hope

Behold, how good and how pleasant it is for brothers to dwell together in unity!
PSALM 133:1

ISRAEL VILLANUEVA CASTILLO: WORD OF GRACE BIBLICAL SEMINARY | MEXICO

Every nation has a national anthem that calls it to unity. *Hatikva* (Hebrew: "The Hope") is Israel's national anthem. The lyrics were written in 1878 by Naftali Herz Imber, a Jewish poet. The music was composed by Samuel Cohen in 1888. It was adopted, *de facto*, in 1948, and officially in 2004. The anthem says, "Our hope will not be lost; the two-thousand-year hope of being a free people in our land, the land of Zion and Jerusalem." What a contrast with what could have been the Jewish official anthem during David's reign!

The unity which the king praises, in which he delights, where he finds an unequaled joy, was present. He invites us to look at a singular event. It is not the superficial unity of a nation. Indeed, the harmonious unity David is contemplating is a spiritual unity.

Today's church also has, in Ephesians 4:2–6, its call to unity. It has its anthem that summons us to spiritual unity: "There is one body and one Spirit, just as also you were called in one hope of your calling; one Lord, one faith, one baptism, one God and Father of all."

Is it your delight to dwell together harmoniously with your brothers Sunday in and Sunday out? Do you delight in serving them? Do you seek through prayer and Bible study how to be more united in your local church? This is not a far hope, like in *Hatikva*. It is a present reality, as David saw it, as Paul saw it, as our Lord Jesus Christ sees it today. It is a spiritual unity you can live in your church today.

Strong Assurance

For the law of the Spirit of life in Christ Jesus has set you free from the law of sin and of death.

ROMANS 8:2

KRISTIAN BRACKETT: THEOLOGICAL BIBLICAL ACADEMY | CROATIA

Few statements draw a stronger response from a Croatian Catholic than, "I know when I die that I will go immediately to heaven." Years of tradition and practice have convinced them that no one can have such assurance. If one's eternal destiny is limited to two options, then there are stark implications. First, my relatives who have died without faith have no hope. Second, all the prayers, masses, and money on behalf of the dead are vain. Third, I must find a way to gain such assurance. Sadly, it is easier to mock and reject this biblical truth than to accept it.

But Paul gives us a reason that believers can be confident in their eternal destiny. They have passed from death to life. They are no longer under the domain of sin. Christ has set them free by faith alone. They now live by a new law—the law of the Spirit. This law produces life. It comes only through Christ Jesus. Therefore, Paul can say with confidence, as he did in the previous verse, "Therefore there is now no condemnation for those who are in Christ Jesus" (Rom. 8:1).

The strong assurance of the believer is possible because of the mighty deliverance the Spirit has worked in Jesus Christ. This is a most precious truth. To reject it is to live in unbelief—in the power of God, the efficacy of Christ's death, and the simplicity of the gospel. How sad when a believer struggles with assurance. Yet, it is sadder still when a "church" robs members of this precious doctrine.

Pause and thank God for the gift of assurance for His children.

Don't Let Sin Fester

He who conceals his transgressions will not prosper, but he who confesses and forsakes them will find compassion.
PROVERBS 28:13

SANTIAGO ARMEL: INSTITUTO DE EXPOSITORES | USA

In recent studies, 33 percent of surveyed pastors admitted to viewing pornography on a regular basis. Only four percent, however, *sought help* or *confessed their sin to someone else*. The statistics are stunning, but the real-life condition of those who do not confess their sin is far worse. Sin is at the door of everyone's life (in more ways than just sexual immorality) and, unfortunately, all give in at some point. Today's proverb tells us that there are two possible responses to an act of sin.

Those who continually disguise, evade, or deny their sin will not prosper. The one who prefers to mask in self-pity, yet stinks of sin, will not find compassion. The consequences of sin without repentance are massive. Sin wants to convince you that it is harmless, that you have control. Yet, after it has deceived you, it destroys you. The loss of your ministry or the destruction of your family is only part of the pain you will feel. You will also offend the One who loves you the most, the One who gave His life on the cross to give you freedom from that dreadful sin.

The second (and biblical) response to sin finds true freedom and compassion. God has ordained that repentance be the antidote to the deadly poison of sin (1 John 1:9). This proverb teaches that the one who confesses his iniquities and departs with diligence from them, will be reconciled to God and others.

Reader, today is the day to deal with sin in your life. Today is the day to confess it and abandon it. Then, you will obtain mercy.

Declare His Glory

Tell of His glory among the nations, His wonderful deeds among all the peoples.

PSALM 96:3

GIDEON MANDA: CENTRAL AFRICAN PREACHING ACADEMY | MALAWI

Psalm 96 is a call to praise Yahweh as Savior and Creator. Verse 3 is part of the response of the community to God for giving His people salvation and for the creation.

Before I was saved, I thought I could earn my way into becoming a child of God by pleasing Him as I engaged in various church activities and events. Blind and lost, I was still actively involved in the church. Oblivious to the truth of God as revealed through His word, I only thanked Him (for anything) when I acquired material possessions. I never thought to express gratitude to Him for the fact that He is the One who created the universe and that He reached out to me through His Son, Jesus Christ. All that changed when He made me alive in Christ Jesus.

Because I know who I am as a child of God, I am motivated to go out and share this good news. The gospel that changed (and is still transforming) my life prompts me to declare the glory of our God and King. This is my response to what God did by granting even someone like me the gift of salvation.

Declaring His glory should be the reaction of every recipient of His grace. Every church, ministry, and Christian must declare God's glory as souls are saved and as they are nourished through the preaching and teaching of the Bible. Our goal in all we do must be to declare God's glory and His marvelous deeds to all the peoples of the world. Stop now, and thank God for His salvation and praise Him for His glory.

The Union of Love and Obedience

If you love Me, you will keep My commandments.
JOHN 14:15

ASTRIT A.: ALBANIA (FULL NAME WITHHELD FOR SECURITY)

This verse is short but contains a massive truth. It is presented by Jesus as a condition. *If* the first part of the sentence is true, *then* the second part will also be true. If we love Him, we will keep His commandments. Love and obedience are inseparable. Where there is no obedience, there is no love. Where there is love, there is obedience.

There is a simple yet profound way that this works. We obey Christ because we love Him. And we love Him because He first loved us (1 John 4:19). Therefore, for the sake of our own obedience, it is critical to grow in our understanding of His love for us. As we meditate on the gospel, as we cherish the good news of great joy for all people, and as we contemplate the matchless love of Christ Jesus, it generates love that results in obedience. So, we need to go to God daily and meditate upon His perfect love, which shines brightest in the sacrifice of our Savior. In Christ we come to understand love; in Christ we come to radiate that love as it is produced in us by God's Spirit. And as a result, we come to obey His commandments.

Take time each day to remember how God has loved you. Let this be your motivation to lovingly obey all that Christ commands.

Motivations to Christlikeness

So then, my beloved, just as you have always obeyed, not as in my presence only, but now much more in my absence, work out your salvation with fear and trembling; for it is God who is at work in you, both to will and to work for His good pleasure.
PHILIPPIANS 2:12–13

S. W.: ASIA (NAME WITHHELD FOR SECURITY)

This is Paul's first charge to believers after developing one of the most glorious pictures of the "mind of Christ" in Philippians 2:5–11. In context, the main charge, "work out your salvation," must be connected to a Christlike humility that Paul has been calling us toward. Here Paul gives three motivations to a Christlike walk of obedience.

First, our Christlikeness must be lived out not in the fear of man, but in the fear of God. This is conveyed through, "just as you have always obeyed, not as in my presence, but now much more in my absence." Our reverence and relationship with our Savior enables a faithfulness that goes beyond human or apostolic accountability.

Second, our Christlikeness is motivated by a sense of our weakness and sinfulness, especially in our tendency toward pride. This is how Paul uses this phrase, "fear and trembling," in other contexts (1 Cor. 2:1–3). Those who know their sinful weakness are driven to depend on their Savior.

Third and finally, our Christlikeness is motivated by God's sovereign faithfulness to us. We only "work out" what He has already "worked in" the more difficult areas of our will, and to do so for His "good pleasure." His sovereign work in regeneration and sanctification enable us to live for Him and love Him more.

What an encouraging charge to us in our daily Christian walk! We will fail even in sanctification apart from Him. We must tune our heart to His pleasure alone, by His strength alone, and all the glory will go to Him alone!

Don't Hold Back!

... speaking to one another in psalms and hymns and spiritual songs, singing and making melody with your heart to the Lord.
EPHESIANS 5:19

ABRAHAM RAMOS: THE EXPOSITOR'S ACADEMY | PHILIPPINES

Congregational singing is one of my favorite parts during a Sunday worship service, second only to the preaching of God's word. Oftentimes, I will stop, close my eyes, and listen to the hundreds of voices filling up our sanctuary walls. Mouths that used to curse and blaspheme God now exalt and magnify Him who rescued them from the domain of darkness, transferring them to the kingdom of His beloved Son (Col. 1:13). Lips that used to hurt and slander now build up others through psalms and hymns and spiritual songs.

Ephesians 5:19–21 describes the results of being Spirit-filled. To be filled with the Holy Spirit is to be yielded to His power, His guidance, and His will. As you submit to His controlling influence, you will be singing (Eph. 5:19), giving thanks (Eph. 5:20), and humbly submitting to others (Eph. 5:21).

A Spirit-filled Christian sings to the praise and glory of his Lord and Savior. He is not lifeless, lacking vigor or excitement. The love of Christ compels him; the Holy Spirit empowers him. He may not be as gifted as others, but that doesn't hinder him from communicating his heartfelt joy and gratitude toward his Savior. Believers sing as an appropriate response to all that the triune God has done for them in Christ. Merely reflecting upon it just doesn't cut it. God's people must sing it.

Are you grateful for what Christ has done for you? Are you humbled by God's grace and mercy toward you in Christ? Are you Spirit-filled? Then don't hold back. Sing!

Canceled Debt

*When you were dead in your transgressions and the
uncircumcision of your flesh, He made you alive together with
Him, having forgiven us all our transgressions, having canceled
out the certificate of debt consisting of decrees against us,
which was hostile to us; and He has taken it out of the way,
having nailed it to the cross.*

COLOSSIANS 2:13–14

E. A.: MIDDLE EAST (NAME WITHHELD FOR SECURITY)

Debt is one word that we try to avoid being tied to. Being in debt is never pleasant; rather it is something we work to be free from. But then, consider a cancelled debt. Those two words will bring joy and happiness to your life.

In these verses from Colossians, Paul recounts that Christians were once in debt—the greatest of debts that deserved eternal hell. Transgressions, disobedience, and sin brings this debt on each of us and it is an amount we cannot repay. Consider the debt of the slave in Matthew 18:24 and you get a glimpse of the infinite debt we owe.

Without Christ, we would spend an eternity in hell settling our debt of sin, but the good news of the gospel is that it has been cancelled. How can this be? The debt is cancelled because Christ Jesus paid it in full when He was nailed to the cross and died in the place of His own at Calvary. This is where we were forgiven. This is where our debt was paid.

Imagine how a repentant criminal would live his life if he were forgiven in a court when he should have been punished for his evil deeds. In like manner, how ought a Christian live when the debt of his sin has been cancelled? Live in thankfulness, rejoice in your salvation, forgive as you have been forgiven, and preach the gospel to those who are still in need of cancelled debt.

Living for Christ, Dying for Christ

For to me, to live is Christ and to die is gain.
PHILIPPIANS 1:21

MARCO BARTHOLOMAE: EUROPEAN BIBLE TRAINING CENTER | GERMANY

This verse explains everything that Paul was living for and was willing to die for.

He was completely convinced that his future was secure in Christ. Nothing was able to separate him from his Lord and Savior, and even if he would die, he would finally be united with the most important person in his life—Jesus Christ. Paul truly longed for this wonderful moment, to be with Christ.

But until then, Paul's entire life—everything he did, everything he thought of, strived for, worshiped, and declared—was Jesus Christ. His entire life, yes, the message of his life, was Jesus Christ and nothing else.

Practically speaking, in the context, this meant that Paul invested his whole life into people. He did this so that they would come to know Jesus Christ as their Savior, in order that they would live a life for Christ alone and understand that dying is truly gain.

If you are a Christian, nothing can separate you from your Lord and Savior Jesus Christ. You can delight in the fact that if your time has come on this earth to pass away, you will be united with Jesus Christ, the most important person in your life.

Until then, let your life be a shining light of Jesus Christ to all people. Go out and declare the precious name of Jesus Christ, who is truly man and truly God, and who alone is able to save sinners. Live a life that is worshiping and glorifying Him alone, because He alone is worthy of all our praise, here on earth and soon for all eternity.

Don't Trust Your Heart

Trust in the Lord *with all your heart and do not lean on your own understanding. In all your ways acknowledge Him, and He will make your paths straight.*

PROVERBS 3:5–6

VITALI ROZHKO: WORD OF GRACE BIBLE INSTITUTE | USA

Our hearts are often the reason our Christian lives become tiresome and ineffective, why our marital relationships turn dry and unpleasant, why our ministry seems burdensome and disappointing, and, why, at times, our whole lives seem to be falling apart. Yes, the reason is often this—we trust our own hearts too much. And here we are warned, the problem is not outside of us, but inside. Why?

God gave us a great gift when He gave us our minds with the ability to think, evaluate, analyze, and interpret. And He did this because He wants us to use our minds to achieve His purposes, to do His will, and to share in His great work. But because of sin, man's heart (thoughts, desires, feelings, and will) was hijacked by satanic lies about self-sufficiency. As a result, instead of relying on God's revelation, we rely on ourselves. Even when we try to do good, ministering to others and serving God, we often lean on our understanding. The heart of our problem is the problem of our heart.

In this text, God Himself—our Heavenly Father—reorients our natural disposition. He "unbends" our natural "bending inward." Here, instead of trusting our own opinions, feelings, or intuitions, we are commanded to trust in God. Instead of putting ourselves at the center of our lives, God is to be first and most important. He is to be the reference point, the highest authority. Why? His ways are better and His understanding is bigger! His every command and promise are expressions of His fatherly love and only He can make our paths straight. Don't trust your heart—trust Him!

Commanded to Forgive

And if he sins against you seven times a day, and returns to
you seven times, saying, "I repent," forgive him.
LUKE 17:4

ISRAEL CORRAL LOPEZ: BEREA SEMINARY | SPAIN

We live in a society where we are encouraged from an early age to fight back if someone hits us. This absurd advice is nothing less than revenge. When you are looking for a job, people tell you that it does not really matter who you have to trample on, you have to look out for yourself and get the job. This is cold-hearted selfishness. And we could go on and on about many other tips and advice that always look for the benefit of oneself over everything and everyone, and yet are against the character of God.

In the words of the Lord Jesus Christ, we find a principle and a simple commandment: Forgive the repentant believer. Therefore, forgiveness is not one option among many; forgiveness does not depend on your mood, or on the gravity of the offense. The problem that makes forgiveness hard is that it is a volitional action that clashes with our sinful human nature. But we must forgive our repentant brother in the faith because it is God Himself who demands it from us.

When a repentant brother comes to you, don't forget this divine commandment. Instead, remember two things: first, God forgave you—not only one sin but all your transgressions. Second, our greatest example, Jesus Christ, forgave others in this manner when at the cross He said, "Father, forgive them; for they do not know what they are doing" (Luke 23:34). The only innocent One, who never committed sin, is the supreme example of forgiveness. Let's imitate Him!

No Thanks? No, Thanks!

In everything give thanks; for this is God's will for you in Christ Jesus.

1 THESSALONIANS 5:18

BRUCE ALVORD: GRACE BIBLE SEMINARY | UKRAINE

This verse doesn't say to give thanks *for* everything but to give thanks *in* everything. How far we are from this! We often feel that we deserve better. But, as the prophet Jeremiah once wrote, "Why should any living mortal, or any man, offer complaint in view of his sins?" (Lam. 3:39). Sadly, we so easily complain about other drivers, things that break, the appearance of others, our own appearance, having to wait, or ... (is the Holy Spirit pointing to something in your heart?).

This may seem like a small thing, but consider the downward spiral described in Romans 1 and its connection to ungratefulness—"For even though they knew God, they did not honor Him as God or *give thanks*" (Rom. 1:21). Complaining was one of the most serious mistakes of the children of Israel as they wandered through the wilderness. Displaying a belief that "life" (that is, the sovereign God of the universe) is cheating you out of what *you* deserve, dishonors the Lord and shortchanges Him the glory and gratitude that *He* deserves.

What do you complain most about? Are you willing, instead, to give God honor and thank Him even in the midst of it, trusting in His gracious salvation and sovereign plan? Remember: complaining is never God's will, but giving thanks in everything most certainly is!

Conformed or Transformed?

Therefore I urge you, brethren, by the mercies of God,
to present your bodies a living and holy sacrifice, acceptable to
God, which is your spiritual service of worship. And do not be
conformed to this world, but be transformed by the renewing
of your mind, so that you may prove what the will of God is,
that which is good and acceptable and perfect.

ROMANS 12:1–2

JORDAN STANDRIDGE: ITALIAN THEOLOGICAL ACADEMY | ITALY

It is a sweet joy to wake up and think of the blessings the gospel brings! If you have been saved, hell has been defeated and you are guaranteed a perfect eternity with Christ in heaven. What a glorious thought. But the second we put our feet on the ground, we remember that each day brings difficulty.

Not only do uncomfortable circumstances come up in our lives, and not only are there people who are difficult to deal with, but one of the greatest obstacles we face each day is the world trying to press and conform us into its mold. This battle is constant throughout our day. But it is a battle worth fighting through resistance and renewal.

We are reminded by Paul that believers are to be holy. Holiness is the way we can present to God a sacrifice of thanksgiving for what He did for us on the cross. This means that we must fight against the world and its lies and temptations. We must not let it squeeze us into its mold! The way to resist this is through the word of God. The word and world are incompatible. God's word is the instrument to transform us in holiness. To be transformed, we must know the word, fill our minds with it, and continually use it in our fight against the world and against our flesh. Only then will we be able to display God's will to the watching world.

Take a moment and ask God if the *world* is conforming you or the *word* is transforming you.

Holiness Through the Word of God

Sanctify them in the truth; Your word is truth.

JOHN 17:17

KOHKI MINAMIDA: JAPAN BIBLE ACADEMY | JAPAN

When we fail to do the right things, when we ignore what we must do, and when we do not walk as we should, we sin against God and do not live in holiness. While sinful behaviors may be lived out because of outright rebellion against God's holy demands, more often than not, these appear in the lives of Christians due to the lack of understanding the truth. Christ, in John 17:17, shows us that for us to be holy, set apart from the world, we need the truth of the word of God and we need it to sanctify us.

Many Japanese churches do not teach this simple truth, that the life characterized by holiness is brought about by the word of God. In our culture, being the same as others so that we won't stand out is extremely important. This seems to have invaded the church. Sadly, it is even true of me at times where I was seeking to be the same as the world around me, though I knew God demanded holiness in my life.

As I gained an understanding of the Scriptures, I began to see the importance of what Christ prays to the Father. It is absolutely necessary for me to know the word of God so that I can live a life characterized by holiness. The power of the word is not just to convert people to have life eternal, but also to make them have a life of holiness. Let us be diligent students of the word, so that our lives can be totally set apart to our God.

Asia

SCHOOLS CLASSIFIED

With the highest concentration of the world's population in Asia, it is no wonder that this is also the region with the largest diversity of false religions. Hinduism, Buddhism, Islam, Shinto, and Confucianism are just some of the dominant religions in the region. Many countries are closed to the gospel, but by God's grace, He is opening more opportunities for training.

TODAY, PRAY FOR

The safety and protection of our workers in this region.

National and local governments to be favorable toward those who are involved in training. Restrictions make training especially challenging.

TMAI leadership as we continue to seek the Lord's will for how we can further penetrate the region with biblical resources and training.

Defeating Despair

Why are you in despair, O my soul? And why have you become disturbed within me? Hope in God, for I shall yet praise Him, the help of my countenance and my God.

PSALM 42:11

MARCUS DENNY: CZECH BIBLE INSTITUTE | CZECH REPUBLIC

Trials, painful and sorrowful as they may be, can never be greater than or totally extinguish the love and hope we have in God. Trials are temporary. The love that God has for His people is eternal.

Despair sets in when we lose sight of this truth and allow our problem to eclipse our God. Observe how even a little hand, when held directly before our eyes, can block out the grandeur of Mt. Everest! When we allow our problem to grow tall in our thinking, then we can lose hope in its shadow. This is why David's command to his soul, though elementary, is profound. One need simply lay aside the hand, and one's view of the mountain is restored.

Are you plagued today by the world, the flesh, or the devil? Are you downcast because of a great trial? Defeat your despair, or the temptation to it, by placing it next to your God. Look at your trial—really look at it. Then look at your God—truly look at Him. Compare His greatness to your problem. Compare the cross Christ bore for you to the cross you currently bear for Him. Compare the length of your trial with the length of eternal bliss that lies before you. Surround yourself with other Christians who have walked a similar path and can point you to these same realities. Then you will hope in God; then you will be led to praise Him!

A Diverse Unity

For just as we have many members in one body and all the members do not have the same function, so we, who are many, are one body in Christ, and individually members one of another.

ROMANS 12:4–5

FILIBERTO ANGELES DORANTES: WORD OF GRACE BIBLICAL SEMINARY | MEXICO

With this illustration, Paul underscores the concept of unity, which in the human body has many parts. The phrase, "many members," shows that this variety of parts comprises a very significant amount in quantity. In other words, there is a great diversity of members with distinct functions. Nevertheless, even though all those parts are different and have distinct roles, they make up a unity. As members of Christ's body, we should keep in mind the right perspective regarding our individual function. As a human body has many members, each with a different role, so each of us in Christ's body has a specific function.

Paul notes how the human body is made up of many members; all are different! However, when Paul says that we "are one body in Christ," he highlights the organic unity of the church. Each member of a church remains in a relationship to the whole that is vital for its existence. Our need for one another calls us to treat others with love and humility.

We should thank God for the display of His grace in others. Do you praise Him for the gifts He's given to others? Do you encourage others toward more fruitfulness according to the way God has designed them? And do you use *your* gifts for their edification? We need one another and we function best only when the various parts are complementing the whole. This is what is intended for the body of Christ!

God's Word Is Important for Your Soul

*Let the word of Christ richly dwell within you, with all
wisdom teaching and admonishing one another with psalms
and hymns and spiritual songs, singing with thankfulness in
your hearts to God.*

COLOSSIANS 3:16

TIMUR R.: RUSSIA (FULL NAME WITHHELD FOR SECURITY)

It's impossible to count the number of words that pass into our
minds in the course of one day. From the varied sources of the
radio, television, the Internet, advertisements, books, and what we
hear people say—each one of these are sources of words that fill our
minds. These words, passing through our minds, offer us a myriad of
topics for our contemplation. What fills our thinking then settles into
our hearts, taking hold of us and shaping our lives. Whatever settles
into our hearts then becomes our object of worship.

In view of this progression, how important it is for us to take in
God's word and to let it richly dwell within us. The teaching of Christ
contains the wisdom that can guard us from making fateful mistakes
with stinging consequences. God's word sweeps from our soul the
filthy garbage that can occupy our thoughts, exchanging it for the
single most fitting object of adoration—Christ.

When the word of Christ takes up residence in you, worship is
unavoidable. Psalms, praises, and spiritual songs will flow from your
heart, for it has been taken captive by the beauty of Christ. When the
word richly dwells in you, then you naturally teach and admonish others for mutual edification. When the word is contemplated, you can't
but help sing with thankfulness to God.

What do *you* open the door of your heart to? What fills your mind?
Let it be Christ and His word, and may it take up a rich residence
there—it is that important for your soul.

The Silent Symphony

The heavens are telling of the glory of God; and their expanse
is declaring the work of His hands.
PSALM 19:1

Aaron Darlington: TMAI Headquarters | Los Angeles, California

The universe is filled with wonder. We are awestruck by the ocean's magnitude, fascinated by ingenuity, and allured by the intoxicating aroma of fresh-roasted coffee. The fantastic world we inhabit boasts unfathomable systems of subterranean caves, impenetrable forests teeming with organisms, and massive ranges of mountain peaks upon which no foot has ever stood. While the sun-illuminated horizons alone are sufficient to rouse admiration, the entirety of space and sky above stretches into a limitless boundary we will never be able to fathom.

The universe, of course, is not just a cosmic playground in which we delight, nor is it merely the picturesque setting of our lives. For all its wonder, we must not forget the origin of its design. It is, above all else, a marvelous message with an unmistakable meaning. Indeed, from the smallest mite of dust to the grandest and most luminous supernova, every ounce of the universe cries out in unanimous attestation of divine authorship.

Take time to delight in the matchless God who created the heavens and the earth. Number the stars, if you can, and consider the immeasurable power and wisdom required to stretch them out across the infinite galaxies. Consider your smallness, frailty, and insufficiency in comparison to His great might. Cast your cares upon His shoulders, lean upon His strength, and worship at His feet.

And no matter how many times you are told that the universe is unplanned, random, and purposeless, just look out the window and see once again that the handiwork of God is as clear as, well, the day.

Purified by God's Word

Vindicate me, O LORD, for I have walked in my integrity, and I have trusted in the LORD without wavering. Examine me, O LORD, and try me; test my mind and my heart. For Your lovingkindness is before my eyes, and I have walked in Your truth.

PSALM 26:1–3

JULIO PACHECO: EVANGELICAL MINISTRIES OF THE AMERICAS | HONDURAS

A clear conscience—one that doesn't accuse of sin—brings peace. In Psalm 26, the psalmist asks God to vindicate him, and he asks because his conscience is at peace. Using three verbs—*examine* me, *try* me, and *test* me—the psalmist expresses that a clear conscience is not a superficial self-examination or a presumptuous declaration of innocence. Rather, it is the result of submission to a thorough analysis in the light of God's word. Paul likewise remarked that it wasn't his own judgment or the judgment of a human court but the Lord's judgment that mattered (1 Cor. 4:3–4).

It is critical for every believer to seek the examination and evaluation of God. We should echo the psalmist's desire to be thoroughly tried and refined, so that in the end we would be purified. We need daily confrontation from the word of God to restore our souls, make us wise, rejoice our hearts, and enlighten our eyes.

If there is sin in your life that you cling to, don't deny it and harden your conscience. Repent of it and trust in God's marvelous forgiveness, having been redeemed by the blood of Christ. If we seek to be refined daily, we will increasingly put off sin and walk in our integrity. As we grow in God's grace, regularly confessing sin and returning to the straight paths of righteousness, we will learn to stand firm, with clear consciences and hearts at ease. And we will, like the psalmist, be free to sing praises in God's house with His congregation.

Help from the Hills

I lift up my eyes to the mountains. From where shall my help come? My help comes from the LORD, who made heaven and earth.

PSALM 121:1–2

GIDEON MANDA: CENTRAL AFRICAN PREACHING ACADEMY | MALAWI

Life is a journey one begins at birth. The journey comes to an end when one's final breath is taken. It is full of challenges and it is hard to cope with. Many in Malawi find it hard to live from day to day. To deal with the fear of death and other challenges of life, many go to witch doctors to find protection. Sadly, this is no protection at all. People find other empty ways to deal with these challenges.

I still remember how as a family we used to live in fear. My father and mother were always trying to look for the best witch doctor so that we had the best protection. We always lived fearing that behind everything in life there was an evil spirit seeking to destroy us. Yet when I put my trust in God through His Son, Jesus Christ, my world changed.

When Christ became my Savior, all fear was gone. Whenever fear gripped me, I always knew one thing—I knew how to lift my heart in prayer to God. I knew that the all-powerful God was always there for me, to protect me and to provide for all my needs. Life was different from that moment when through Christ, by grace, God became my Father. I learned to cast all my cares on Him because He cares.

Are you controlled by fear? Do the challenges of life press in on you? Look outside of yourself, and up to God. Help is found in Him, hope is found in His Son Jesus Christ. Cast every burden onto Him.

Evangelism Requires an Excellent Reputation

*Keep your behavior excellent among the Gentiles, so that in
the thing in which they slander you as evildoers, they may
because of your good deeds, as they observe them, glorify God
in the day of visitation.*

1 PETER 2:12

OLEG KALYN: GRACE BIBLE SEMINARY | UKRAINE

When Jesus gave the Great Commission to His disciples, He called them to be His witnesses "to the remotest part of the earth" (Acts 1:8). We understand that being witnesses of Christ Jesus is directly related to preaching the gospel to the nations around us. But it also includes another very important element: the way we live our lives and respond to the world.

Having this truth in mind, Peter urges his readers to "keep your behavior excellent among the Gentiles," knowing that it has a tremendous impact for the gospel. It is difficult to be loving and kind when slandered and treated as "evildoers." Yet, Peter teaches that it is essential to our gospel witness. Believers are to maintain excellent behavior so that their testimonies are clear refutations to the accusations that will inevitably come. God may even use their godly testimonies to change the hearts of the Gentiles, whereby the very people who slandered them may join them in glorifying God "in the day of visitation."

How do you respond to slander and attack? Do you respond like the world? Or do you respond with godly behavior that makes Christ and the Christian life attractive? Would the unbelieving world be led to glorify God because of your deeds?

These are challenging questions that God desires us to consider. This text is a call to live our lives with excellence, even in the face of slander. May we strive for faithfulness in this area for the sake of reaching the lost and glorifying God!

The Source of Motivation

But I do not consider my life of any account as dear to myself,
so that I may finish my course and the ministry which I
received from the Lord Jesus, to testify solemnly of the gospel
of the grace of God.

ACTS 20:24

VITALI ROZHKO: WORD OF GRACE BIBLE INSTITUTE | USA

Someone once noted that life is ministry and ministry is life. This description fits the apostle Paul, whose life and ministry has impacted generations of Christians. What was the driving force of his life? What motivated him? What gave him strength to get up and move forward with such rigor, confidence, and passion in spite of many dangers and much persecution? Was it his strong will? Personal discipline? Positive attitude? High IQ? Super human abilities?

According to this one statement from Paul's pastoral speech to the Ephesian elders, it was one thing—*the gospel of the grace of God.* Yes, this one thing—the good news of Jesus Christ, the Son of God, who humbled Himself in human flesh, who lived a perfect life and died a perfect death for His people, who rose from the dead and now reigns, who intercedes for His own before the Father, and who will come again as the King of kings and Lord of lords to establish His eternal kingdom—this gospel was the motivation for Paul. Christ Himself was Paul's greatest treasure, biggest passion, and the love of his heart and ministry. From this verse we see the gospel of grace was not just a lofty concept or idea. The gospel of grace and grace of the gospel were the very life of this man.

What then is the love of our hearts? What is the root of our passion? What motivates us in ministry at home, at work, and at church? Are we motivated by the gospel like Paul? May nothing else but Christ and His gospel move our hearts and motivate our ministry.

A Christian Paradox

At that time Jesus said, "I praise You, Father, Lord of heaven and earth, that You have hidden these things from the wise and intelligent and have revealed them to infants."

MATTHEW 11:25

THOMAS HOCHSTETTER: EUROPEAN BIBLE TRAINING CENTER | GERMANY

In God's economy, there exists a number of paradoxical realities: that God is Three-in-One; that Jesus is fully man and fully God; that God is fully sovereign and man is fully responsible. To our limited understanding and experience these things seem to contradict each other. But in reality, they do not. They coexist in equal parts and bring us all the more to worship God for His "otherness."

There is another paradox that puzzles the mind of mankind. That paradox is you, Christian.

The world tends to value the rich, the mighty, the influencers, the famous, the intellectual, the beautiful, and the successful. In short: the free thinkers and the independent. But that is not how God thinks and works.

Jesus lets us know that those who will hear Him and be saved are not the ones this world would have picked. After rebuking people group after people group for their unbelief, He switches His tone to praise:

"I praise You, Father … that You have hidden these things from the wise and intelligent and have revealed them to infants."

Jesus does not contrast the "wise" and the "stupid." He contrasts the godless and the God-fearing. The God-fearing are like "infants," in that they are dependent on a higher mind. The wise and pompous of this world do not reckon with God because they think of themselves as self-sufficient and independent, relying on their sin-tainted understanding.

Next time someone suggests that your dependence on God is weakness, know that Jesus praises His Father for you. Dependence is not weakness. It is a mark of a child of God.

Go be a paradox!

Turn Back and Repent

Therefore repent and return, so that your sins may be wiped away.

ACTS 3:19

David González: Berea Seminary | Spain

R epentance is a term that is increasingly rejected in our society. Talking about the need of repentance is antagonistic and offensive in our culture. Most people think that they are right and they do not need to repent for anything. Like the crowd who clung to Peter and John, people are more interested in the power of the creature than in the Creator. They reject the holy and righteous One, and defend sin and evil.

On the contrary, the Bible clearly declares that repentance is a required response for salvation. It is the only way your sins can be wiped away. When Peter proclaimed this, he was not intimidated by the opposition of the crowd but persuaded by the power of God. Though the crowd did not want to hear about repentance, Peter responded to them with this great message: "repent and return." Change your mind, stop sinning, and turn back to God, because He commands all people everywhere to repent from their sins.

Maybe you are not a Christian, so you need to confess your sin and your rebellion against God. It is not enough to have regret or sorrow for sin; you must genuinely repent from your sin and turn to God. If you are a Christian, consider Peter's conviction in God's word. Do not be afraid of the opposition you will face. Find comfort in God's will. Proclaim repentance. Do not be carried along by modern influences—confront people with their sin, and call them to repentance and belief in Christ.

He Sees Your Service

For God is not unjust so as to forget your work and the love which you have shown toward His name, in having ministered and in still ministering to the saints.

HEBREWS 6:10

EDWIN MAKIWA: CHRIST SEMINARY | SOUTH AFRICA

The book of Hebrews was written to help Christians grow in the faith. The author of Hebrews is encouraging his audience to spiritual maturity through obedience. There are two things in this verse which God faithfully remembers about His servants: He takes note of our individual deeds and He also takes notes of the motives for our deeds.

God is not unjust to forget our service to Him. The verse follows an essential warning against spiritual immaturity and fundamental directives on attaining complete maturity. It also gives great encouragement to believers who are seeking to stand firm in the faith in the center of a corrupt and rebellious age.

The author knew that God was not unjust and that those who trust in Him alone will never be dissatisfied by Him. In our lives there are times when we need instruction and admonishment, but God within His sovereignty knows that there are also times when we need reassurance.

What a glorious, wonderful reminder and assurance, to be told that the Creator's eyes will never miss any good deed we do. Nor will He be uninformed or ignorant of any labor of love that is shown to Him through a compassionate, loving ministry that is engaged toward His people.

Let this verse stir and strengthen your heart to give yourself to greater service to other believers. God sees and is glorified. What greater motive do you need?

Moving beyond Friendly Nods and Smiles

Therefore, accept one another, just as Christ also accepted us to the glory of God.
ROMANS 15:7

ALBERTO SOLANO: INSTITUTO DE EXPOSITORES | USA

One of the major themes of Romans is *acceptance*. Acceptance goes beyond a friendly nod and a smile. It means to open your home and invite others in. It means to open yourself up to allow others to get to know you, and you get to know them. It denotes a kind of friendship that is seen by actions and not just words. So, how do we *accept one another* at church?

First, *accepting one another* is not limited to people of our choosing. Tall, short, dark, light, rich, poor—in God's redemptive plan, He does not limit His salvific work to a specific kind of people; God saves "from every nation and all tribes and peoples and tongues" (Rev. 7:9). As Christians, we are to accept and love *everyone* that God calls into the church, regardless of their race and background.

Second, *accepting one another* means seeing other Christians as loved and accepted by Christ. It is a terrible thing to reject someone that Christ Himself has accepted and purchased with His own blood (Acts 20:28). We should love others for the love of Christ, and regard others "as more important than yourselves" for the glory of God (Phil. 2:3).

Finally, *accepting one another* does not mean that we should accept sin. When you see a fellow believer in sin, confront him in love and "in a spirit of gentleness" (Gal. 6:1). Part of *accepting one another* means helping one another grow in holiness and Christlikeness.

How *accepting* have you been at church? Think through practical ways that you can move beyond mere friendly nods and smiles.

The Blessing of the Persecuted

*But as for me, I will hope continually, and will praise You yet
more and more.*
PSALM 71:14

S. W.: ASIA (NAME WITHHELD FOR SECURITY)

The author of this Psalm is unknown, but revealed as an older
man (Psa. 71:9) who faces wicked men that seek to destroy his
reputation and life (Psa. 71:4, 10–11). In the midst of the onslaught of
persecution, his main appeal is for God to be near to him (Psa. 71:12),
by hastening to help him. The first plea for help that he seeks is for his
enemies to be judged by God (Psa. 71:13). The second plea for help is
found in our verse, where he asks for a hopeful heart of praise.

We must pause and consider how different this is from the modern evangelical perspective on persecution. We might agree with the
psalmist in his request for justice upon his enemies. But the second
plea seems antithetical to the spirit of today. Should not persecuted believers ask for physical restoration and blessing? We are con-
victed when the psalmist asks instead for a heart that would praise
God more—a heart that would wait and hope continually. This is like
the undoubting heart of faith that James exhorts us to have in trials
(James 1:6).

The psalmist also asks for a heart that would be caused (the language emphasizes God *causing* this praise) to praise God more than
before the trial. Rather than disillusionment, the trial of persecution
should remind us of God's sovereignty, faithfulness, love, mercy, forgiveness, and so much more!

This is a sweet reminder to me in ministry, where persecution and
opposition are a growing reality for me and faithful brethren. God
will use even persecution to bless us—not physically, but spiritually—
by showing us a bigger picture of His kingdom purposes and faithfulness.

The Spiritual Recorder

For when Gentiles who do not have the Law do instinctively the things of the Law, these, not having the Law, are a law to themselves, in that they show the work of the Law written in their hearts, their conscience bearing witness and their thoughts alternately accusing or else defending them.

ROMANS 2:14–15

MARKO PETEK: THEOLOGICAL BIBLICAL ACADEMY | CROATIA

Merely possessing the Law of God does not secure diplomatic immunity from it. God requires total obedience to His Law. A sinner, who follows some standard and expects the same from others, knows he falls short.

To crush the self-righteous confidence of religious people, Paul explains that even those without God's Law have a conscience that demands compliance to its standards. Like an inspector, the conscience verifies if a person is compliant to the law in his heart. Even the most corrupt sinner has his own standards and feels an internal pressure to follow that law. Furthermore, the conscience that has been placed within him by God is like a video recorder that captures every detail of every man's journey. It will serve as evidence against him in the court of God.

Even though a person may be ignorant of the Law of God, the existence of his own personal law reveals that he has been created by the Creator. Because his law reflects God's Law, he is under the jurisdiction of the King of the universe. Like a small child, he may try to cover his eyes in order to not be seen by God, but he cannot change the reality of his accountability to God.

But the accusations of conscience only prove that every man is a lawbreaker. Therefore, we need protection from God's justice that our own obedience cannot provide. The protection we need is found only in the righteousness of Jesus Christ our Savior.

Have you sought this righteousness from Christ? Are you relying on His perfect obedience to the Law in your place? If so, then praise Him today for it!

The Essence of God's Law

Love does no wrong to a neighbor; therefore love is the fulfillment of the law.
ROMANS 13:10

TIMUR R.: RUSSIA (FULL NAME WITHHELD FOR SECURITY)

What is the essence of God's Law? How would you define it in one sentence? According to our verse, the essence of the Law and all of its rules comes down to learning how to love God and consequently our neighbor. This is exactly the goal the Creator pursued in issuing commandments. The heart of His Law is love for God and for neighbor.

It's a sad state when the heart is torn out of God's Law and only bare conformity to rules and commands remains. This was the form in which the Law existed for Saul. While he knew the minutest detail of the Law, studied it, and even observed it outwardly, nevertheless he did not understand its essence. Therefore he was filled with malice and hatred, persecuting those whom the Law prescribed to love, all the while thinking he was fulfilling it. Saul perpetrated a great evil against those who were to be loved, and he committed this evil in the name of God and His Law.

We, born-again Christians, can find ourselves in similar situations. We can do evil to our neighbors, while forgetting what constitutes the essence of obedience to God's law. We can also deprive the Law of its genuine content by straining to observe rules based on a righteousness we ourselves have concocted. But the essence of obedience to God is the love for Him and for neighbor. The fulfillment of the Law flows out of such love.

How is your love for your neighbors—those closest around you? Ask God for enabling grace to love from the heart so you can fulfill His Law.

The Gospel of First Importance

For I delivered to you as of first importance what I also received, that Christ died for our sins according to the Scriptures, and that He was buried, and that He was raised on the third day according to the Scriptures.

1 CORINTHIANS 15:3–4

R. N.: MIDDLE EAST (NAME WITHHELD FOR SECURITY)

"WARNING! DANGER AHEAD!" Have you ever seen a sign like this? It means that we should pay attention, proceed cautiously, and keep away from any dangerous areas. God also warns of danger ahead—much greater than that of a treacherous road—for sinners who do not heed the gospel message. Man is unable to rid himself of the sin and guilt that creates hostility and separation between holy God and sinful man.

The Scriptures—both the witness of the Old Testament and the message of the New Testament—tell us about this gospel. This is what Paul writes of in the opening verses of 1 Corinthians 15. According to him, it is a message of first importance, and this includes the often-overlooked resurrection of Christ. The resurrection of Christ is central to the Christian faith and a major way that Christ glorified Himself. The resurrection demonstrates the victory of the Savior and the salvation He accomplished.

This gospel is the only way God prepared for sinners to be saved. Jesus Christ came to this earth to pay the price for sin. But the story of salvation does not end with Christ's death. The resurrection proves His victory over sin and death. The grave was unable to hold Christ. He was resurrected back to life, having completed the work of salvation. The resurrection of Christ holds a promise for the resurrection of others also.

There are many who need to hear this message of the crucified and resurrected Savior. Are you delivering this most important message to others? Have you believed in it yourself?

The End Is Glory

... through whom also we have obtained our introduction by faith into this grace in which we stand; and we exult in hope of the glory of God.

ROMANS 5:2

FILIBERTO ANGELES DORANTES: WORD OF GRACE BIBLICAL SEMINARY | MEXICO

It is only by Jesus Christ's work that we have unrestricted access, through faith, to God. We are like a great king's sons and daughters, who alone may approach the king without fear. This is a happy result of our justification. No one could achieve this privilege on his own merits. This introduction into grace has been obtained only through faith in Christ. The access to this grace is not transitory or limited in duration. Rather, we remain permanently in this grace. We are saved through faith, but it is by grace that we stand firm in that position.

Not only do we have the privilege of access now, but we also exult in the future expectation of God's glory! Entering grace is only the beginning. The end is marvelous glory. The believer's ultimate destiny is to share in the glory of God. Our future glorification, when we are given bodies suitable for eternal praise and heavenly fellowship, will consummate the work of grace in our lives. This is the hope in which we rejoice!

We have peace with God because we have been justified in the past. We have entrance to His grace at any time we may need it in the present. And we have the expectancy of God's glory in the future. These are truths that should stoke the fire of our souls on a daily basis. This is what we were made for. "For I am confident of this very thing," says Paul to that first generation of believers, "that He who began a good work in you will perfect it until the day of Christ Jesus" (Phil. 1:6).

Near to the Brokenhearted

The Lord *is near to the brokenhearted and saves those who are crushed in spirit.*

PSALM 34:18

Astrit A.: Albania (full name withheld for security)

God never rejects a person who is humble before Him. Those who are brokenhearted should be greatly encouraged that God is near to them. Those who are crushed in spirit should expect His comfort and rescue. Pride and arrogance will always be opposed by God, but He gives grace to the humble. It is His nature to lift up the lowly and to bring down the lofty. O, God, give us a contrite heart and a crushed spirit so that we may receive the help we so desperately need!

David expressed this truth in another psalm: "The sacrifices of God are a broken spirit; a broken and a contrite heart, O God, You will not despise" (Psa. 51:17). Few things are more precious in the eyes of God than a repentant sinner who has come to Him broken and crushed to receive forgiveness and mercy. He is a God merciful and gracious, who forgives iniquity and transgression and sin. He is a God who lifts up the poor man from the ash heap and makes him to be a prince among the people.

We thank you, God, that You do not turn us away when we come to You humble and broken, seeking Your help. We cannot stand on our own, and so we praise You for lifting us up and rescuing us in our time of need. Your grace is greater than all our sin.

Submission to Authorities

Every person is to be in subjection to the governing authorities.
For there is no authority except from God, and those which
exist are established by God.

ROMANS 13:1

JUREM RAMOS: THE EXPOSITOR'S ACADEMY | PHILIPPINES

A number of political events have recently shocked the world. Underdog candidates and secession votes in America and Europe succeeded despite the predictions of polling experts. Certain candidates in the Philippines and other countries have likewise won despite the widespread opposition in media perception. Many have reacted to these events with protests and riots. Some Christians may be enthusiastic while others are grieved, but the Bible calls all of us to follow the same command: *Every person is to be in subjection to the governing authorities.*

Biblical exceptions for passive resistance (Dan. 3, 6; Acts 4:17–20) aside, Paul's general rule in Romans 13:1 toward governing authorities is to be in subjection to them. This means to recognize one's place under someone else in God's established hierarchy. In the Philippines, these authorities include everyone from the president down to the traffic enforcer. No Christian is exempted from obeying this command, because government is a divine institution given by God to establish order in the world. Secular rulers are His instruments, ministers for the good of believers, and avengers carrying out God's wrath on wrongdoers (Rom. 13:4).

So, the next time you are pulled over by a traffic enforcer for using your cellphone while driving, or for not fastening your seatbelt (two of the things many Filipino drivers notoriously disregard), remember that God put them in authority to protect you. The laws they enforce aim to spare you from a disaster that might otherwise have sent you to your final destiny instead of to your intended destination! And when we submit to the governing authorities, we honor the God who established them.

Living in the Presence of the Lord

O God, You are my God; I shall seek You earnestly; my soul
thirsts for You, my flesh yearns for You, in a dry and weary
land where there is no water.

PSALM 63:1

ANIBAL ELEAZAR AGUILAR: EVANGELICAL MINISTRIES OF THE AMERICAS | HONDURAS

King David found himself in the Judean wilderness, fleeing from his son Absalom, who had conspired against him and taken the throne of Israel (2 Sam. 15–17). However, in the midst of this pain and suffering caused by his own son's betrayal, David's foremost desire wasn't to take back the throne but to be in the presence of his beloved God, and to delight in His glory and power. The king loved and valued God more than his reign and riches.

Instead of complaining or becoming embittered by his situation, David's heart was with the Lord. "The king," he resolves, "will rejoice in God" (Psa. 63:11). He could lose everything else, but he couldn't bear to lose his communion with the Almighty. Longing to be back in Jerusalem, worshiping God, he compares his languishing soul to the surrounding landscape—dry and arid. For this reason, he ardently desired the refreshing presence of the Lord.

Emma, a believer with scarce economic resources, has been in a wheelchair and confined to her bed for more than twenty years due to chronic arthritis. I visited her one day this summer and it was stifling hot. She was lying in bed and there was no sort of ventilation. I asked her how she could stand it, and she said, "I think about God's word. It helps me with the pain and refreshes my body." As she was speaking, her words expressed thankfulness while her countenance reflected peace and joy, the fruit of an intimate communion with the Lord.

Are you suffering? Don't fall into bitterness, depression, or hopelessness. Take refuge in the presence of the Lord.

Christ Crucified

For I determined to know nothing among you except Jesus Christ, and Him crucified.

1 CORINTHIANS 2:2

DAVID ROBLES: BEREA SEMINARY | SPAIN

Everywhere around the world there is a great need for pastors who just preach Christ and Him crucified. These days, especially in the West, there are many ministers in churches who have become "experts" in family, administration, relationships, building programs, meetings, pursuing a reputation in the community, and so on. This is sad. Instead, the greatest need of the moment is to be determined, as Paul was, to know nothing except Jesus Christ, and Him crucified. The minister of God needs to be a preacher of Christ and His word. Christ must be the center and supreme subject of his preaching and living.

Many attract crowds by preaching man-pleasing sermons. The gospel of self-esteem and self-love is reigning in too many places. Eloquence and human wisdom are at the center of much proclamation around the globe. But none of these gospel counterfeits will either save anyone or edify God's people.

The church must return to the bold and simple preaching of Christ, and Him crucified. Each one of us needs to be involved in this commission. Churches and Christians need to be praying and supporting those who devote their lives to preaching Christ and training others to do likewise. Preachers must preach, not with persuasive words of wisdom, but in fear and weakness and the demonstration of the power of the Holy Spirit, so that people's faith is not resting on the wisdom of men, but on the power of God (1 Cor. 2:3–5). We preach Christ, and Him crucified! Reader, do you have this same determination as Paul?

Signs of Decay

*[The apostles said] to you, "In the last time there will be mock-
ers, following after their own ungodly lusts." These are the ones
who cause divisions, worldly-minded, devoid of the Spirit.*

JUDE 18–19

VIKTOR Z.: RUSSIA (FULL NAME WITHHELD FOR SECURITY)

When something starts to decay, certain signs are noticeable.
Similarly, when spiritual life starts to decay, there are noticeable
signs—signs that point to greater issues.

What are these noticeable signs of decay? First, there is profane
speech. This can display itself in self-exaltation or moral impurity.
In our passage, Jude calls people who use such language "mockers."
They are those who mock and treat people with disdain. If such
language comes from your lips or you hear the same language from
members of your church, then you need to look beneath this behavior
to the heart. Remember, nothing can change unless the Holy Spirit
works in the heart and helps kill the desires of the flesh.

A second sign of decay is conduct that destroys unity. Jude uses a
word that indicates disagreement with teaching in the church, which
is meant to build up believers in their "most holy faith" (Jude 20).
Unfortunately, someone displaying this conduct may try to justify
themselves saying that they are fighting for the truth, defending the
doctrines, and battling legalism. However, instead of contending for
the faith, they are contentious and simply hurting the church. In reality, their behavior and words exalt themselves instead of bringing
glory to God and edifying the church.

If you believe in God's care for your congregation, then you will
work for its edification and pray for struggling believers. If you know
someone who is showing these signs of decay, talk with him—encourage, exhort, admonish, reprove—and do so in love, so he doesn't hurt
his own soul and also the souls of other brothers and sisters.

Proclaim the Truth

And do not take the word of truth utterly out of my mouth,
for I wait for Your ordinances.
PSALM 119:43

L. J.: ASIA (NAME WITHHELD FOR SECURITY)

We are living in an ever-changing world where biblical truths are distorted rapidly. Even Christians are sometimes tempted to waver in taking a stand for true values and principles instructed in the Bible. How especially challenging for servants of God to proclaim God's truth from the pulpit without fearing any backlash from the congregation!

The longest Psalm in the Bible, Psalm 119, unashamedly declares the excellencies of the word of God. The text under consideration carries the earnest request from the psalmist for boldness to proclaim the word of God to the people around him. The psalmist, without being intimidated by reproaches (Psa. 119:42), pleads that he would never lack God's word to respond. He is not looking to his self-generated ideas, but only to the true word of God. The psalmist rests on the hope that God's truth will finally triumph.

I was reading about the challenge faced by a minister, who was proclaiming that Christian women ought to be family-oriented when most of the women in his congregation were focused on building careers. Some were offended, but God's word prevailed, convicting many women to reconsider their priorities. Many left their jobs to serve their family first.

Do you proclaim God's truth fearlessly, knowing that His truth will ultimately triumph? You can ask for wisdom from above so that you may have a ready defense from Scripture. Proclaim the truth!

Through One Man

Therefore, just as through one man sin entered into the world, and death through sin, and so death spread to all men, because all sinned.

ROMANS 5:12

GIDEON MANDA: CENTRAL AFRICAN PREACHING ACADEMY | MALAWI

God created man to be procreative, and as we give birth to off-spring we pass to them and to their children our natures. These inherent natures, because of the first disobedience of Adam, are depraved and sinful. When Adam sinned, the whole human race sinned and his fallenness was passed on to all his descendants. It is present from the moment we are conceived, and apart from Christ we cannot know God because we are dead in our wretched state as sinners.

This concept makes sense to Malawians because our traditional worldview correlates with the idea that when one person angers "God" (not Yahweh), the entire village will suffer the consequences. Adam represents mankind in as far as sin is concerned, and because of this connection to Adam, all have sinned.

Imagine what it would be like if every nation was required to obtain a savior of its own—no country would have been able to find one. But through Christ, God's salvation plan was made complete. He deserves all glory, honor, and praise for providing a Savior who gives eternal life to people who are dead in their sins, people from all tribes and nations of the world.

This is why we need to spread the gospel and make disciples of *all* nations. No culture, no tribe, nor group of people can claim to be free from sin, because we are all descendants of Adam. Every tribe and every nation has to hear the good news of salvation given by the Father. Stop and pray that from *all* nations, those *in Adam*, can be saved *in Christ*.

Basking in the Glory of the Impartial God

Or is God the God of Jews only? Is He not the God of Gentiles also? Yes, of Gentiles also.
ROMANS 3:29

RAFAEL SALAZAR: EVANGELICAL MINISTRIES OF THE AMERICAS | HONDURAS

Both the evangelization of sinners and the fraternal coexistence of Christians have the same obstacle: personal pretentiousness and exaggerated self-importance. In the first-century Roman church, some of the Jewish Christians struggled with a prejudiced view of the gospel, salvation, and God. It became an issue that diminished the sanctifying power of the gospel and the missionary power of the church. So, Paul had to resolve this issue by affirming that the Gentile had as much right as the Jew to turn to God.

God judges the sinner impartially and finds him guilty, but He also saves the sinner and declares him justified in the same manner. No matter the reputation of the sinner, good or bad, to God all are guilty sinners; and for each of them, there is only one solution: to be justified by faith in Jesus. The God of the gospel universally and impartially manifests His saving power to sinners, regardless of their merit so that no one may boast.

Beloved brothers and sisters, bask in the glory of God, humbly proclaiming the gospel to believers and unbelievers. Don't diminish the power of the gospel, but boast in it. Boast in our Savior and proclaim the gospel without reservation or discrimination. Girolamo Savonarola, an Italian forerunner of the Reformation, said that you can go to paradise if you want to, because your Savior, Christ, has gone there, but know that it is not by your own nature or by your own virtue that you will reach that place. Praise God for sending His Son to die so that we—Jews *and* Gentiles—might live!

Getting It Right

But as for you, speak the things which are fitting
for sound doctrine.
TITUS 2:1

ENRIQUE GODOY CASTILLON: WORD OF GRACE BIBLICAL SEMINARY | MEXICO

In this letter, Paul instructs his disciple and co-laborer, Titus, to correct the wrong doctrines and practices that had crept into the churches of Crete. First, Titus was to establish elders (Titus 1:5). These qualified men (Titus 1:6–9) were essential to the work because they were to hold "fast the faithful word" (Titus 1:9). The same need exists today in every church. It is necessary for the church to have biblically qualified men who teach sound doctrine and counter false teaching. Sound doctrine is healthy and needful for churches; false teaching is fatal (2 Tim. 4:3).

There is never any shortage of false teaching and error. Dangerous doctrines and erroneous interpretations assault the church on a daily basis. Therefore, Paul soberly addresses Titus: "But as for you"—in contrast with false teachers—"speak the things which are fitting for sound doctrine." Doctrine that is sound means that it is without pollution. It is truth that is effectively taught and correctly interpreted, bringing health and nourishment to Christ's church.

We must never overlook the importance of sound doctrine, of careful and meticulous interpretation of God's word, of efforts to get it right and cut it straight. Sound doctrine guards us from error. It produces true, spiritual growth in our lives. May we never disregard those faithful and qualified men whom God has called to preach His word and speak the truth. Let others have their ears tickled, if they must, but let us pursue the hard truths that are fitting for sound doctrine.

The Nature of Our Love

And He said to him, "'YOU SHALL LOVE THE LORD YOUR GOD WITH ALL YOUR HEART, AND WITH ALL YOUR SOUL, AND WITH ALL YOUR MIND.'"
MATTHEW 22:37

KOHKI MINAMIDA: JAPAN BIBLE ACADEMY | JAPAN

A lawyer, an expert in the Jewish law, once came to Jesus with a question to test Him, stemming from his hateful heart. He asked, "Which is the greatest commandment in the Law?" Jesus had no problem answering this question. In fact, there is no one who is more fit to provide the answer to this question. Jesus simply declared that it was to love the Lord your God with a true and total love, with all of one's heart, soul, and mind. This is really an exclusive love that is based upon one's commitment to God.

This is an important truth for all Christians. The concept of love that we hear and see today is completely different from the teaching of Christ. What is sinful and twisted has been taught as if it is true love, and what is truly loving according to the Bible is considered as sinful or hateful.

This is, sadly, especially true in Japan. The concept of love is absolutely different from what Jesus describes here. Even at church, people consider "love" as emotionally based feelings that can change and shift at any moment. But we must pay close attention to and heed the words of Christ. Loving God is not an emotionally based love, nor is it a form of sinful acceptance. Loving God is an exclusive and willful love that is true and total. And that is how we must love Him in our own daily walk, wherever He has placed us in life.

Is your understanding of love more like Christ's or the world's? Resolve today to love God with total allegiance.

The Righteousness of Another

*Now to the one who works, his wage is not credited as a
favor, but as what is due. But to the one who does not work,
but believes in Him who justifies the ungodly, his faith is
credited as righteousness.*

ROMANS 4:4–5

CESARE ALBANESI: ITALIAN THEOLOGICAL ACADEMY | ITALY

One of the battle cries of the Reformation was the doctrine of justification by faith alone. God justifies the one who has faith in Jesus, and He does so on the basis of the credited righteousness of Christ. We believe, embrace, and rejoice in this truth. We are justified because of Jesus, not our own works.

However, there are times when we forget this truth and live as if we can obtain favor from God on the ground of our works, and not on the basis of Jesus' righteousness. Instead of resting in Jesus' work, we can live as if our salvation depended on our good works. We may strive to please God, keep ourselves busy in ministry, try to reach our goals, and work hard so that we can earn His favor. We can profess we are saved by faith and then live as if we are saved by works.

But we did not obtain our salvation and God's favor because of our works. Even in the present, we do not obtain favor or righteousness before God because of what we do. Our daily relationship with the Lord is based on the continuous work of Jesus and His perfect righteousness. We stand justified before God not because of our goodness, but because of Jesus' righteousness. And only through Him can our imperfect obedience be accepted in God's sight.

Friend, remind yourself today that the only way you can be accepted by God is by placing your faith in Jesus alone. Rejoice in the perfect righteousness of Jesus that is yours through faith in Him.

Gracious Saving Faith

For by grace you have been saved through faith; and that not
of yourselves, it is the gift of God; not as a result of works, so
that no one may boast.

EPHESIANS 2:8–9

ALOIS KLEPACEK: CZECH BIBLE INSTITUTE | CZECH REPUBLIC

A recent edition of a Czech Baptist magazine reflects and reveals the crisis and root problem that exists in the Christian community here. It states that we do not have to believe in God's grace to be saved, just in Jesus himself. This is presented as maximum common ground for all Czech churches within this denomination. No further truths are needed or are to be imposed.

Today we are meditating on a sola of the Reformation, *sola gratia*—grace alone. The amazing truth in this text about God's grace stresses the initiative of God in our salvation. He is the one who must change our hearts and give us the ability to believe and have saving faith. We are dead in our sins (Eph. 2:1–3), unable to meet God's standard and His will for our lives. In reality, we want nothing to do with God and we do not seek Him, nor believe in Him (Rom. 3:11). By nature, we hate Him and we face His wrath (Rom. 1:18).

Faith must be granted to us. If a person is not given faith, there is no hope for him. He will never understand his sin or God's righteousness. He will never comprehend who Jesus is, nor appreciate what He did. He will never trust Jesus for his salvation. No one is able to receive and understand the biblical Jesus without God's sovereign work (Mark 4:10–12).

Praise God we have been given this faith. *He* is the one who seeks us, regenerates us from our dead condition (Eph. 2:4–5), and gives us saving faith.

Malawi

CENTRAL AFRICAN PREACHING ACADEMY

The Republic of Malawi is located in southern Africa, on the western shores of Lake Malawi. As with other African nations facing poverty and a lack of resources, the prosperity gospel is leading many away from the purity of the true gospel. In response, Central African Preaching Academy (CAPA) is training men to faithfully preach the gospel and bring true hope to those in physical and spiritual poverty.

TODAY, PRAY FOR

Wisdom for the leadership of CAPA. The bureaucracy and corruption of the country can create challenges for training.

The gospel to reach many who are deceived by the false gospel of prosperity.

The physical sustenance of Malawian pastors. With such widespread poverty, it is difficult for pastors to provide for the needs of their family.

Love Must Be Tough

Fervently love one another from the heart.
1 PETER 1:22

BRUCE ALVORD: GRACE BIBLE SEMINARY | UKRAINE

Far and away the favorite sport of most Ukrainians is soccer. I love it, too, and played goalie as a youth. The only way to be decent at this position is to fling your body farther and stretch your appendages longer than is normally natural for a human being. It's that kind of strenuous, full-out, leave-nothing-on-the-field effort that Peter is talking about in this verse. The word describing how we should love each other is "fervently," which means "to stretch out." Like a goalie who flings himself wildly to the side and stretches to block the last-minute shot and save the game, so too our love should involve an all-out, intense strain. It denotes a willingness to sacrifice our own desires, comforts, and conveniences in order to accomplish what love would do for others.

How is your game? Are you expending great effort to minister to your spouse, children, parents, teammates, etc.? Or are you just standing between the goal posts, not wanting to get your uniform dirty or a scrape on your elbow? The Lord highly prizes fervent love, and His "well done" will make all the glory associated with winning the *World* Cup look like an old, crumpled *Dixie* cup in comparison.

The Gospel Never Changes

For if Abraham was justified by works, he has something to boast about, but not before God. For what does the Scripture say? "ABRAHAM BELIEVED GOD, AND IT WAS CREDITED TO HIM AS RIGHTEOUSNESS."

ROMANS 4:2–3

S. W.: ASIA (NAME WITHHELD FOR SECURITY)

Beginning in Romans 3, Paul has been speaking to the Jews and demonstrating to them that justification by faith was not a new truth but was clearly established in the Old Testament. Why is this important? Because the gospel, in its content and application, never changes. Sinful men are only justified through faith, looking to a faithful God who saves. Paul uses Abraham, the Father of Israel, in this text to prove this very point.

First, Paul considers if Abraham was justified by works, as some of the Judaizers and Pharisees might claim. If he had a righteousness of his own he would be able to boast before men. The qualifier that Paul adds, "but not before God," shows the foolishness of such self-righteousness.

Second, Paul then settles the case with Scripture, by quoting Genesis 15:6. Abraham believed God's promise of blessing through his seed, and this faith was credited to him as righteousness. So, he could not boast—instead he fell on his face before God (Gen. 17:3). Ultimately, the promise to Abraham was fulfilled in Christ Jesus the Messiah, the Seed who would bless all the nations (Gal. 3:16).

May we be encouraged to preach this one singular gospel of faith in Christ, until all the nations truly experience the blessings promised in Him! The gospel never changes—go today and tell someone this good news.

The Cure for Anxieties

[Cast] all your anxiety on Him, because He cares for you.
1 PETER 5:7

VITALI ROZHKO: WORD OF GRACE BIBLE INSTITUTE | USA

There are real anxieties in the lives of Christians, and their anxieties are many. Believers are not immune to pain, stress, uncertainties, and heartaches. Yet, God is there. His presence and provision in times of trouble is real. But Christians must avail themselves of the solution God provides to relieve our anxieties—casting them upon the Lord.

How do you cast your anxieties on God? First, *recognize* the presence of anxiety. You should grab and own your anxiety. Behind most of your (and everyone's) anxieties there is a specific thought or perspective that must be identified. You should investigate your concerns or fears, noting what thought patterns or beliefs you are following that give rise to fears or worry.

Second, *remind* yourself who God is. Your little heart needs big thoughts about God. Speak the truth about God to your heart. Remember that God is in control. He has a mighty hand. He is near and able. He does care. He knows the *when*, *how*, and *why* of every anxiety. Meditating often on God will help melt away your anxieties.

Third, *resort* to prayer. God is near; talk to Him. Let your heart cry "Abba Father!" Pour your heart out before Him. Turn to Him like a child who runs to his father when hurt, uncertain, or afraid. Note, you must cast *all* anxieties—big and small; deep and momentary; anxieties about your past, present, and future—on Christ! Do not hide them or ignore them, nor try carrying them on your own or dumping them on other people. In casting your anxieties on Him there is true peace and healing for your soul.

Count the Cost

And He summoned the crowd with His disciples, and said
to them, "If anyone wishes to come after Me, he must deny
himself, and take up his cross and follow Me."

MARK 8:34

DANIJEL KUHAR: THEOLOGICAL BIBLICAL ACADEMY | CROATIA

Even those closest to Jesus may not understand what it means to truly follow Him. Jesus' radical call to discipleship demands the high price of total commitment, which all of His followers must be willing to pay.

It is not enough to merely confess Christ with our words (Mark 8:27–29); we must also follow Him with our lives (Mark 8:34-38). To follow Jesus Christ will often cost the disciple everything. He must be *willing* to give up everything and must also submit every aspect of his life to Christ. Jesus expects His disciples to be ready to lose their lives for Him and for the gospel, if necessary. The readiness to do this demonstrates the genuineness of the disciple's commitment (Mark 8:35–38).

Many evangelical churches in the former Yugoslavia have forgotten Jesus' radical call to discipleship. Instead, the gospel message has been reduced to: "God is love and has a wonderful plan for you," or, "Jesus can help you solve your problems," or, "Accept Jesus in your life." Sadly, as a consequence, many in the church do not even understand the gospel message and what it means to follow Jesus.

Nevertheless, God graciously continues to raise up for Himself true disciples who are willing to serve Christ and pay the high cost of total commitment that Jesus demands. Theological Biblical Academy is part of this body of true disciples that God has raised up. Many within can testify of their experience and how often Christ's call to discipleship brings division in families. We all need to be ready to pay that high cost and to say with Paul: "For to me, to live is Christ and to die is gain" (Phil. 1:21).

Have you, reader, counted this cost? Are you following Jesus with just your lips, or also your whole life? Pray for grace to count the cost and follow Christ.

December 5

The Sovereign Mercy of God

Just as it is written, "JACOB I LOVED, BUT ESAU I HATED."
What shall we say then? There is no injustice with God, is
there? May it never be! For He says to Moses, "I WILL HAVE
MERCY ON WHOM *I* HAVE MERCY, AND *I* WILL HAVE COMPASSION
ON WHOM *I* HAVE COMPASSION.*"*
ROMANS 9:13–15

EVIS CARBALLOSA: EVANGELICAL MINISTRIES OF THE AMERICAS | HONDURAS

Sovereignty is the supreme and independent exercise of authority. God is the only being that possesses that absolute authority, and His authority is completely independent from any other being. The authority of God is not capricious, but rather based in the totality of His perfections—including His justice, holiness, compassion, and love.

As the Almighty, God has the right to choose anything He wants to include in His eternal plan, including people. God chooses human beings for salvation independent of anything in them, because all men are "dead in [their] trespasses and sins" (Eph. 2:1), and are therefore incapable of seeking out God.

Paul makes the point that it was not Jacob whose decision was determinative, but God's. God chose Jacob and passed over Esau. This choice was not a reflection of Jacob's merit, but of God's mercy. Jacob wasn't better than Esau, but God sovereignly chose him. This in no way means that God is unjust, but shows that God acts in accordance with His own perfections. His mercy and His election are sovereign.

God's choice of Jacob over Esau was no capricious decision. It was the manifestation of His sovereign grace. The question isn't *why did God reject Esau*, but rather *why did He love Jacob*. This was an act of mercy.

This text reminds us that salvation is a gift of God's sovereign grace. No one deserves to be saved, but God has determined to be merciful. We see that remarkable determination in the words of our Lord Jesus Christ, who used His supreme and independent authority to lay down His own life for those He loved (John 10:18).

355

The Power of Jesus Christ

The news about Him spread throughout all Syria; and they brought to Him all who were ill, those suffering with various diseases and pains, demoniacs, epileptics, paralytics; and He healed them.

MATTHEW 4:24

NENAD PESUT: EUROPEAN BIBLE TRAINING CENTER | GERMANY

Nothing was impossible for our Savior. No disease or pain was too severe for Him to heal. Some of the diseases Jesus healed were a direct result of sin. Some people were demon-possessed, others were handicapped—Jesus had compassion on them all. That's why the news about Jesus spread quickly, even into regions where Jesus wasn't doing miracles. These signs not only proved that He was the Messiah, promised by the prophets, but also corroborated the things He taught.

After Jesus had finished His redemptive work on earth and the foundation of the church had been laid by the apostles, such miracles were no longer necessary. But the greatest miracle, worked by our Lord Jesus even today, is that He heals our spiritual diseases, infirmities, and pain—namely sin.

So, be compassionate with the lost, like our Lord Jesus. Tell them about the One who alone can open up and heal their hardened hearts. At the end of Matthew's gospel, He assures us: "All authority has been given to Me in heaven and on earth" (Matt. 28:18); and He has promised you, "I am with you always, even to the end of the age" (Matt. 28:20). We don't have to be afraid of anything, because the Lord Jesus is with us, the Lord "who pardons all your iniquities, who heals all your diseases, who redeems your life from the pit" (Psa. 103:3–4).

I'm always encouraged and edified when I contemplate the greatness and the power of our Lord Jesus Christ. This verse in Matthew gives a foretaste of how glorious the future with Jesus will be, where there will be no more sorrow or pain.

December 7

Burning Coals

BUT IF YOUR ENEMY IS HUNGRY, FEED HIM, AND IF HE IS THIRSTY,
GIVE HIM A DRINK; FOR IN SO DOING YOU WILL HEAP BURNING COALS
ON HIS HEAD.

ROMANS 12:20

GIDEON MANDA: CENTRAL AFRICAN PREACHING ACADEMY | MALAWI

As sinners, our natural response to an enemy is to retaliate. But here, Paul emphasizes the need to conquer evil with good as he quotes Proverbs 25:21–22. In living a transformed life in Christ, we should be on guard, ensuring that we are not overcome by evil but rather conquer evil with good.

Where I come from in Malawi, there is a saying: "When someone hits you, you have to hit them back." Growing up, some parents would be the ones encouraging such behavior. By retaliating, you may gain respect, both from the individual as well as from onlookers. However, in many cases the opposite proved to be true—seeds of vengeance bore more fruits of animosity and hatred than they did of respect.

What Paul teaches in this text would not only gain someone true respect, but it also has the ability to cause many to follow Christ as their hearts melt when met with kindness instead of reprisal. Pride and revenge strain and sever relationships; Paul's teaching seeks to build and repair relationships.

The concept of feeding your hungry enemy and offering a drink to your thirsty foe sounds strange, unconventional, and foolish to many; yet out of His wisdom, God calls us to turn the other cheek. Our part is to trust Him and lovingly obey His commands. This is the duty of every Christian to his/her enemy, to return good for evil. Who is your enemy? Write down five ways you can practically do them good and return good for evil.

Loving the One God

Hear, O Israel! The LORD is our God, the LORD is one!
DEUTERONOMY 6:4

JUAN ANTONIO ORTEGA MONTOYA: WORD OF GRACE BIBLICAL SEMINARY | MEXICO

Jewish teachers have long considered this text the heart of the whole Law. In fact, this confession is so important that obedient Jews even in our own time recite it at least twice a day. Known as the *Shema*, which means "hear," it has played a foundational role in Jewish thought for thousands of years.

This verse teaches that there is only one God. The Lord alone is God, and there is no other. This is by no means in opposition to the doctrine of the Trinity; rather, it emphasizes the self-consistency and oneness of the Lord, who alone is God.

God requires His people to love Him wholeheartedly. Just as God is one, so we His people are to be of one mind and one heart, loving no other gods, and loving the Lord completely. We are not to love Him simply more than any other god, or worship Him as the greatest of the gods. Rather, we are to worship Him only, and love Him in a way that we love nothing else. Our thoughts should be captivated by Him and His word, and our lives spent in joyful obedience to Him.

The call to remember God's oneness is a call to refocus our hearts on God. The *Shema* calls us to turn away from the many things that vie for our attention and affection. It is a call to restore the Lord to the center of our lives, to esteem Him above all else, and to give Him in our own hearts His rightful place as God.

Praise to the Creator

*I will give thanks to You, for I am fearfully and wonderfully
made; wonderful are Your works, and my soul knows it very well.*

PSALM 139:14

FREDERICK PAULO TOMACDER: THE EXPOSITOR'S ACADEMY | PHILIPPINES

David was in awe of God's infinite knowledge and His all-pervading presence. He realized that nothing about him escapes the mind of God and that there is nowhere that he can go where God is not present. This is because God is his Creator, Designer, and Sustainer. David was in God's mind even before his conception. His very life was written in God's book even before he was born. He, with the rest of mankind, is indeed "fearfully and wonderfully made"!

As the pinnacle of God's creative act, human beings are unique in all of creation. We bear God's image and likeness. We are given authority to rule over other creatures, and the responsibility to cultivate this good earth. We are set apart by these things.

Our intellect, creativity, emotions, passion, and complexity evoke awe and wonder. But they are not just a source of amazement. Human beings, unlike animals and plants, can process the beauty of God's design and respond to Him in praise and thanksgiving!

So, if you find yourself dry and without reason to magnify God, you don't need to look far. Reflect on your very life. Be in awe of God's design of the human body, in the systems and processes that keep you alive. Reflect on your daily experiences, and marvel at how He directs them into a grand story of goodness.

And, when you are tempted to live life according to your rules, remember the Creator who wove every fiber of your being for His glory. The life you have is a gift of grace, and it must rightfully be an offering of praise.

What Are You Seeking?

Therefore if you have been raised up with Christ, keep seeking the things above, where Christ is, seated at the right hand of God. Set your minds on the things above, not on the things that are on earth.

COLOSSIANS 3:1–2

ANDREY GORBAN: WORD OF GRACE BIBLE INSTITUTE | USA

The Christian's whole life is Christ. The thought of a life without Him should not only sound foreign to the man or woman of God, but altogether miserable. The desire to be with God should be an overwhelming one; so much so, in fact, that death is seen as gain for those who love God (Phil. 1:21). This is what the apostle Paul points to as he encourages the Colossian believers to consider, on a deeper level, what it means to long for Christ.

In considering the fact that one has "been raised," the obvious conclusion is that this is the result of being born again, of receiving a new life. This person who has been given this enormous gift, must then, out of a deep love for Christ, intentionally set his mind to where He is. The Lord is presently at the right hand of the Father, so what other place could possibly be better or more appealing for the Christian? This seeking, this desiring, this longing, will be all-consuming, as the Christian understands that Christ is his or her whole life (Gal. 2:20).

The language of setting one's mind on something is reminiscent of the fact that we are to "[take] every thought captive" (2 Cor. 10:5). The world in which we live offers much by way of distraction, but the love of Christ, the reality of one's identity in Him, and the desire to be with Him prompts the Christian to gladly seek where He is and to think of Him. This world is fleeting, but an eternity with King Jesus is imminent.

Is your mind set on Christ? Seek Him above!

The Wisdom of Christ and His Word

I say this so that no one will delude you with
persuasive argument.
COLOSSIANS 2:4

DAVID ROBLES: BEREA SEMINARY | SPAIN

This text is warning us against being deceived by persuasive human wisdom. Instead, we know Christ, in whom are all the treasures of wisdom and knowledge (Col. 2:2–3).

The primary industry in Spain is tourism. After France and the USA, Spain receives the most international visitors. In 2016, more than 75 million people visited Spain, almost double its population. When you are a tourist anywhere in the world, it is easy to be deceived by the local "picaresca" who con and steal from unsuspecting foreigners. Not knowing the language and culture leaves any visitor as an easy prey for these "picaros."

Sadly, many believers are like spiritual tourists. Christians who have not been firmly rooted and built up in Christ (Col. 2:7) are at risk of being easily deceived by human wisdom, holding to merely a form of godliness. Today, many churches and believers are in jeopardy of being taken captive through philosophy and empty deception, by wisdom that follows the traditions of men and the elementary principles of the world (Col. 2:8), rather than Christ and His word.

How do I raise my children? How do I treat my spouse? What should I do with my life? What kind of job should I pursue? How do I handle my emotions? How do I handle my finances? How should I consider others and myself? These and other life questions will be answered differently by human wisdom than by Christ and His word. Do not be deceived with persuasive arguments, but instead be firmly rooted and built up in Christ and His word. They are all you need!

Take Courage

These things I have spoken to you, so that in Me you may have peace. In the world you have tribulation, but take courage; I have overcome the world.

JOHN 16:33

ROMAN K.: RUSSIA (FULL NAME WITHHELD FOR SECURITY)

This verse contains the antidote to despair, depression, and weariness. Christ warns His disciples about the many difficulties that would await them immediately after His departure. However, He gives them this magnificent promise, which has supported His followers throughout the whole history of the church.

Christ says that the disciples have an unshakeable foundation for boldness and courage in the face of affliction—Christ Himself and His victory. The source of true boldness is not to be found anywhere in the world or in the disciples themselves, but only in Christ and His completed work and victory over the world. The world is defeated and presents no spiritual danger for the redeemed.

Christ clearly hinted at the transient nature of all earthly affliction. Nothing, not even the worst possible trial a Christian can experience in this earthly life, can follow him into eternity. When you take a step back and consider this reality, it puts all trials in perspective.

Christ's call comes to us as well. We must be courageous in the face of the dangers and afflictions in this world. Ponder the complete victory of Christ at Calvary. Look at all circumstances from the point of view of eternity—then nothing will be able to shake or destroy your faith. Encourage another believer with these words; tell them to take courage, for our Savior has overcome the world!

The Importance of Your Work to Missions

Therefore we ought to support such men, so that we may be fellow workers with the truth.

3 JOHN 8

ERIC WEATHERS: TMAI HEADQUARTERS | LOS ANGELES, CALIFORNIA

How important is your work to missions? Seeing my 20-year corporate career as through a rearview mirror, I wonder how much more fulfilling ministry could have been if I had known a fellow businessman named Gaius.

Jesus preached the Great Commission to 11 men (Matt. 28:16–20). Their responsibility was to go and make disciples of all nations. They had to teach people to obey everything Jesus taught. These men needed help. Great news—a short time later, in Acts 2 and 1 Corinthians 15, there were at least 3,511 disciple makers.

Now it is your turn. Like successful businesses, mission work requires a well-orchestrated supply chain. Meet Gaius, a businessman and fellow worker with the truth. John commends Gaius' help of missionaries and strangers (3 John 5), and in our verse today, he exhorts Gaius to support those who have gone out for the sake of Christ. John prayed that God would continue prospering Gaius "in all respects," which would include his vocational success.

The redeemed in the marketplace must underwrite pastoral training centers, professors, translation efforts, and future pastors' tuition. Trained expositors go nowhere without believers fulfilling God's call to send and support them (Rom. 10:13–15).

This is how people like you and me and Gaius participate in missions. Fellow workers in the truth are obliged to underwrite the Great Commission with their God-given wealth. They are the redeemed who support missionaries—they work together with them for the sake of the truth. Hence, John calls you "fellow workers with the truth."

Your work is a critical link conjoined to others in the supply chain, all engineered to fulfill the Great Commission in your lifetime.

He Brought Us Forth

In the exercise of His will He brought us forth by the word of truth, so that we would be a kind of first fruits among His creatures.

JAMES 1:18

NORMAN SEFALA: CHRIST SEMINARY | SOUTH AFRICA

All people are born separated from God and destined to destruction in hell's fire, where they will feel the might of the wrath of God, where there will be no chance to escape. This is our destiny, unless God intervenes.

In the exercise of His will, God brought us forth from our destined place of destruction; the good news of the gospel assures us that we can be made right with God by the blood of His own Son, Jesus Christ, that was shed for our sins. We are thus no longer in danger of destruction in hell's fire, and by Jesus' resurrection God gave us new life and dedicated us to Himself alone—a kind of first fruits, distinct from the rest of His creation.

Now that we have been brought forth from our wretched state, we no longer need to try to appease God by performing any other rites and rituals associated with our cultures and indigenous religions, like offering animal sacrifices in the hope that they will cleanse us of our sins and curses. Neither should we try to reach God through our ancestors, as that is tantamount to rejecting His free gift of eternal life through faith in His Son, Jesus Christ. "For there is one God, and one mediator also between God and men, the man Christ Jesus, who gave Himself as a ransom for all, the testimony given at the proper time" (1 Tim. 2:5–6).

If you have been saved, give thanks to God, for He brought you forth *in the exercise of His will*. Rejoice in being a kind of first fruits of the coming harvest.

Deeds That Deny

They profess to know God, but by their deeds they deny Him, being detestable and disobedient and worthless for any good deed.

TITUS 1:16

JORDAN STANDRIDGE: ITALIAN THEOLOGICAL ACADEMY | ITALY

Do you *know God*? Do you *actually know Him*?

Many claim to know God but the question to ask is: Is it possible to think that we know God and not actually know him?

We can know with confidence that anyone who does not believe in Christ does not know God, and needs the gospel. But it becomes much more difficult when we interact with people who profess to know the God of the Bible.

While many may walk into our churches and sit in our pews week after week, and make some form of profession, Paul provides a clue to test if someone's profession of faith is real. The test that reveals if someone knows God is, what are their deeds?

Deeds do not save people, but they do reveal whether God has saved them or not. People whose deeds include regular habits of sin, an unwillingness to forgive, or who willfully go on disobeying God's clear biblical commands, demonstrate by their deeds that their professions are empty and that they do not know God.

Before you think of another person, the first step is to stop and make sure that you truly know the Lord. One way to know is to reflect on your deeds and actions. Do they reveal a heart that loves God or a heart that despises Him? Do they reveal a heart that *knows* God or merely *knows about* Him?

A Word of Warning

He will say, "I tell you, I do not know where you are from;
DEPART FROM ME, ALL YOU EVILDOERS."
LUKE 13:27

ASTRIT A.: ALBANIA (FULL NAME WITHHELD FOR SECURITY)

Throughout history, during the time of the Old Testament and also now in the church age, the people of God have been accompanied by others who think such a connection makes them believers as well. And often it is difficult to distinguish them from true believers, because they seem to agree with sound doctrine and can even articulate basic truths of the faith. Nevertheless, in the final judgment all such people will be revealed for who they truly are. And so these words of our Lord directed to such people are truly terrifying. For such, eternal punishment is reserved!

Therefore, this ought to cause all believers to examine themselves to determine whether they truly are a part of the kingdom of God. Assurance that we are indeed children of God only comes from the Spirit of God and from our walk with God. Trials that come into our lives are all for our good so that we can grow and so that the genuineness of our faith can be demonstrated. The true believer will grow in faith over time. The change that has happened within him will be clear through his good works.

Let us thank God for every challenging situation in our lives, which gives us both the opportunity to grow and also to verify our faith. Let us thank God for His salvation. Let us persevere so that on that day we will hear those wonderful words: "Well done, good and faithful slave ... enter into the joy of your master" (Matt. 25:23).

Loving without Delay

*Be devoted to one another in brotherly love; give preference to
one another in honor.*

ROMANS 12:10

Cornelius Rivera: Evangelical Ministries of the Americas | Honduras

Loving others as our own siblings is not easy. Even within the same household, taking the initiative to love can be difficult, as our human natures interfere. But this verse is preceded by the call to submit to God in light of all that He has done for us (Rom. 12:1). Such is the prerequisite to lovingly serve the household of Christ (Rom. 12:3–9).

The question then becomes: Will I serve and exercise my spiritual gifts, reflecting brotherly love? If so, do I wait until someone shows that love to me? Not according to this verse! It bids me to be the first to love, not as a response for others loving me. This is the intent of the phrase, "give preference." The verb means "to take the lead," suggesting that we honor others by giving them preference and loving them first.

Did not the Lord Jesus love us first? "This is My commandment," He said, "that you love one another, just as I have loved you" (John 15:12). He made love the identifying mark of His disciples, saying, "All men will know that you are My disciples, if you have love for one another" (John 13:35).

To the Thessalonians, Paul wrote, "As to the love of the brethren, you have no need for anyone to write to you.... But we urge you, brethren, to excel still more" (1 Thess. 4:9–10). And they did excel all the more in love, for when a need arose in Jerusalem, they begged for the favor to participate (2 Cor. 8:1–5). May we likewise lovingly serve the brethren without delay!

Fuel for Service

Not lagging behind in diligence, fervent in spirit, serving the Lord.

ROMANS 12:11

S. W.: ASIA (NAME WITHHELD FOR SECURITY)

Paul has been giving a series of exhortations focusing on our service in the body of Christ in Romans 12:4–13. Here he deals with the natural tendency we have as frail people to be exhausted and to give up in loving and serving our fellow brothers and sisters. How do we keep from the tendency toward frustration in the often-unrewarding toil of ministry? Paul gives three exhortations to spur us on in the work of the Lord.

First, he urges us to not lag behind in diligence. The idea is to not be slow in zeal, but to do things quickly. This is a confrontation to the laziness or procrastination that creeps into the life of the discouraged Christian. We must recognize that our time is short and ultimately a stewardship from the Lord.

Second, Paul urges us to be fervent, or literally to *boil,* "in spirit." In the original (by use of the article in Greek), Paul may be referring to the Holy Spirit rather than our spirit. Our focus should not be on externals, but on the spiritual fruit that only God can produce.

Third, we must be dedicated to "serving the Lord." Ministry is through Him and for Him—only this perspective will keep us going strong. He is the Master of the church and we are but servants.

William Carey faithfully toiled in India for seven years before rejoicing in 1800 over the first believer, Krishna Pal. That kind of patience is only possible by rooting ourselves in faithfulness to Christ and trusting Him for the harvest. Be fueled and renewed in your service to Christ and His people.

December 19

What's Your Ministry Mindset?

But Jesus called them to Himself and said, "You know that the rulers of the Gentiles lord it over them, and their great men exercise authority over them. It is not this way among you, but whoever wishes to become great among you shall be your servant."
MATTHEW 20:25–26

OSCAR VILLA: THE EXPOSITOR'S ACADEMY | PHILIPPINES

How did Jesus transform the way His disciples thought about ministry? In Israel at this time, the Jews lived under Gentile rulers who were known to forcefully overpower and subdue others. Jesus' disciples saw how power, prominence, and rank made leaders great in the eyes of the people. When the disciples began to follow Jesus, they brought into the ministry these ideas regarding position, influence, and authority. They thought that being Jesus' first disciples meant that they were entitled to privileged and powerful positions (Matt. 20:21).

Jesus identified their sinful tendency to conform Christian ministry to the world's selfish and self-centered system. He told them that dominating others and wielding authority was incompatible with what His disciples were to do. In stark contrast to their craving for position and power was Jesus' call to selflessness in servanthood (Matt. 23:1–12). He exemplified this servanthood in His submission to God's will (Matt. 12:18), suffering and dying as a ransom for many (Matt. 20:28).

Many today have allowed the world to shape ministry. Many Filipino pastors have made corporate giants their standard of success, and leaders of industry their exemplars of leadership. Some view their ministries like businesses, running their local churches like corporations. There are workers whose shelves are filled with books by authors who have no biblical foundations. Some seminary students pursue theological training because they crave the recognition and respect of others.

How much of your thinking about the ministry has been shaped by the world? How should Jesus' words and work change the way you think and go about your ministry? Will you embrace the privilege to serve others?

Salvation Means Love in Action

Do not love the world nor the things in the world. If anyone loves the world, the love of the Father is not in him.

1 JOHN 2:15

ALOIS KLEPACEK: CZECH BIBLE INSTITUTE | CZECH REPUBLIC

It is generally known that during the peak of communism, the Czech church grew stronger and was more unified. But after communism lost its strength, the church grew weaker and weaker. New distractions and possibilities from this world caught the attention of many Christians.

Though Christians have been given new life, which provides the ability to resist sin, the tension of the Christian life demonstrates that the presence of sin has not yet been eliminated. It is the power of sin that was broken. This means Christians have the ability to resist temptation, so we need to be warned against falling into sin.

Today's passage speaks to this warning. After giving an assurance to his audience, John now warns the saints not to take their salvation for granted by loving the world. For if we love the world, the love of the Father is not in us.

It is important to realize that when John speaks about the world, he is referring to the world system and the things of this present life. This world screams loudly every day for our attention over the things of God. It wants us to love it more than God. As we know, this is one of the main sins of our day. People love creation and the creature more than the Creator (Rom. 1:25). Unbelievers are obsessed by and devoted to this present world, which is perishing. We must not fix our hope and love in the same place.

As Christians, let us make sure our hearts are never set on what this world loves, but on what God loves. This will demonstrate that the Father's love is in us.

December 21

Sound Ministry Requires Love

If I speak with the tongues of men and of angels, but do not have love, I have become a noisy gong or a clanging cymbal.
1 CORINTHIANS 13:1

IGOR BODUN: GRACE BIBLE SEMINARY | UKRAINE

When I was a young boy, before the collapse of the Soviet Union, I was part of the Young Soviet Pioneers. As a pioneer, I had a special responsibility: I was the drummer for our unit. I was given a drum to play, and a good friend of mine was given a pipe. And when we played at an event, we could be heard almost everywhere in our village. Yet our drumming and piping were only empty sounds, just noise with no lasting profit for our audience. When all was done, we hung our instruments back on the wall, and life went on as before.

During the first century, the church at Corinth was making a lot of "noise" as well. The believers were entrusted with spiritual gifts (1 Cor. 1:7) to be used in ministering to others. However, Paul discovered one extremely important shortcoming: a *lack of love* for God and for each other. The absence of love resulted in division, quarrels, selfishness, arrogance, and more. Without love, their church services were not focused on the gospel or its true promotion.

We also need to guard against losing love and becoming mere noise makers. We shouldn't allow religious knowledge, endless activities, and professionalism to push out love and leave us spiritually empty.

Love is the most important gift and the *first fruit* of the Holy Spirit (Gal. 5:22). This fruit of the Holy Spirit is "the engine" for the blessed ministry of the church. Please check whether love is in its place! Don't just be a noisy drummer in your community.

Exclusive Love for the One True God

You shall love the Lord *your God with all your heart and with all your soul and with all your might.*

DEUTERONOMY 6:5

Juan Antonio Ortega Montoya: Word of Grace Biblical Seminary | Mexico

We cannot separate this verse from the one preceding it, which begins with the confession that the Lord alone is God. For if there is no God but the Lord, that means that He alone created the world, that He alone blesses, protects, provides, and saves. Whom else should we or could we love? He ought to occupy our exclusive love, which includes both devotion and obedience. This passage, in fact, conveys the covenant relationship between Israel and the Lord God, with "love" carrying the idea of covenant obligation and legal demand.

Love and obedience are everywhere connected in Scripture. For example, Jesus tells His disciples to make more disciples of every nation and to teach them to obey everything that He commands (Matt. 28:18–20). Elsewhere, Jesus says, "If you love me, you will keep My commandments" (John 14:15). So, as we consider Jesus as Lord, as the one true God of creation, we ought to love and obey Him.

The love that God expects is wholehearted, encompassing every aspect of who we are—our minds, our strength, our time, and our very souls. Our daily priority is to seek out those areas in our lives that are not fitting for the kind of love that Jesus, our wonderful God and Savior, deserves. What area of your life and of your soul do you need to realign in loving obedience to Him today? Is it your thought life? Is it a relationship? Is it the way you spend your time? Is it the way you treat others? Whatever it may be, ask God today to incline your heart to love Him more through greater obedience today.

The Word Incarnate

And the Word became flesh, and dwelt among us, and we saw
His glory, glory as of the only begotten from the Father, full
of grace and truth.

JOHN 1:14

GIAMPAOLO NATALE: ITALIAN THEOLOGICAL ACADEMY | ITALY

This verse speaks of the Incarnation, and it is the climax of John's prologue. There have been references to the Incarnation in Chapter One, but this is now a picture *par excellence* of what the Incarnation is. This Word, the *Logos*, the Agent of creation, was made flesh and dwelt among us. Jesus' existence didn't begin with His conception; He was God and was with God since from the beginning. But He became man.

The Incarnation is crucial for those who want to be reconciled with God. Although the postmodern mind will never accept this truth, the word of God clearly teaches that Jesus was both truly human and truly divine at the same time.

The Incarnation is one of God's many inscrutable designs that make "foolish the wisdom of the world" (1 Cor. 1:20). It is also neglected and under attack today by many who would call themselves "Christians." A proper understanding of the Incarnation of Christ, however, is key to understanding the gospel; it is also important to preserve the purity of sound doctrine. We must never put aside or minimize this doctrine. Whenever we preach or speak about Christ, we should always remember the importance of the Incarnation, through which God entered into humanity to save men from their sins: "For the Son of Man has come to seek and to save that which was lost" (Luke 19:10).

Gifts of Worship

After coming into the house they saw the Child with Mary His mother; and they fell to the ground and worshiped Him. Then, opening their treasures, they presented to Him gifts of gold, frankincense, and myrrh.

MATTHEW 2:11

ADAN RUBEN FUENTES BARRERA: WORD OF GRACE BIBLICAL SEMINARY | MEXICO

I once received a surprise from a stranger that I had only spoken with over the phone. For whatever reason, he decided to give a gift to my family. It was not the economic value but his display of love that made the impact. There is something pleasing about receiving a gift. Gifts certainly bring joy, especially when the one receiving the gift recognizes the kind intention of the one giving it.

When Jesus was born in Bethlehem, He and His family received strangers who came bearing gifts. The focus of the scene is not on Mary or the wise men. Instead, the focus is on the little boy, Jesus. The wise men recognized Jesus to be the promised King of the Jews, so they traveled a great distance to honor Him with their gifts. Though the gifts were valuable, their true value lay in the worship that was offered to Jesus through them.

As believers, we are no longer strangers and enemies to God. We do not need to travel far distances in order to bring Him gifts. Because of this little boy, Jesus, and all that He accomplished in His life, death, and resurrection, we are now a part of His family. How much more should we, then, give Him gifts! How much more should we desire to be pleasing in His eyes! Though we do not offer gold, frankincense, or myrrh, we should nonetheless offer gifts to God. We are urged to present our very bodies to God as gifts (Rom. 12:1–2). Let your obedience to Christ today be a gift from a heart of worship.

God's Love for the World

For God so loved the world, that He gave His only begotten
Son, that whoever believes in Him shall not perish,
but have eternal life.

JOHN 3:16

ASTRIT A.: ALBANIA (FULL NAME WITHHELD FOR SECURITY)

This is perhaps the most universally well-known Bible verse, and for good reason! God's love for the world is truly a thing to behold. For those of us in Christ, we realize that it surpasses all human understanding and logic. The sacrificial love of a Father who sends His only begotten Son to bring eternal life to a dying world through *His own death*—it is too much! It amazes us and leaves us with our mouths open in astonishment.

Today, we as believers celebrate and remember the amazing truth that God sent His only begotten Son. He did not send Him as a conquering king or as a triumphant warrior. He sent Him as a humble, lowly, helpless baby, in the midst of the filth and stench of animals and human sin. From the beginning to the very end, Jesus' was a life of humiliation. The One who alone should have been worshiped as God came in the likeness of sinful flesh (Rom. 8:3) so that He might redeem us from the curse of our sin. What a Savior we have!

This Christmas let us gaze deeply at Christ and marvel at His humility, His love, His sacrifice. Let us worship the triune God for the matchless gift of our Savior. And let us never become too familiar with the simple truth of Christmas that God so loved the world, that He gave His only begotten Son, that whoever believes in Him shall not perish, but have eternal life.

Plural Godly Leadership

*For this reason I left you in Crete, that you would set in order
what remains and appoint elders in every city as I directed you.*

TITUS 1:5

GIDEON MANDA: CENTRAL AFRICAN PREACHING ACADEMY | MALAWI

Paul asked Titus to set in order what remained and appoint leaders in the church so that ministry would run smoothly. This highlights the need for leaders in the church. The role of elders/overseers/bishops in the church is crucial.

Elders are a group of men who are appointed to lead God's flock as they preach and teach the word of God. They are meant to establish the pattern of faith for the people to follow, while imitating the example of the Chief Shepherd, Jesus Christ.

Although Scripture clearly calls for plural leadership, many pastors in Malawi seek to manage God's work single-handedly, and as a result the work of the Lord suffers. In order to ensure their personal interests, some senior pastors even appoint members of their families into leadership. This is not honoring to the Lord, as it does not honor and follow His word.

The process of selecting elders should be done by seeking God's guidance in prayer. Clear criteria are given in the New Testament, with 1 Timothy 3:1–7 and Titus 1:5–9 being key passages that provide details on the essential qualifications of an elder. Elders ought to work willingly and discharge their responsibility with reverence. We ought to pray continuously for church leaders.

Think of the leadership at your church. Pray for them, that God would bless them, grow them, and use them. Next time you see them, thank them for their ministry labor.

Whom Are You Trusting?

Wait for the Lord; be strong and let your heart take courage; yes, wait for the Lord.

PSALM 27:14

Sergey M.: Russia (full name withheld for security)

When we, as believers, encounter more and more difficult trials, each one of us must have strong faith in the Lord and unshakeable trust in Him. Such was the case in the life of David. In Psalm 27, David describes a situation when he was faced with many enemies (Psa. 27:2–3, 12). David, however, as a true believer in God, obtained courage and strength by trusting the Lord. Surrounded by enemies, he is sure that the Lord will defend him. Counting on this, David says to himself, "Wait for the Lord; be strong and let your heart take courage; yes, wait for the Lord."

In our country, it is often said: "Trust in the Lord, but don't slip up." This saying, though it may sound biblical, misses the point. The emphasis in this saying is on man. However, the Bible places the emphasis differently. Although we are responsible to act wisely and rightly without straying, we are called to trust not in ourselves but in the Lord! "Don't slip up, but trust in the Lord!" would be more biblical.

The words from David are ones we need to hear today. Wait on the Lord! God will always help on time. Wait on the Lord and take courage! Wait on the Lord and strengthen your heart with hope in Him! You can always rely on Him—rely only on Him and on no one else. He will never let you down. He who trusts in the Lord will never find himself in a hopeless situation.

Unashamed of the Gospel

For I am not ashamed of the gospel, for it is the power of God for salvation to everyone who believes, to the Jew first and also to the Greek. For in it the righteousness of God is revealed from faith to faith; as it is written, "BUT THE RIGHTEOUS MAN SHALL LIVE BY FAITH."

ROMANS 1:16–17

FERNANDO JAIMES: INSTITUTO DE EXPOSITORES | USA

It is common to hear people talk about how they fear sharing the gospel in certain contexts, because of the antagonism that they may suffer. A biblical antidote for this dread is a healthy dose of fear toward God, which enables you to not be ashamed of the gospel.

In today's passage, Paul indicates that man cannot attain a righteous status apart from God and the gospel. Men are utterly lost and cannot be saved except through God's good news. What are unbelievers being saved from? Paul says outside this righteous gospel, nothing but the wrath of God ought to be expected (Rom. 1:18). The gospel has a unique focus on God's wrath. Because of His anger toward sinners, God had to transfer His wrath toward His adopted children onto His only begotten Son, and then crush that Son.

Until we grow in being unashamed of the gospel and specifically gain a glimpse of the horrors of God's wrath, we will never begin to see the horror and beauty of the cross, which *motivates our evangelism.* When we know what awaits the wicked, we are motivated to evangelize individuals and masses of unbelievers. We are motivated to evangelize people in our community and churches when we realize that many have deceived themselves into thinking that they are part of God's people, yet they are not.

Are you unashamed? Then remember your duty and go preach the gospel so that others are persuaded and saved from the wrath of God. The person who truly understands the fate of the sinner will be motivated to preach the gospel without hesitation (Acts 17:30–31).

Doers and Hearers

But prove yourselves doers of the word, and not merely hearers
who delude themselves.
JAMES 1:22

DAVID ROBLES: BEREA SEMINARY | SPAIN

E very believer is called to be a doer of the word of God, and not
merely a hearer. This is a huge warning, because if you are only a
hearer, then you are deceiving yourself.

Sadly, self-deception is quite common in every society these days.
This is nothing new. In fact, the human heart has always tended to
deceive itself because of our fallen nature. We can witness this in several ways and different contexts. You can always find those who pro-
crastinate at work, those who always look busy but never accomplish
anything. They may say that they are working, but if you do not see
the fruit and results of their labor, they are just deceiving themselves.

Likewise, there are those who consider themselves Christians because they grew up in a Christian family, were born in a "Christian
country," or regularly attend a Christian church. But they are deceiving themselves.

True Christians follow Christ and His word. Yes, they rejoice in
reading and hearing His word. They receive with humility what the
Bible says, no matter what others say. But then, they are characterized
by applying it by God's grace and the Spirit's empowerment to their
own lives.

Are you deceiving yourself? Are you a faithful hearer of the word
of God, *and* an effectual doer of the word for God's glory?

A Song of Praise

*Then Moses…sang this song to the L*ORD*, and said… "The L*ORD
is my strength and song, And He has become my salvation."
EXODUS 15:1-2

DANIEL GUMPRECHT: TMAI HEADQUARTERS | LOS ANGELES, CALIFORNIA

"Do we sing as much as the birds do? Yet what have birds to sing about, *compared with us?*" These probing questions posed by C. H. Spurgeon strike hard—Christians of all people have reason to sing. Indeed, we have been *created to praise* and *saved to praise*!

But if we are honest, sometimes it can be hard to praise. Perhaps trials have compounded or the busy routine of life has emptied your heart of praise. Perhaps the twin dangers of familiarity or forgetfulness have struck—and you don't remember what God has delivered you from. Consider then the song of Moses, sung after God's deliverance of Israel in the Exodus. This song, like a wonderful template, provides three reasons for praise.

Praise God for *who He is* (Exod. 15:1-3). Stop and reflect on the character of God. He is our strength and our song. He is a warrior who fights for His people. He has become our salvation.

Praise God for *what He has done* (Exod. 15:4-11). Look back and marvel at salvation accomplished. For Moses, this was a physical deliverance from slavery to Pharaoh. For Christians, this is a spiritual deliverance from slavery to sin. Think on your testimony and how God acted to save you in Christ.

Praise God for *what He will do* (Exod. 15:12-18). Moses looks to the future and God's plan for Israel. So, Christian, look ahead to the hope of salvation. God will bring His children safely home to heaven where they will dwell with Him forever—yea, He will reign forever!

As this year comes to an end, reflect on God's care in your life and follow Moses' example. Like the saints in heaven, sing this song of Moses and the song of the Lamb (Rev. 15:2-4).

December 31

Former Soviet Union

GRACE BIBLE SEMINARY | UKRAINE

RUSSIA (SCHOOL NAME CLASSIFIED)

WORD OF GRACE BIBLE INSTITUTE (FOR RUSSIAN SPEAKERS)

When the Soviet Union dissolved in 1991, the future of religious freedom looked bright. Over time, however, many of the religious rights that were once granted gave way to increased government regulations as the Orthodox Church and Islam gained ground. Today, much of the former Soviet nations are becoming increasingly opposed to Christianity and in countries like Uzbekistan, Turkmenistan, and Tajikistan, there is open hostility.

TODAY, PRAY FOR

Increased religious freedom for believers in the former Soviet Union.

Wisdom for believers as they contend with hostile societies and governments.

Bold and courageous church leaders who will be willing to pay the high price for faithfulness to God's word.

Scripture Index

THE
MASTER'S ACADEMY
INTERNATIONAL

Our Mission

TMAI is committed to fulfilling the Great Commission by training indigenous church leaders to be approved pastor-teachers, able to equip their churches to make biblically sound disciples.

Who We Are

TMAI is an association of like-minded training centers that equip and train church leaders in their home countries around the world. Each member school is independently led, yet all are united in their common doctrinal convictions and commitment to TMAI's core values. Additionally, each member school is staffed with at least two graduates of The Master's Seminary.

Membership in TMAI is based on adherence to strict standards of excellence and stewardship, which include financial, academic, and theological criteria. In addition to upholding these standards for its member schools, TMAI provides vital funding for its member schools through the generosity of like-minded donors. As TMAI looks to expand into additional countries in the coming years, we invite you to pray for this ministry and consider how you might give to the Lord's work in training church leaders worldwide.

www.tmai.org | info@tmai.org | 818.909.5570
13248 Roscoe Blvd, Sun Valley, CA 91352